T0014085

HOW TO BE QUEER

ANCIENT WISDOM FOR MODERN READERS

■ ■ ■ ■

For a full list of titles in the series, go to
https://press.princeton.edu/series/ancient-wisdom-for-modern-readers.

How to Be Queer: An Ancient Guide to Sexuality by Sappho, Plato, and Other Lovers

How to Get Over a Breakup: An Ancient Guide to Moving On by Ovid

How to Make Money: An Ancient Guide to Wealth Management by Pliny & Co.

How to Focus: A Monastic Guide for an Age of Distraction by John Cassian

How to Be Healthy: An Ancient Guide to Wellness by Galen

How to Care about Animals: An Ancient Guide to Creatures Great and Small by Porphyry and Friends

How to Flourish: An Ancient Guide to Living Well by Aristotle

How to Do the Right Thing: An Ancient Guide to Treating People Fairly by Seneca

How to Grieve: An Ancient Guide to the Lost Art of Consolation inspired by Marcus Tullius Cicero

How to Have a Life: An Ancient Guide to Using Our Time Wisely by Seneca

How to Say No: An Ancient Guide to the Art of Cynicism by Diogenes and the Cynics

How to Tell a Story: An Ancient Guide for Aspiring Writers by Aristotle

How to Stop a Conspiracy: An Ancient Guide for Saving a Republic by Sallust

How to Be a Farmer: An Ancient Guide to Life on the Land by Many Hands

How to Innovate: An Ancient Guide to Creative Thinking by Aristotle

HOW TO BE QUEER

■ ■ ■ ■

An Ancient Guide to Sexuality

Sappho, Plato, and Other Lovers

Selected, translated, and introduced
by Sarah Nooter

PRINCETON UNIVERSITY PRESS
PRINCETON AND OXFORD

Published by Princeton University Press
41 William Street, Princeton, New Jersey 08540
99 Banbury Road, Oxford OX2 6JX
press.princeton.edu

Library of Congress Cataloging-in-Publication Data

Names: Nooter, Sarah, editor.
Title: How to be queer : an ancient guide to sexuality / the wisdom of many bodies ; selected, translated, and introduced by Sarah Nooter.
Description: Princeton, New Jersey : Princeton University Press, [2024] | Series: Ancient wisdom for modern readers | Includes bibliographical references.
Identifiers: LCCN 2023044952 (print) | LCCN 2023044953 (ebook) | ISBN 9780691248615 (hardback ; alk. paper) | ISBN 9780691248608 (ebook)
Subjects: LCSH: Classical literature. | Homosexuality in literature. | Sex in literature. | Homosexuality—Greece. | Homosexuality—Rome. | Sex customs—Greece. | Sex customs—Rome.
Classification: LCC PA3014.S47 H69 2024 (print) | LCC PA3014.S47 (ebook) | DDC 883.01093538—dc23/eng/20231206
LC record available at https://lccn.loc.gov/2023044952
LC ebook record available at https://lccn.loc.gov/2023044953

British Library Cataloging-in-Publication Data is available

Editorial: Rob Tempio and Chloe Coy
Production Editorial: Sara Lerner
Text Design: Pamela L. Schnitter
Jacket Design: Heather Hansen
Production: Erin Suydam
Publicity: Tyler Hubbert and Carmen Jimenez
Copyeditor: Jennifer Harris

Jacket image: *Erastes* (lover) and *eromenos* (beloved) kissing. Tondo of an Attic red-figured cup. Courtesy of the Louvre Museum, Paris, France.

This book has been composed in Stempel Garamond

Printed in the United States of America

1 3 5 7 9 10 8 6 4 2

CONTENTS

INTRODUCTION

The past decade has seen a revolution in sexuality, and counterrevolutionary opposition in turn. Still, sexual fluidity is now mainstream, the *Guardian* announced in 2019:

> Last year, "pansexual" briefly became the online dictionary Merriam-Webster's most searched word of the day after the singer Janelle Monáe defined herself as a pansexual and "queer-ass motherfucker."

And yet the Greeks got there long ago, often taking up the theme of sexuality with little angst and much wit, insight, and depth. Sometimes they wrote in the mode of pure eroticism, sometimes in terms of profound emotion, and sometimes in the casual, simple sense of lust. Confronting Greek thinking on sexuality reveals that we have quite literal guides among ancient authors as we navigate the "new" forms of being that are finding their place in our modern society.

This contribution to the *Ancient Wisdom for Modern Readers* series is intended to act as a resource for readers

interested in ancient conceptions of sexuality and in finding connections across time to their own queer experiences. It can also be used as a resource offering imaginative paradigms for a full and erotic life. It aims to present, and bring together, a plurality of the instances of non-heteronormativity that exist in the archaic and classical Greek texts that we still possess. What we find is a great abundance of forms of love, life, sexuality, and selfhood.

However, this volume also does *not* do a few things. It does not suggest that ancient Greece was a utopia of tolerance. It does not paint a holistic picture of ancient Greek social mores. It does not seek to outline the strictures and biases that limited the sexual life of ancient people. Nor is the aim to explain the elitism of male citizens and ancient prejudices against men seen as effeminate, sexual passivity in general, and women more widely. It does not treat questions and controversies around ancient practices of pederasty.[1] It was by and large understood that young men, often called "boys," were attractive to older men, much as young women, often called "girls," were seen in many quarters as being at peak desirability.

Archaic and classical Greece (the eighth to the fourth centuries BCE) offers glimpses of queer love and life in both poetry (mostly archaic) and prose (mostly classical). Since much of the poetry in this volume derives from fragments of lyric poetry, many selections present short, interlacing narratives of same-sex encounters and relationships, or expressions of sexual longing and identification.

A few examples, however, stretch as late as the Hellenistic poet Theocritus (third century BCE) and give more detailed accounts of queer desire and devotion.

The book also includes short excerpts from the stage in works of Euripides and Aristophanes that feature experimental takes on gender, and longer prose passages from Plato's and Xenophon's dialogues that portray and discuss eroticism. It closes with sequences from Plutarch's (first-to-second century CE) *Life of Alcibiades* that reflect back on this lost world. Throughout, the book gestures at how discussions of queer thought are threaded across time: excerpts that frame the (intense but not necessarily erotic) relationship of Achilles and Patroclus in Homer's *Iliad* are joined by discussion of the pair framed explicitly as lovers in Aeschylus's *Myrmidons* and Plato's *Symposium*; several poems by Sappho are paired with Anacreon's brief, erotic portrait of a girl from Lesbos, who is understood by many readers to be Sappho. A section of Anacreon's lustful poems ends with Theocritus's epigram on Anacreon, which indicates the importance of remembering his pleasure in boys.

The *Oxford English Dictionary* states that the term "queer . . . denotes a sexual or gender identity that does not correspond to established ideas of sexuality and gender, especially heterosexual norms." The word "queer" seems to move outward from there. In the words of Eve Kosofsky Sedgwick, queer "can refer to: the open mesh of possibilities, gaps, overlaps, dissonances and resonances, lapses and excesses of meaning when the constituent elements of

anyone's gender, of anyone's sexuality aren't made (or *can't* be made) to signify monolithically."[2] My use of the term here is deliberately anachronistic, since we can be sure that the identities that we recognize today do not line up with those acknowledged in antiquity. In fact, the identities of the 2020s hardly line up with those of just a decade ago. One purpose of this volume is to invite readers to loosen their ideas of what is "queer" and what is "straight." The boundary between them is not so stable; nor should it be.

This volume is not restricted to readers who consider themselves queer and the texts presented here are not concerned with imposing categories or limning identities. Instead, they are deeply engaged with detailing and exploring erotic instances and experiences—what the Greeks called *eros*. The word *eros* can mean a range of things: romantic affection, intense desire, the feeling of being *in love*, or the deity who provokes these feelings. In this book, I translate it as "desire," "love," and "Eros," depending on the context, and at times simply print the term "*eros*," to show that the term itself is being discussed. *Eros* is above all a feeling so powerful that it is understood as divine, an affective force that draws people away from what is demanded of them by institutions and establishments, and toward an experience of fervent vitality. This volume is divided into sections that isolate certain encounters with *eros*, modes of queer love, desire, and sex.

The book moves through its texts also in a loose chronology, starting from the oldest Greek text we have (Homer's

Iliad) and ending with fourth-century prose (Xenophon, Plato) and a much later text that reflects back on this period (Plutarch's *Life of Alcibiades*). I have tried to preserve some sense of the verse when translating poetry, and have labored to keep the language lucid. There are many names and figures, mythological and historical, that pass through these pages. I identify only those in the notes that seem critical to understanding the sense of the passages. Some of these texts, particularly the lyric poems, come to us in fragmented form; empty brackets and ellipses indicate that sections of text are missing. The Greek texts found here are largely derived from the editions published by Oxford, often but not always from their Oxford Classical Text imprint. Exceptions are the texts of Plutarch, Theocritus, and Xenophon, for which I used the Greek found in the Loeb editions.[3] In several cases, supplements or slight emendations have been made to the Greek for the sake of clarity and consistency across the volume.

Reader, whatever your own sense of your own identity, sexuality, or place in the world, I hope that you will find this volume by turns buoyant, playful, and passionate. If there is one thing the Greeks can teach us, it is that the erotic and queer are a source of life and a cause for celebration.

HOW TO BE QUEER

1 TWO OF US: BEYOND EROS

Homer's Iliad, *composed in the mid-700s BCE, shows one of the most intense and loving relationships between two men in world literature. Though it is never made clear in the epic that this relationship is sexual, many later Greek authors read it this way. These passages from the* Iliad *show the most passionate moments between the pair: first Patroclus admonishes Achilles for his uncaring attitude toward the Greeks and his insatiable anger against Agamemnon, leader of the Greek army, who had taken the enslaved girl, Briseis, from Achilles after a quarrel. Patroclus begs for Achilles' armor, so that he can go into battle and help the Greeks, but Achilles longs to triumph in war with Patroclus alone. Nonetheless, he allows Patroclus to wear his armor into battle, only to have him die at Hector's hands. The final sections focus on Achilles' inconsolable grief after Patroclus's death.*

16.1–100

Ὣς οἳ μὲν περὶ νηὸς ἐϋσσέλμοιο μάχοντο·
Πάτροκλος δ᾽ Ἀχιλῆϊ παρίστατο ποιμένι λαῶν
δάκρυα θερμὰ χέων ὥς τε κρήνη μελάνυδρος,
ἥ τε κατ᾽ αἰγίλιπος πέτρης δνοφερὸν χέει ὕδωρ.
τὸν δὲ ἰδὼν ᾤκτιρε ποδάρκης δῖος Ἀχιλλεύς,
καί μιν φωνήσας ἔπεα πτερόεντα προσηύδα·
τίπτε δεδάκρυσαι Πατρόκλεες, ἠΰτε κούρη
νηπίη, ἥ θ᾽ ἅμα μητρὶ θέουσ᾽ ἀνελέσθαι ἀνώγει
είανοῦ ἁπτομένη, καί τ᾽ ἐσσυμένην κατερύκει,
δακρυόεσσα δέ μιν ποτιδέρκεται, ὄφρ᾽ ἀνέληται·
τῇ ἴκελος Πάτροκλε τέρεν κατὰ δάκρυον εἴβεις.
ἠέ τι Μυρμιδόνεσσι πιφαύσκεαι, ἢ ἐμοὶ αὐτῷ,
ἦέ τιν᾽ ἀγγελίην Φθίης ἐξέκλυες οἶος;
ζώειν μὰν ἔτι φασὶ Μενοίτιον Ἄκτορος υἱόν,
ζώει δ᾽ Αἰακίδης Πηλεὺς μετὰ Μυρμιδόνεσσι;
τῶν κε μάλ᾽ ἀμφοτέρων ἀκαχοίμεθα τεθνηώτων.
ἦε σύ γ᾽ Ἀργείων ὀλοφύρεαι, ὡς ὀλέκονται
νηυσὶν ἔπι γλαφυρῇσιν ὑπερβασίης ἕνεκα σφῆς;

Homer, *Iliad*

And so they were fighting around the well-benched ships.
But Patroclus approached Achilles, shepherd of men,
weeping hot tears, like a spring of black depths
that pours dark water down from the sheer rocks.
Swift-footed, godlike Achilles looked at him and felt pity,
and speaking said these winged words,
"Why do you cry, Patroclus, like some silly girl
who runs to her mother and begs to be picked up,
grasping at her robe, getting in her way,
and looking up at her with tears in her eyes until she is picked up?
Just like this girl, Patroclus, you shed tender tears.
Do you have something to tell the Myrmidons? Or just me?
Or have you alone heard some message from Phthia?
Do they not say that your father Menoetius, Actor's son, still lives,
and that Peleus, son of Aeacus, my father, is alive among the Myrmidons?
We would indeed be very distressed by the death of either of them.
Or do you weep for the Argives, that they are being destroyed
by the hollow ships on account of their own transgressions?

ἐξαύδα, μὴ κεῦθε νόῳ, ἵνα εἴδομεν ἄμφω.
Τὸν δὲ βαρὺ στενάχων προσέφης Πατρόκλεες ἱππεῦ·
ὦ Ἀχιλεῦ Πηλῆος υἱὲ μέγα φέρτατ' Ἀχαιῶν
μὴ νεμέσα· τοῖον γὰρ ἄχος βεβίηκεν Ἀχαιούς.
οἳ μὲν γὰρ δὴ πάντες, ὅσοι πάρος ἦσαν ἄριστοι,
ἐν νηυσὶν κέαται βεβλημένοι οὐτάμενοί τε.
βέβληται μὲν ὃ Τυδεΐδης κρατερὸς Διομήδης,
οὔτασται δ' Ὀδυσεὺς δουρικλυτὸς ἠδ' Ἀγαμέμνων,
βέβληται δὲ καὶ Εὐρύπυλος κατὰ μηρὸν ὀϊστῷ.
τοὺς μέν τ' ἰητροὶ πολυφάρμακοι ἀμφιπένονται
ἕλκε' ἀκειόμενοι· σὺ δ' ἀμήχανος ἔπλευ Ἀχιλλεῦ.
μὴ ἐμέ γ' οὖν οὗτός γε λάβοι χόλος, ὃν σὺ φυλάσσεις
αἰναρέτη· τί σευ ἄλλος ὀνήσεται ὀψίγονός περ
αἴ κε μὴ Ἀργείοισιν ἀεικέα λοιγὸν ἀμύνῃς;
νηλεές, οὐκ ἄρα σοί γε πατὴρ ἦν ἱππότα Πηλεύς,
οὐδὲ Θέτις μήτηρ· γλαυκὴ δέ σε τίκτε θάλασσα
πέτραι τ' ἠλίβατοι, ὅτι τοι νόος ἐστὶν ἀπηνής.

Speak and do not keep it back in your mind, so that we both may know."
With a deep sigh, horseman Patroclus, you answered him,
"O Achilles, son of Peleus, greatest of the Achaeans,
do not be angry. For such great hardship presses upon the Achaeans.
Indeed all of them, as many who were the best before,
now lie in the ships, battered and wounded.
Strong Diomedes, son of Tydeus, has been hit,
and Odysseus, glorious with the spear, has been wounded and Agamemnon too,
and even Eurypylus has been struck by an arrow in his thigh.
The doctors, who know of medicine, are tending to their wounds
to heal them. But you are implacable, Achilles.
May such anger as this never take hold of me, which you so cherish,
you paragon of grim virtue. What will any of our descendants ever gain from you,
if you do not defend the Argives from shameful ruin?
Cruel man, I do not think that the horseman Peleus was your father,
nor was Thetis your mother. No, the gleaming sea bore you
and the sheer rocks, so hard is your heart.

εἰ δέ τινα φρεσὶ σῇσι θεοπροπίην ἀλεείνεις
καί τινά τοι πὰρ Ζηνὸς ἐπέφραδε πότνια μήτηρ,
ἀλλ' ἐμέ περ πρόες ὦχ', ἅμα δ' ἄλλον λαὸν ὄπασσον
Μυρμιδόνων, ἤν πού τι φόως Δαναοῖσι γένωμαι.
δὸς δέ μοι ὤμοιιν τὰ σὰ τεύχεα θωρηχθῆναι,
αἴ κ' ἐμὲ σοὶ ἴσκοντες ἀπόσχωνται πολέμοιο
Τρῶες, ἀναπνεύσωσι δ' Ἀρήϊοι υἷες Ἀχαιῶν
τειρόμενοι· ὀλίγη δέ τ' ἀνάπνευσις πολέμοιο.
ῥεῖα δέ κ' ἀκμῆτες κεκμηότας ἄνδρας ἀϋτῇ
ὤσαιμεν προτὶ ἄστυ νεῶν ἄπο καὶ κλισιάων.
Ὣς φάτο λισσόμενος μέγα νήπιος· ἦ γὰρ ἔμελλεν
οἷ αὐτῷ θάνατόν τε κακὸν καὶ κῆρα λιτέσθαι.
τὸν δὲ μέγ' ὀχθήσας προσέφη πόδας ὠκὺς Ἀχιλλεύς·
ὤ μοι διογενὲς Πατρόκλεες οἷον ἔειπες·
οὔτε θεοπροπίης ἐμπάζομαι ἥν τινα οἶδα,
οὔτέ τί μοι πὰρ Ζηνὸς ἐπέφραδε πότνια μήτηρ·

But if in your mind there is some prophecy you are avoiding discussing,
or something from Zeus that your mother has revealed to you,
then at least send me forth swiftly, and supply me with the rest of the army
of the Myrmidons, in case I can be some small light to the Danaans.
And give me your armor to strap onto my shoulders,
in the hopes that the Trojans might, thinking I'm you, back off
from the fighting, and the warlike sons of the Achaeans might catch
their breath, for they are worn out. There's so little breathing space in war.
Easily we who are not tired out can push back men wearied
from the war-cry to their city, away from our ships and tents."
So he spoke, beseeching him vehemently, fool that he was. For it was fated
that it was his own evil death and fate for which he begged.
Swift-footed Achilles, deeply upset, replied,
"O Zeus-born Patroclus, what a thing you have said!
I am not heeding any prophecy that I know of,
nor has my mother reported anything at all to me from Zeus.

ἀλλὰ τόδ᾽ αἰνὸν ἄχος κραδίην καὶ θυμὸν ἱκάνει,
ὁππότε δὴ τὸν ὁμοῖον ἀνὴρ ἐθέλῃσιν ἀμέρσαι
καὶ γέρας ἂψ ἀφελέσθαι, ὅ τε κράτεϊ προβεβήκῃ·
αἰνὸν ἄχος τό μοί ἐστιν, ἐπεὶ πάθον ἄλγεα θυμῷ.
κούρην ἣν ἄρα μοι γέρας ἔξελον υἷες Ἀχαιῶν,
δουρὶ δ᾽ ἐμῷ κτεάτισσα πόλιν εὐτείχεα πέρσας,
τὴν ἂψ ἐκ χειρῶν ἕλετο κρείων Ἀγαμέμνων
Ἀτρεΐδης ὡς εἴ τιν᾽ ἀτίμητον μετανάστην.
ἀλλὰ τὰ μὲν προτετύχθαι ἐάσομεν· οὐδ᾽ ἄρα πως ἦν
ἀσπερχὲς κεχολῶσθαι ἐνὶ φρεσίν· ἤτοι ἔφην γε
οὐ πρὶν μηνιθμὸν καταπαυσέμεν, ἀλλ᾽ ὁπότ᾽ ἂν δὴ
νῆας ἐμὰς ἀφίκηται ἀϋτή τε πτόλεμός τε.
τύνη δ᾽ ὤμοιιν μὲν ἐμὰ κλυτὰ τεύχεα δῦθι,
ἄρχε δὲ Μυρμιδόνεσσι φιλοπτολέμοισι μάχεσθαι,
εἰ δὴ κυάνεον Τρώων νέφος ἀμφιβέβηκε
νηυσὶν ἐπικρατέως, οἳ δὲ ῥηγμῖνι θαλάσσης
κεκλίαται, χώρης ὀλίγην ἔτι μοῖραν ἔχοντες
Ἀργεῖοι, Τρώων δὲ πόλις ἐπὶ πᾶσα βέβηκε
θάρσυνος· οὐ γὰρ ἐμῆς κόρυθος λεύσσουσι μέτωπον
ἐγγύθι λαμπομένης· τάχα κεν φεύγοντες ἐναύλους
πλήσειαν νεκύων, εἴ μοι κρείων Ἀγαμέμνων

But this terrible pain comes to my heart and soul,
since that man was willing to deprive an equal
and take back my prize, for he overstepped in his power.
A terrible pain this is for me, and I have suffered in
my soul.
That girl whom the sons of the Achaeans picked out for
me as prize,
when by my spear I took and sacked that well-walled
city,
it was she that lord Agamemnon, son of Atreus, took
from my hands, as if I were some lowly vagrant.
But we will let these things be in the past. For not at all
did I mean
to rage unceasingly in my heart. But I did say
that I would not pause from my wrath at any point
before
the war-cry and the war itself reached my ships.
So then, put my famous armor on your shoulders,
and be a leader for the war-loving Myrmidons as they
fight,
if indeed the dark cloud of Trojans thickly surrounds
our ships, and the Argives are pushed back against
the surf
of the sea, with just a small portion of land left,
and the whole city of the Trojans presses on boldly.
For they do not see the top of my helmet
flashing nearby. Soon they would be fleeing and filling
their waterways with corpses, if lord Agamemnon

ἤπια εἰδείη· νῦν δὲ στρατὸν ἀμφιμάχονται.
οὐ γὰρ Τυδεΐδεω Διομήδεος ἐν παλάμῃσι
μαίνεται ἐγχείη Δαναῶν ἀπὸ λοιγὸν ἀμῦναι·
οὐδέ πω Ἀτρεΐδεω ὀπὸς ἔκλυον αὐδήσαντος
ἐχθρῆς ἐκ κεφαλῆς· ἀλλ' Ἕκτορος ἀνδροφόνοιο
Τρωσὶ κελεύοντος περιάγνυται, οἳ δ' ἀλαλητῷ
πᾶν πεδίον κατέχουσι μάχῃ νικῶντες Ἀχαιούς.
ἀλλὰ καὶ ὧς Πάτροκλε νεῶν ἄπο λοιγὸν ἀμύνων
ἔμπεσ' ἐπικρατέως, μὴ δὴ πυρὸς αἰθομένοιο
νῆας ἐνιπρήσωσι, φίλον δ' ἀπὸ νόστον ἕλωνται.
πείθεο δ' ὥς τοι ἐγὼ μύθου τέλος ἐν φρεσὶ θείω,
ὡς ἄν μοι τιμὴν μεγάλην καὶ κῦδος ἄρηαι
πρὸς πάντων Δαναῶν, ἀτὰρ οἳ περικαλλέα κούρην
ἂψ ἀπονάσσωσιν, ποτὶ δ' ἀγλαὰ δῶρα πόρωσιν.
ἐκ νηῶν ἐλάσας ἰέναι πάλιν· εἰ δέ κεν αὖ τοι
δώῃ κῦδος ἀρέσθαι ἐρίγδουπος πόσις Ἥρης,
μὴ σύ γ' ἄνευθεν ἐμεῖο λιλαίεσθαι πολεμίζειν
Τρωσὶ φιλοπτολέμοισιν· ἀτιμότερον δέ με θήσεις·
μὴ δ' ἐπαγαλλόμενος πολέμῳ καὶ δηϊοτῆτι
Τρῶας ἐναιρόμενος προτὶ Ἴλιον ἡγεμονεύειν,

had known gentle ways. But now they battle around
the camp.
For not in the hands of Diomedes, son of Tydeus,
does the spear rage to save the Danaans from ruin,
nor yet have I ever heard the son of Atreus's voice
shouting
from his hateful head. But the shout of man-slaying
Hector
urging on the Trojans breaks all around me, and with
their war-cry
they hold all the plain as they conquer the Achaeans in
battle.
And so, Patroclus, enter the fray fiercely to save the ships
from destruction, lest they burn them with blazing fire
and take away our beloved return to home.
But listen to me so that I can place the purpose of my
plan in your mind,
that you may win great honor and glory for me
on behalf of the Danaans, and then they will send back
again
that stunning girl and also offer many glorious gifts.
But when you have driven them from the ships, come
back again.
If the husband of Hera should grant it that you win glory,
do not strive to win the war with the war-loving Trojans
without me. You would make me dishonored.
And do not, glorying in war and the battle-cry,
slaying the Trojans, take the lead against Ilium,

μή τις ἀπ' Οὐλύμποιο θεῶν αἰειγενετάων
ἐμβήῃ· μάλα τούς γε φιλεῖ ἑκάεργος Ἀπόλλων·
ἀλλὰ πάλιν τρωπᾶσθαι, ἐπὴν φάος ἐν νήεσσι
θήῃς, τοὺς δ' ἔτ' ἐᾶν πεδίον κάτα δηριάασθαι.
αἳ γὰρ Ζεῦ τε πάτερ καὶ Ἀθηναίη καὶ Ἄπολλον
μήτέ τις οὖν Τρώων θάνατον φύγοι ὅσσοι ἔασι,
μήτέ τις Ἀργείων, νῶϊν δ' ἐκδῦμεν ὄλεθρον,
ὄφρ' οἶοι Τροίης ἱερὰ κρήδεμνα λύωμεν.

18.78–116

Τὴν δὲ βαρὺ στενάχων προσέφη πόδας ὠκὺς Ἀχιλλεύς·
μῆτερ ἐμή, τὰ μὲν ἄρ μοι Ὀλύμπιος ἐξετέλεσσεν·
ἀλλὰ τί μοι τῶν ἦδος ἐπεὶ φίλος ὤλεθ' ἑταῖρος
Πάτροκλος, τὸν ἐγὼ περὶ πάντων τῖον ἑταίρων
ἶσον ἐμῇ κεφαλῇ; τὸν ἀπώλεσα, τεύχεα δ' Ἕκτωρ
δῃώσας ἀπέδυσε πελώρια θαῦμα ἰδέσθαι
καλά· τὰ μὲν Πηλῆϊ θεοὶ δόσαν ἀγλαὰ δῶρα
ἤματι τῷ ὅτε σε βροτοῦ ἀνέρος ἔμβαλον εὐνῇ.
αἴθ' ὄφελες σὺ μὲν αὖθι μετ' ἀθανάτῃς ἁλίῃσι
ναίειν, Πηλεὺς δὲ θνητὴν ἀγαγέσθαι ἄκοιτιν.
νῦν δ' ἵνα καὶ σοὶ πένθος ἐνὶ φρεσὶ μυρίον εἴη

lest one of the everlasting gods from Olympus
steps in. For far-shooting Apollo, at least, loves them
well.
But turn back whenever you have given light to the ships,
and let them still battle on the plain.
O father Zeus and Athena and Apollo,
if only it might be that not one of the Trojans escape
death,
and not one of the Argives, but that you and I might
avoid destruction
so that we alone would dissolve the holy battlements of
Troy!"

. . . . .

Groaning heavily, swift-footed Achilles answered her,
"Mother, the Olympian one fulfilled my prayers.
But what pleasure is left to me when he is dead, my
beloved companion
Patroclus, whom I valued above all other companions,
equally to myself? I have lost him. Hector has slain him
and stripped him of my mighty armor, a wonder to
behold,
the gleaming gifts that the gods gave to Peleus
on that day when they placed you in the bed of a
mortal man.
If only you had stayed with the gods of the sea,
and Peleus had taken a mortal wife,
then you wouldn't now have ceaseless pain in your breast

παιδὸς ἀποφθιμένοιο, τὸν οὐχ ὑποδέξεαι αὖτις
οἴκαδε νοστήσαντ', ἐπεὶ οὐδ' ἐμὲ θυμὸς ἄνωγε
ζώειν οὐδ' ἄνδρεσσι μετέμμεναι, αἴ κε μὴ Ἕκτωρ
πρῶτος ἐμῷ ὑπὸ δουρὶ τυπεὶς ἀπὸ θυμὸν ὀλέσσῃ,
Πατρόκλοιο δ' ἕλωρα Μενοιτιάδεω ἀποτίσῃ.
Τὸν δ' αὖτε προσέειπε Θέτις κατὰ δάκρυ χέουσα·
ὠκύμορος δή μοι τέκος ἔσσεαι, οἷ' ἀγορεύεις·
αὐτίκα γάρ τοι ἔπειτα μεθ' Ἕκτορα πότμος ἑτοῖμος.
Τὴν δὲ μέγ' ὀχθήσας προσέφη πόδας ὠκὺς Ἀχιλλεύς·
αὐτίκα τεθναίην, ἐπεὶ οὐκ ἄρ' ἔμελλον ἑταίρῳ
κτεινομένῳ ἐπαμῦναι· ὃ μὲν μάλα τηλόθι πάτρης
ἔφθιτ', ἐμεῖο δὲ δῆσεν ἀρῆς ἀλκτῆρα γενέσθαι.
νῦν δ' ἐπεὶ οὐ νέομαί γε φίλην ἐς πατρίδα γαῖαν,
οὐδέ τι Πατρόκλῳ γενόμην φάος οὐδ' ἑτάροισι
τοῖς ἄλλοις, οἳ δὴ πολέες δάμεν Ἕκτορι δίῳ,
ἀλλ' ἧμαι παρὰ νηυσὶν ἐτώσιον ἄχθος ἀρούρης,
τοῖος ἐὼν οἷος οὔ τις Ἀχαιῶν χαλκοχιτώνων
ἐν πολέμῳ· ἀγορῇ δέ τ' ἀμείνονές εἰσι καὶ ἄλλοι.
ὡς ἔρις ἔκ τε θεῶν ἔκ τ' ἀνθρώπων ἀπόλοιτο

for the loss of your child, whom you will never again
receive
returning home, since my heart no longer bids me
to live and remain among men, unless Hector
first, beaten by my spear, loses his life,
and pays the price for the death of Patroclus, son of
Menoetius."
And Thetis replied to him, pouring out tears,
"You will indeed die soon, my child, since you have
declared this.
For immediately after Hector, your death will hang
over you."
Swift-footed Achilles, much distressed, answered her,
"Then immediately may I die, since I was not there to
protect
my companion from being killed. Far away indeed from
his fatherland
did he perish, for he needed me to be his protector from
ruin.
So now I will not go back to my beloved fatherland,
and I was not at all a light for Patroclus nor for my other
friends, many of whom have been vanquished by brilliant
Hector,
but instead I sat by the ships, a useless burden on the
earth,
I who am such as no other of the bronze-clad Achaeans
in war, though there are others who excel in the assembly.
Thus may strife among gods and men be gone,

καὶ χόλος, ὅς τ' ἐφέηκε πολύφρονά περ χαλεπῆναι,
ὅς τε πολὺ γλυκίων μέλιτος καταλειβομένοιο
ἀνδρῶν ἐν στήθεσσιν ἀέξεται ἠΰτε καπνός·
ὡς ἐμὲ νῦν ἐχόλωσεν ἄναξ ἀνδρῶν Ἀγαμέμνων.
ἀλλὰ τὰ μὲν προτετύχθαι ἐάσομεν ἀχνύμενοί περ,
θυμὸν ἐνὶ στήθεσσι φίλον δαμάσαντες ἀνάγκῃ·
νῦν δ' εἶμ' ὄφρα φίλης κεφαλῆς ὀλετῆρα κιχείω
Ἕκτορα· κῆρα δ' ἐγὼ τότε δέξομαι ὁππότε κεν δὴ
Ζεὺς ἐθέλῃ τελέσαι ἠδ' ἀθάνατοι θεοὶ ἄλλοι.

19.303–27

αὐτὸν δ' ἀμφὶ γέροντες Ἀχαιῶν ἠγερέθοντο
λισσόμενοι δειπνῆσαι: ὃ δ' ἠρνεῖτο στεναχίζων·
λίσσομαι, εἴ τις ἔμοιγε φίλων ἐπιπείθεθ' ἑταίρων,
μή με πρὶν σίτοιο κελεύετε μηδὲ ποτῆτος
ἄσασθαι φίλον ἦτορ, ἐπεί μ' ἄχος αἰνὸν ἱκάνει·
δύντα δ' ἐς ἠέλιον μενέω καὶ τλήσομαι ἔμπης.
  ὣς εἰπὼν ἄλλους μὲν ἀπεσκέδασεν βασιλῆας,
δοιὼ δ' Ἀτρεΐδα μενέτην καὶ δῖος Ὀδυσσεὺς
Νέστωρ Ἰδομενεύς τε γέρων θ' ἱππηλάτα Φοῖνιξ
τέρποντες πυκινῶς ἀκαχήμενον· οὐδέ τι θυμῷ
τέρπετο, πρὶν πολέμου στόμα δύμεναι αἱματόεντος.
μνησάμενος δ' ἁδινῶς ἀνενείκατο φώνησέν τε·

and fury too, which makes even a wise man aggrieved,
and, much sweeter than honey dripping down
in the chests of men, grows like smoke.
So even now did Agamemnon, lord of men, infuriate me.
But, though it still pains me, I will let this be in the past,
and tame the dear heart in my chest by necessity.
And now I go to meet the murderer of that beloved man,
Hector. And I will accept the goddess of death
    whensoever
Zeus and the other deathless gods may wish it so."

. . . . . .

Around Achilles the elders of the Achaeans gathered,
begging him to eat. But he refused them, groaning,
"I beg you, if any of my dear comrades might comply,
do not bid me so soon to satiate my heart
with food and drink, since terrible grief sits upon me.
For I will wait till sunset and hold out even so."
  So he spoke and the others kings dispersed,
but the two sons of Atreus and divine Odysseus
    remained,
and Nestor and Idomeneus and the old man, Phoenix,
    horse-driver,
trying to cheer him, so deeply pained. But there was
    nothing
to cheer his heart until he might sink into the maw of
    bloody war.
And thinking back, he heaved a deep sigh and spoke,

ἦ ῥά νύ μοί ποτε καὶ σὺ δυσάμμορε φίλταθ' ἑταίρων
αὐτὸς ἐνὶ κλισίῃ λαρὸν παρὰ δεῖπνον ἔθηκας
αἶψα καὶ ὀτραλέως, ὁπότε σπερχοίατ' Ἀχαιοὶ
Τρωσὶν ἐφ' ἱπποδάμοισι φέρειν πολύδακρυν Ἄρηα.
νῦν δὲ σὺ μὲν κεῖσαι δεδαϊγμένος, αὐτὰρ ἐμὸν κῆρ
ἄκμηνον πόσιος καὶ ἐδητύος ἔνδον ἐόντων
σῇ ποθῇ· οὐ μὲν γάρ τι κακώτερον ἄλλο πάθοιμι,
οὐδ' εἴ κεν τοῦ πατρὸς ἀποφθιμένοιο πυθοίμην,
ὅς που νῦν Φθίηφι τέρεν κατὰ δάκρυον εἴβει
χήτεϊ τοιοῦδ' υἷος· ὃ δ' ἀλλοδαπῷ ἐνὶ δήμῳ
εἵνεκα ῥιγεδανῆς Ἑλένης Τρωσὶν πολεμίζω·
ἠὲ τὸν ὃς Σκύρῳ μοι ἔνι τρέφεται φίλος υἱός,
εἴ που ἔτι ζώει γε Νεοπτόλεμος θεοειδής.

22.385–90

ἀλλὰ τί ἤ μοι ταῦτα φίλος διελέξατο θυμός;
κεῖται πὰρ νήεσσι νέκυς ἄκλαυτος ἄθαπτος
Πάτροκλος· τοῦ δ' οὐκ ἐπιλήσομαι, ὄφρ' ἂν ἔγωγε
ζωοῖσιν μετέω καί μοι φίλα γούνατ' ὀρώρῃ·
εἰ δὲ θανόντων περ καταλήθοντ' εἰν Ἀΐδαο
αὐτὰρ ἐγὼ καὶ κεῖθι φίλου μεμνήσομ' ἑταίρου.

"Truly it used to be that you, ill-fated and most beloved
of comrades,
you yourself would lay out a lovely dinner in this tent
with speed and skill, whenever the Achaeans rushed
to bring doleful Ares against the horse-taming Trojans.
But now you lie torn up, and my heart
abstains from drink and food, though they are nearby,
because of my longing for you. For I could not suffer any
worse,
not even were I to learn that my father had wasted away,
he who I suppose now sheds tender tears in Phthia,
since he is missing such a son as me. For I am off in a
foreign land,
making war with the Trojans on account of ghastly
Helen;
or even if it were he who is raised in Scyros as my
own son,
if he is even still alive—godlike Neoptolemus."

▪ ▪ ▪ ▪ ▪

"But why does my own heart debate these things
with me?
For by the ships lies his corpse, unmourned, unburied—
Patroclus. I will not forget him, so long as I remain
among the living and my own knees can leap.
And even if the dead forget the dead in Hades,
yet even there I will remember my dear companion."

23.35–107

Αὐτὰρ τόν γε ἄνακτα ποδώκεα Πηλεΐωνα
εἰς Ἀγαμέμνονα δῖον ἄγον βασιλῆες Ἀχαιῶν
σπουδῇ παρπεπιθόντες ἑταίρου χωόμενον κῆρ.
οἳ δ' ὅτε δὴ κλισίην Ἀγαμέμνονος ἷξον ἰόντες,
αὐτίκα κηρύκεσσι λιγυφθόγγοισι κέλευσαν
ἀμφὶ πυρὶ στῆσαι τρίποδα μέγαν, εἰ πεπίθοιεν
Πηλεΐδην λούσασθαι ἄπο βρότον αἱματόεντα.
αὐτὰρ ὅ γ' ἠρνεῖτο στερεῶς, ἐπὶ δ' ὅρκον ὄμοσσεν·
οὐ μὰ Ζῆν', ὅς τίς τε θεῶν ὕπατος καὶ ἄριστος,
οὐ θέμις ἐστὶ λοετρὰ καρήατος ἆσσον ἱκέσθαι
πρίν γ' ἐνὶ Πάτροκλον θέμεναι πυρὶ σῆμά τε χεῦαι
κείρασθαί τε κόμην, ἐπεὶ οὔ μ' ἔτι δεύτερον ὧδε
ἵξετ' ἄχος κραδίην ὄφρα ζωοῖσι μετείω.
ἀλλ' ἤτοι νῦν μὲν στυγερῇ πειθώμεθα δαιτί·
ἠῶθεν δ' ὄτρυνον ἄναξ ἀνδρῶν Ἀγάμεμνον
ὕλην τ' ἀξέμεναι παρά τε σχεῖν ὅσσ' ἐπιεικὲς

▪ ▪ ▪ ▪ ▪

Meanwhile, the kings of the Achaeans led the lord, the swift-footed
son of Peleus, to brilliant Agamemnon, having worked hard
to win over the heart in him that grieved for his companion.
But when they came to the tent of Agamemnon,
straightaway they ordered the clear-voiced heralds
to set up a great tripod on the fire, in case they might persuade
the son of Peleus to wash off the bloody gore of battle.
But he staunchly refused, and swore an oath on it,
"Not, by Zeus, who is the highest and best of the gods,
shall it be lawful for cleansing water to come near my head
before Patroclus has been placed on the fire and a tomb has been raised,
and my hair has been cut off, since not again a second time
will such grief sit in my heart, so long as I remain among the living.
But now then let us be convinced to turn to our hateful meal.
At dawn, Agamemnon, lord of men, send men
to gather and bring back wood and whatever is fitting

νεκρὸν ἔχοντα νέεσθαι ὑπὸ ζόφον ἠερόεντα,
ὄφρ' ἤτοι τοῦτον μὲν ἐπιφλέγῃ ἀκάματον πῦρ
θᾶσσον ἀπ' ὀφθαλμῶν, λαοὶ δ' ἐπὶ ἔργα τράπωνται.
῝Ως ἔφαθ', οἳ δ' ἄρα τοῦ μάλα μὲν κλύον ἠδὲ πίθοντο.
ἐσσυμένως δ' ἄρα δόρπον ἐφοπλίσσαντες ἕκαστοι
δαίνυντ', οὐδέ τι θυμὸς ἐδεύετο δαιτὸς ἐΐσης.
αὐτὰρ ἐπεὶ πόσιος καὶ ἐδητύος ἐξ ἔρον ἕντο,
οἳ μὲν κακκείοντες ἔβαν κλισίην δὲ ἕκαστος,
Πηλεΐδης δ' ἐπὶ θινὶ πολυφλοίσβοιο θαλάσσης
κεῖτο βαρὺ στενάχων πολέσιν μετὰ Μυρμιδόνεσσιν
ἐν καθαρῷ, ὅθι κύματ' ἐπ' ἠϊόνος κλύζεσκον·
εὖτε τὸν ὕπνος ἔμαρπτε λύων μελεδήματα θυμοῦ
νήδυμος ἀμφιχυθείς· μάλα γὰρ κάμε φαίδιμα γυῖα
῞Εκτορ' ἐπαΐσσων προτὶ Ἴλιον ἠνεμόεσσαν·
ἦλθε δ' ἐπὶ ψυχὴ Πατροκλῆος δειλοῖο
πάντ' αὐτῷ μέγεθός τε καὶ ὄμματα κάλ' ἐϊκυῖα
καὶ φωνήν, καὶ τοῖα περὶ χροῒ εἵματα ἕστο·
εὕδεις, αὐτὰρ ἐμεῖο λελασμένος ἔπλευ Ἀχιλλεῦ.
οὐ μέν μευ ζώοντος ἀκήδεις, ἀλλὰ θανόντος·

for a corpse to have when he passes into the gloomy
darkness below,
so that tireless fire may burn him up, quickly
snatching him from our eyes, and then these men may
turn back to their work."
So he spoke, and the others heard and obeyed him.
Quickly each man prepared and ate his dinner,
and no soul lacked at all for his fair share of food.
But when they had put away their desire for food and
drink,
then each man went to his tent to lie down,
but the son of Peleus lay on the beach of the loud-
roaring sea,
groaning deeply among the many Myrmidons,
in a clearing where the waves dashed against the shore.
When sleep snatched him, freeing him from the cares of
his heart,
pleasantly engulfing him—for indeed in his mind he was
still chasing
Hector to windy Ilium with his gleaming limbs—
then did the soul of wretched Patroclus come to him,
in every way like to the man himself, in build and
lovely eyes
and in voice, and he wore still the very same clothes.
"You sleep, for indeed you have forgotten me, Achilles.
When I was alive, you were not so uncaring, just now
that I am dead.

θάπτέ με ὅττι τάχιστα πύλας Ἀΐδαο περήσω.
τῆλέ με εἴργουσι ψυχαὶ εἴδωλα καμόντων,
οὐδέ μέ πω μίσγεσθαι ὑπὲρ ποταμοῖο ἐῶσιν,
ἀλλ᾽ αὔτως ἀλάλημαι ἀν᾽ εὐρυπυλὲς Ἄϊδος δῶ.
καί μοι δὸς τὴν χεῖρ᾽· ὀλοφύρομαι, οὐ γὰρ ἔτ᾽ αὖτις
νίσομαι ἐξ Ἀΐδαο, ἐπήν με πυρὸς λελάχητε.
οὐ μὲν γὰρ ζωοί γε φίλων ἀπάνευθεν ἑταίρων
βουλὰς ἑζόμενοι βουλεύσομεν, ἀλλ᾽ ἐμὲ μὲν κὴρ
ἀμφέχανε στυγερή, ἥ περ λάχε γιγνόμενόν περ·
καὶ δὲ σοὶ αὐτῷ μοῖρα, θεοῖς ἐπιείκελ᾽ Ἀχιλλεῦ,
τείχει ὕπο Τρώων εὐηφενέων ἀπολέσθαι.
ἄλλο δέ τοι ἐρέω καὶ ἐφήσομαι αἴ κε πίθηαι·
μὴ ἐμὰ σῶν ἀπάνευθε τιθήμεναι ὀστέ᾽ Ἀχιλλεῦ,
ἀλλ᾽ ὁμοῦ ὡς ἐτράφημεν ἐν ὑμετέροισι δόμοισιν,
εὖτέ με τυτθὸν ἐόντα Μενοίτιος ἐξ Ὀπόεντος
ἤγαγεν ὑμέτερόνδ᾽ ἀνδροκτασίης ὕπο λυγρῆς,
ἤματι τῷ ὅτε παῖδα κατέκτανον Ἀμφιδάμαντος
νήπιος οὐκ ἐθέλων ἀμφ᾽ ἀστραγάλοισι χολωθείς·
ἔνθά με δεξάμενος ἐν δώμασιν ἱππότα Πηλεὺς

Bury me as quickly as possible so that I may pass through
the gates of Hades.
The souls, shades of dead men, keep far away from me
and do not allow me yet to mingle with them across the
river,
but in vain I wander about the well-gated house of
Hades.
Give me your hand. I grieve, for never again
will I return from Hades, once you have given me my
due in fire.
For when I was alive, we sat apart from our dear
comrades
and made our plans, but hateful fate has consumed me,
the death that was my fate already at my birth.
Even for you yourself, Achilles, like to the gods, it is
destined
that you will die beneath the walls of wealthy Troy.
But I will ask and enjoin for one more thing, in case you
may obey:
do not place my bones apart from yours, Achilles,
but together, even as we were raised in your house,
since when I was small Menoitius brought me from
Opoeis
to your land, due to my baneful act of manslaughter
on that day when I killed the child of Amphidamus,
stupidly, not meaning to, angered by a game of dice.
Then the horseman Peleus, taking me into his home,

ἔτραφέ τ' ἐνδυκέως καὶ σὸν θεράποντ' ὀνόμηνεν·
ὣς δὲ καὶ ὀστέα νῶϊν ὁμὴ σορὸς ἀμφικαλύπτοι
χρύσεος ἀμφιφορεύς, τόν τοι πόρε πότνια μήτηρ.
Τὸν δ' ἀπαμειβόμενος προσέφη πόδας ὠκὺς Ἀχιλλεύς·
τίπτέ μοι ἠθείη κεφαλὴ δεῦρ' εἰλήλουθας
καί μοι ταῦτα ἕκαστ' ἐπιτέλλεαι; αὐτὰρ ἐγώ τοι
πάντα μάλ' ἐκτελέω καὶ πείσομαι ὡς σὺ κελεύεις.
ἀλλά μοι ἆσσον στῆθι· μίνυνθά περ ἀμφιβαλόντε
ἀλλήλους ὀλοοῖο τεταρπώμεσθα γόοιο.
Ὣς ἄρα φωνήσας ὠρέξατο χερσὶ φίλῃσιν
οὐδ' ἔλαβε· ψυχὴ δὲ κατὰ χθονὸς ἠΰτε καπνὸς
ᾤχετο τετριγυῖα· ταφὼν δ' ἀνόρουσεν Ἀχιλλεὺς
χερσί τε συμπλατάγησεν, ἔπος δ' ὀλοφυδνὸν ἔειπεν·
ὢ πόποι ἦ ῥά τίς ἐστι καὶ εἰν Ἀΐδαο δόμοισι
ψυχὴ καὶ εἴδωλον, ἀτὰρ φρένες οὐκ ἔνι πάμπαν·
παννυχίη γάρ μοι Πατροκλῆος δειλοῖο
ψυχὴ ἐφεστήκει γοόωσά τε μυρομένη τε,
καί μοι ἕκαστ' ἐπέτελλεν, ἔϊκτο δὲ θέσκελον αὐτῷ.

raised me with care and named me your attendant.
So too let the same vessel surround the bones of us two,
a golden amphora, the one that your majestic mother
    gave you."
  And answering him, swift-footed Achilles said,
"Why, my trusty friend, have you come here
to enjoin these things of me? But indeed I will do
all of this for you and obey as you command.
But come to me now! For just a little while, let us hold
one another and take comfort in our dreadful grief."
  So he spoke and stretched out his own hands,
but could not grasp him. The soul like smoke
vanished beneath the earth with a shriek. Astonished,
    Achilles awoke,
striking at the air with his hands, and he spoke this word
    of lament:
"Oh horror, that even in the house of Hades there exists
some sort of soul and phantom, but there is no mind
    within it at all.
For all night long, the soul of wretched Patroclus
stood by me, wailing and lamenting,
and he enjoined me to do each thing, and he seemed
    wondrously like him."

23.138–53

Οἳ δ’ ὅτε χῶρον ἵκανον ὅθί σφισι πέφραδ’ Ἀχιλλεὺς
κάτθεσαν, αἶψα δέ οἱ μενοεικέα νήεον ὕλην.
ἔνθ’ αὖτ’ ἄλλ’ ἐνόησε ποδάρκης δῖος Ἀχιλλεύς·
στὰς ἀπάνευθε πυρῆς ξανθὴν ἀπεκείρατο χαίτην,
τήν ῥα Σπερχειῷ ποταμῷ τρέφε τηλεθόωσαν·
ὀχθήσας δ’ ἄρα εἶπεν ἰδὼν ἐπὶ οἴνοπα πόντον·
Σπερχεί’ ἄλλως σοί γε πατὴρ ἠρήσατο Πηλεὺς
κεῖσέ με νοστήσαντα φίλην ἐς πατρίδα γαῖαν
σοί τε κόμην κερέειν ῥέξειν θ’ ἱερὴν ἑκατόμβην,
πεντήκοντα δ’ ἔνορχα παρ’ αὐτόθι μῆλ’ ἱερεύσειν
ἐς πηγάς, ὅθι τοι τέμενος βωμός τε θυήεις.
ὣς ἠρᾶθ’ ὃ γέρων, σὺ δέ οἱ νόον οὐκ ἐτέλεσσας.
νῦν δ’ ἐπεὶ οὐ νέομαί γε φίλην ἐς πατρίδα γαῖαν
Πατρόκλῳ ἥρωϊ κόμην ὀπάσαιμι φέρεσθαι.
Ὣς εἰπὼν ἐν χερσὶ κόμην ἑτάροιο φίλοιο
θῆκεν, τοῖσι δὲ πᾶσιν ὑφ’ ἵμερον ὦρσε γόοιο.

. . . . .

When they came far enough to the place that Achilles had settled on,
they set down his body and immediately heaped up a plentiful pile of wood.
But then swift-footed, brilliant Achilles decided on something else again,
and, standing apart from the pyre, cut off a lock of his fair hair,
which he had kept flourishing for the river Sperchius.
But now, saddened, he spoke, looking toward the wine dark sea:
"Sperchius, in vain did my father Peleus pray to you
that if I were to return to there, my beloved fatherland,
he could cut my hair for you and perform a holy hecatomb,
and on the same spot sacrifice fifty male sheep at your waters,
where there is a sacred precinct and fragment altar for you.
So did the old man pray, but you did not fulfill his intent.
So now since I will not return to my beloved fatherland,
I would rather give this hair to the hero Patroclus to have."
Speaking thus, he placed the hair into the hands
of his beloved friend, and stirred up the desire for lament in everyone.

23.217–25

παννύχιοι δ᾽ ἄρα τοί γε πυρῆς ἄμυδις φλόγ᾽ ἔβαλλον
φυσῶντες λιγέως· ὃ δὲ πάννυχος ὠκὺς Ἀχιλλεὺς
χρυσέου ἐκ κρητῆρος ἑλὼν δέπας ἀμφικύπελλον
οἶνον ἀφυσσόμενος χαμάδις χέε, δεῦε δὲ γαῖαν
ψυχὴν κικλήσκων Πατροκλῆος δειλοῖο.
ὡς δὲ πατὴρ οὗ παιδὸς ὀδύρεται ὀστέα καίων
νυμφίου, ὅς τε θανὼν δειλοὺς ἀκάχησε τοκῆας,
ὣς Ἀχιλεὺς ἑτάροιο ὀδύρετο ὀστέα καίων,
ἑρπύζων παρὰ πυρκαϊὴν ἁδινὰ στεναχίζων.

24.1–12

Λῦτο δ᾽ ἀγών, λαοὶ δὲ θοὰς ἐπὶ νῆας ἕκαστοι
ἐσκίδναντ᾽ ἰέναι. τοὶ μὲν δόρποιο μέδοντο
ὕπνου τε γλυκεροῦ ταρπήμεναι· αὐτὰρ Ἀχιλλεὺς
κλαῖε φίλου ἑτάρου μεμνημένος, οὐδέ μιν ὕπνος
ᾕρει πανδαμάτωρ, ἀλλ᾽ ἐστρέφετ᾽ ἔνθα καὶ ἔνθα
Πατρόκλου ποθέων ἀνδροτῆτά τε καὶ μένος ἠΰ,
ἠδ᾽ ὁπόσα τολύπευσε σὺν αὐτῷ καὶ πάθεν ἄλγεα
ἀνδρῶν τε πτολέμους ἀλεγεινά τε κύματα πείρων·

. . . . .

And so all night the winds fell as one upon the flames of
the fire,
blowing shrilly. And all night swift-footed Achilles
used a two-handled cup to draw wine from the golden pot
and poured it on the ground, and wet the earth,
calling upon the soul of wretched Patroclus.
Just as a father mourns for his own son who was just
married, and burns
his bones, a boy whose death has brought grief to his
wretched parents,
so did Achilles mourn, burning the bones of his friend,
falling about the funeral pyre and weeping unceasingly.

. . . . .

The gathering dispersed, and each man went back to his
swift ships,
scattering. They took care of their dinner
and enjoyed sweet sleep. But Achilles
wept, thinking of his beloved friend. And sleep,
though all-conquering, did not hold him but instead he
tossed this way
and that, longing for the manhood and noble might of
Patroclus,
and he replayed as many things as he had suffered with him,
when they had gone through the wars of men and the
grievous waves.

τῶν μιμνησκόμενος θαλερὸν κατὰ δάκρυον εἶβεν,
ἄλλοτ᾽ ἐπὶ πλευρὰς κατακείμενος, ἄλλοτε δ᾽ αὖτε
ὕπτιος, ἄλλοτε δὲ πρηνής· τοτὲ δ᾽ ὀρθὸς ἀναστὰς
δινεύεσκ᾽ ἀλύων παρὰ θῖν᾽ ἁλός·

Fr. 228a

ΑΧΙΛΛ. σέβας δὲ μηρῶν ἁγνὸν οὐκ ἐπηιδέσω,
ὦ δυσχάριστε τῶν πυκνῶν φιλημάτων.

Fr. 229a

ΑΧΙΛΛ. μηρῶν τε τῶν σῶν ηὐσέβησ᾽ ὁμιλίαν
κλαίων.

Fr. 231a

ΑΧΙΛΛ. καὶ μήν, φιλῶ γάρ, ἀβδέλυκτ᾽ ἐμοὶ τάδε.

And remembering these things he let fall warm tears,
and lay now on his side, and now again
on his back, and now on his stomach. And then he
would rise
and roam about, wandering along the shore of the sea.

Aeschylus, *Myrmidons*

Aeschylus's play, Myrmidons, *was performed in the early fifth century BCE, but exists now only in fragments. The play appears to be the first part of a trilogy based on the* Iliad. *The fragments presented here show Achilles in mourning for Patroclus, as we see him in the final books of the* Iliad. *In Aeschylus's play, unlike in Homer's epic, the two were not just loving comrades, but were clearly lovers.*

Achilles: You did not hold as sacred my reverence for
your thighs,
o you ingrate for countless kisses!

. . . . .

Achilles: I revered the intimacy of your thighs,
weeping.

. . . . .

Achilles: And yet, since I love him, these things are not
revolting to me.

179b–180a

Καὶ μὴν ὑπεραποθνῄσκειν γε μόνοι ἐθέλουσιν οἱ ἐρῶντες, οὐ μόνον ὅτι ἄνδρες, ἀλλὰ καὶ αἱ γυναῖκες. τούτου δὲ καὶ ἡ Πελίου θυγάτηρ Ἄλκηστις ἱκανὴν μαρτυρίαν παρέχεται ὑπὲρ τοῦδε τοῦ λόγου εἰς τοὺς Ἕλληνας, ἐθελήσασα μόνη ὑπὲρ τοῦ αὑτῆς ἀνδρὸς ἀποθανεῖν, ὄντων αὐτῷ πατρός τε καὶ μητρός, οὓς ἐκείνη τοσοῦτον ὑπερεβάλετο τῇ φιλίᾳ διὰ τὸν ἔρωτα, ὥστε ἀποδεῖξαι αὐτοὺς ἀλλοτρίους ὄντας τῷ ὑεῖ καὶ ὀνόματι μόνον προσήκοντας, καὶ τοῦτ᾽ ἐργασαμένη τὸ καὶ ὀνόματι μόνον προσήκοντας, καὶ τοῦτ᾽ ἐργασαμένη τὸ ἔργον οὕτω καλὸν ἔδοξεν ἐργάσασθαι οὐ μόνον ἀνθρώποις ἀλλὰ καὶ θεοῖς, ὥστε πολλῶν πολλὰ καὶ καλὰ ἐργασαμένων εὐαριθμήτοις δή τισιν ἔδοσαν τοῦτο γέρας οἱ θεοί, ἐξ Ἅιδου ἀνεῖναι πάλιν τὴν ψυχήν, ἀλλὰ τὴν ἐκείνης ἀνεῖσαν ἀγασθέντες τῷ ἔργῳ· οὕτω καὶ θεοὶ τὴν περὶ τὸν ἔρωτα σπουδήν τε καὶ ἀρετὴν μάλιστα τιμῶσιν.

Ὀρφέα δὲ τὸν Οἰάγρου ἀτελῆ ἀπέπεμψαν ἐξ Ἅιδου, φάσμα δείξαντες τῆς γυναικὸς ἐφ᾽ ἣν ἧκεν, αὐτὴν δὲ οὐ

Plato, *Symposium*

Plato wrote the Symposium *in the early fourth century BCE about a party that supposedly directly followed the victory of the playwright Agathon in a dramatic competition called the City Dionysia in 412 BCE. Plato shows each man at the party making a speech in praise of Eros, or love. What follows here is the end of the speech delivered by Phaedrus.*

Moreover, only people who are in love are willing to die for someone, and not only men but women too. Alcestis, daughter of Pelias, offers sufficient proof of this point to the Greek people, for she alone was willing to die on behalf of her husband, though his mother and father still lived. By so much did she outpace them in devotion due to her love that she revealed them to be strangers to their own son, related only in name. When she had done this, she seemed to have performed so noble a deed—and not just in view of men but also of the gods—that of the many people who have accomplished fine things, she received a prize from the gods that very few get: to have their souls come back from Hades. Yet they brought hers back out of admiration for her act of love. So greatly, above all else, do the gods honor zeal and virtue in matters of love.

But Orpheus son of Oeagrus they sent back unsatisfied from Hades, showing only the ghost of the woman for whom he'd come, but not giving her over, since he seemed soft in that, being a musician, he did not have the courage

δόντες, ὅτι μαλθακίζεσθαι ἐδόκει, ἅτε ὢν κιθαρῳδός, καὶ οὐ τολμᾶν ἕνεκα τοῦ ἔρωτος ἀποθνῄσκειν ὥσπερ Ἄλκηστις, ἀλλὰ διαμηχανᾶσθαι ζῶν εἰσιέναι εἰς Ἅιδου. τοιγάρτοι διὰ ταῦτα δίκην αὐτῷ ἐπέθεσαν, καὶ ἐποίησαν τὸν θάνατον αὐτοῦ ὑπὸ γυναικῶν γενέσθαι, οὐχ ὥσπερ Ἀχιλλέα τὸν τῆς Θέτιδος ὑὸν ἐτίμησαν καὶ εἰς μακάρων νήσους ἀπέπεμψαν, ὅτι πεπυσμένος παρὰ τῆς μητρὸς ὡς ἀποθανοῖτο ἀποκτείνας Ἕκτορα, μὴ ποιήσας δὲ τοῦτο οἴκαδε ἐλθὼν γηραιὸς τελευτήσοι, ἐτόλμησεν ἑλέσθαι βοηθήσας τῷ ἐραστῇ Πατρόκλῳ καὶ τιμωρήσας οὐ μόνον ὑπεραποθανεῖν ἀλλὰ καὶ ἐπαποθανεῖν τετελευτηκότι· ὅθεν δὴ καὶ ὑπεραγασθέντες οἱ θεοὶ διαφερόντως αὐτὸν ἐτίμησαν, ὅτι τὸν ἐραστὴν οὕτω περὶ πολλοῦ ἐποιεῖτο.

Αἰσχύλος δὲ φλυαρεῖ φάσκων Ἀχιλλέα Πατρόκλου ἐρᾶν, ὃς ἦν καλλίων οὐ μόνον Πατρόκλου ἀλλ᾽ ἅμα καὶ τῶν ἡρώων ἁπάντων, καὶ ἔτι ἀγένειος, ἔπειτα νεώτερος πολύ, ὥς φησιν Ὅμηρος. ἀλλὰ γὰρ τῷ ὄντι μάλιστα μὲν ταύτην τὴν ἀρετὴν οἱ θεοὶ τιμῶσιν τὴν περὶ τὸν ἔρωτα, μᾶλλον μέντοι θαυμάζουσιν καὶ ἄγανται καὶ εὖ ποιοῦσιν ὅταν ὁ ἐρώμενος τὸν ἐραστὴν ἀγαπᾷ, ἢ ὅταν ὁ ἐραστὴς τὰ παιδικά. θειότερον γὰρ ἐραστὴς παιδικῶν· ἔνθεος γάρ ἐστι. διὰ ταῦτα καὶ τὸν Ἀχιλλέα τῆς Ἀλκήστιδος μᾶλλον ἐτίμησαν, εἰς μακάρων νήσους ἀποπέμψαντες.

to die on account of love like Alcestis had, but contrived instead to enter Hades while still alive. Accordingly, they punished him for these things and brought about his death at the hands of women, in contrast to Achilles, son of Thetis, whom they honored and sent to the islands of the blessed. For, although he had learned from his mother that he would die once he killed Hector, but that if he didn't he would get to go home and grow old there, he dared nonetheless to come to the aid of his lover Patroclus and to avenge him, and not only to die for him but to die right after his lover died. The gods were exceedingly pleased by this and especially honored him for holding his lover in such great esteem.

But Aeschylus wrote nonsense when he said that Achilles was in fact the lover of Patroclus,[1] since he was not only more beautiful than Patroclus but was also more so than all the heroes together, and was still beardless, since he was much younger, as Homer says. For in truth the gods honor this virtue above all others, that which concerns love. Indeed they are in awe and delighted and beneficent whenever a beloved is fond of his lover, more so than when a lover feels the same for his sweetheart. For a lover is more like to the gods than his sweetheart; he is full of divine feeling. For this reason, the gods honored Achilles more than Alcestis, and sent him to the islands of the blessed.

5.202–17

ἦ τοι μὲν ξανθὸν Γανυμήδεα μητίετα Ζεὺς
ἥρπασεν ὃν διὰ κάλλος ἵν' ἀθανάτοισι μετείη
καί τε Διὸς κατὰ δῶμα θεοῖς ἐπιοινοχοεύοι,
θαῦμα ἰδεῖν, πάντεσσι τετιμένος ἀθανάτοισι,
χρυσέου ἐκ κρητῆρος ἀφύσσων νέκταρ ἐρυθρόν.
Τρῶα δὲ πένθος ἄλαστον ἔχε φρένας, οὐδέ τι ᾔδει
ὅππῃ οἱ φίλον υἱὸν ἀνήρπασε θέσπις ἄελλα·
τὸν δὴ ἔπειτα γόασκε διαμπερὲς ἤματα πάντα.

2 COME AND GET YOUR LOVE: SNATCHING BOYS

Early poetry presents the phenomenon of the boy "snatched" by a god because of his surpassing beauty, showing that the attraction of men to other men was recognized in early literature as a basis for erotic and reciprocal (if uneven) relationships. This section includes the snatching of Ganymede by Zeus in the Homeric Hymn to Aphrodite *and a portrait of the relationship of Poseidon and Pelops in the epinician ode known as* Olympian 1 *by the classical poet Pindar.*

Homeric Hymn to Aphrodite

In truth, wise Zeus carried off fair-haired Ganymede
due to his beauty so that he might dwell among the
  immortals
and pour wine for the gods in the house of Zeus,
a wonder to behold, honored by all the immortals,
as he draws red nectar from a golden jug.
But terrible grief took hold of the heart of Troas, since he
  had no idea
where the divine storm had carried off his beloved son,
so he mourned continually every day.

καί μιν Ζεὺς ἐλέησε, δίδου δέ οἱ υἷος ἄποινα
ἵππους ἀρσίποδας, τοί τ' ἀθανάτους φορέουσι.
τούς οἱ δῶρον ἔδωκεν ἔχειν· εἶπεν δὲ ἕκαστα
Ζηνὸς ἐφημοσύνῃσι διάκτορος Ἀργειφόντης,
ὡς ἔοι ἀθάνατος καὶ ἀγήρως ἶσα θεοῖσιν.
αὐτὰρ ἐπεὶ δὴ Ζηνὸς ὅ γ' ἔκλυεν ἀγγελιάων
οὐκέτ' ἔπειτα γόασκε, γεγήθει δὲ φρένας ἔνδον,
γηθόσυνος δ' ἵπποισιν ἀελλοπόδεσσιν ὀχεῖτο.

Olympian 1.36–87

υἱὲ Ταντάλου, σὲ δ' ἀντία προτέρων φθέγξομαι,
ὁπότ' ἐκάλεσε πατὴρ τὸν εὐνομώτατον
ἐς ἔρανον φίλαν τε Σίπυλον,
ἀμοιβαῖα θεοῖσι δεῖπνα παρέχων,
τότ' Ἀγλαοτρίαιναν ἁρπάσαι,

δαμέντα φρένας ἱμέρῳ, χρυσέαισί τ' ἀν' ἵπποις
ὕπατον εὐρυτίμου ποτὶ δῶμα Διὸς μεταβᾶσαι·
ἔνθα δευτέρῳ χρόνῳ
ἦλθε καὶ Γανυμήδης
Ζηνὶ τωὔτ' ἐπὶ χρέος.

And Zeus pitied him, and gave him as recompense for
his son
high-stepping horses, who had once carried the
immortals.
These he granted to Troas as a gift. The messenger
Hermes
explained all of this to him, on the orders of Zeus,
that his son would be immortal and ageless, equal to
the gods.
And when he had heard this account from Zeus,
he no longer mourned, but rejoiced in his heart,
and joyfully was borne by the storm-footed horses.

Pindar

Son of Tantalus,[1] I will tell a different tale than my
forebears,
that when your father summoned divine guests
to his well laid table and to lovely Sipylus,
providing meals to share with the gods,
then Poseidon of the shining trident snatched you,

overcome in his wits by desire, and on golden horses
he whisked you away to the house on high of widely
honored Zeus,
where, at a later time,
Ganymede came too,
to assuage the same ache in Zeus.

ὡς δ᾽ ἄφαντος ἔπελες, οὐδὲ
  ματρὶ πολλὰ μαιόμενοι φῶτες ἄγαγον,
ἔννεπε κρυφᾷ τις αὐτίκα φθονερῶν γειτόνων,
ὕδατος ὅτι τε πυρὶ ζέοισαν εἰς ἀκμάν
μαχαίρᾳ τάμον κατὰ μέλη,
τραπέζαισί τ᾽ ἀμφὶ δεύτατα κρεῶν
σέθεν διεδάσαντο καὶ φάγον.

ἐμοὶ δ᾽ ἄπορα γαστρίμαργον μακάρων τιν᾽ εἰπεῖν·
  ἀφίσταμαι·
ἀκέρδεια λέλογχεν θαμινὰ κακαγόρους.
εἰ δὲ δή τιν᾽ ἄνδρα θνατὸν Ὀλύμπου σκοποί
ἐτίμασαν, ἦν Τάνταλος οὗτος· ἀλλὰ γὰρ καταπέψαι
μέγαν ὄλβον οὐκ ἐδυνάσθη, κόρῳ δ᾽ ἕλεν
ἄταν ὑπέροπλον, ἅν τοι πατὴρ ὕπερ
κρέμασε καρτερὸν αὐτῷ λίθον,
τὸν αἰεὶ μενοινῶν κεφαλᾶς βαλεῖν εὐφροσύνας ἀλᾶται.

ἔχει δ᾽ ἀπάλαμον βίον τοῦτον ἐμπεδόμοχθον
μετὰ τριῶν τέταρτον πόνον, ἀθανάτους ὅτι κλέψαις
ἁλίκεσσι συμπόταις
νέκταρ ἀμβροσίαν τε
δῶκεν, οἷσιν ἄφθιτον

But when you disappeared, and men had sought
you out
but could not bring you back to your mother,
then right away one of your envious neighbors said in
secret
that you were cut limb from limb
when the water had come to a peak boil,
and that, at the tables set for feasts, for the final course,
they divided up and ate your flesh.

But for me, there is no way
to call any of the blessed gods a glutton. I stand back.
Loss falls thick and fast on gossipers.
And anyhow if the watchers from Olympus ever
honored
any mortal man, it was Tantalus.
But he could not digest
his great wealth—insatiably, defiantly, he grasped
at the ruin that the father hung over him: such heft.
Always eager to cast
it off his head, he wanders apart, far from all festivities.

He has this hapless life, thick with pain,
with a fourth labor added to three more, since he stole
from the immortals to give
to his friends
the nectar and ambrosia
by which the gods had made him

θῆκαν. εἰ δὲ θεὸν ἀνήρ τις
  ἔλπεταί τι λαθέμεν ἔρδων, ἁμαρτάνει.
τοὔνεκα προῆκαν υἱὸν ἀθάνατοί οἱ πάλιν
μετὰ τὸ ταχύποτμον αὖτις ἀνέρων ἔθνος.
πρὸς εὐάνθεμον δ' ὅτε φυὰν
λάχναι νιν μέλαν γένειον ἔρεφον,
ἑτοῖμον ἀνεφρόντισεν γάμον

Πισάτα παρὰ πατρὸς εὔδοξον Ἱπποδάμειαν
σχεθέμεν. ἐγγὺς ἐλθὼν πολιᾶς ἁλὸς οἶος ἐν ὄρφνᾳ
ἄπυεν βαρύκτυπον
Εὐτρίαιναν· ὁ δ' αὐτῷ
πὰρ ποδὶ σχεδὸν φάνη.
τῷ μὲν εἶπε· Φίλια δῶρα
  Κυπρίας ἄγ' εἴ τι, Ποσείδαον, ἐς χάριν
τέλλεται, πέδασον ἔγχος Οἰνομάου χάλκεον,
ἐμὲ δ' ἐπὶ ταχυτάτων πόρευσον ἁρμάτων
ἐς Ἆλιν, κράτει δὲ πέλασον.
ἐπεὶ τρεῖς τε καὶ δέκ' ἄνδρας ὀλέσαις
μναστῆρας ἀναβάλλεται γάμον

undying. (If any man expects
to evade the notice of a god in his actions, he is mistaken.)
On account of all of this, the immortals sent back again
his son Pelops to be among the short-lived tribe of men.
And when, in the bloom of youth,
soft hair gave a dark shadow to his chin,
he turned his mind readily to marriage,

to win the renowned Hippodameia
from her Pisan father. Coming near to the gray sea, all alone in the darkness,
he called upon the deep-thundering
sea-god with the great trident. And the god appeared,
close at hand, just by his foot.
And Pelops said to him, "Come, Poseidon, if ever at all
the lovely gifts of Cypris were realized in pleasure between us,
bind fast the bronze sword of Oinomaus, father of this girl,
and convey me on the swiftest of chariots
to Elis, and bring me to power.
For he has already killed thirteen men,
her suitors, to put off the marriage

θυγατρός. ὁ μέγας δὲ κίνδυνος ἄναλκιν οὐ φῶτα
λαμβάνει.
θανεῖν δ’ οἷσιν ἀνάγκα, τά κέ τις ἀνώνυμον
γῆρας ἐν σκότῳ καθήμενος ἕψοι μάταν,
ἁπάντων καλῶν ἄμμορος; ἀλλ’ ἐμοὶ μὲν οὗτος ἄεθλος
ὑποκείσεται· τὺ δὲ πρᾶξιν φίλαν δίδοι.
ὧς ἔννεπεν· οὐδ’ ἀκράντοις ἐφάψατο
ἔπεσι. τὸν μὲν ἀγάλλων θεός
ἔδωκεν δίφρον τε χρύσεον πτεροῖσίν τ’ ἀκάμαντας
ἵππους.

of his daughter. Great risk does not take hold of a
cowardly man.
For those of us destined to die, why should we sit in
the shadows
seething over a nameless old age in vain,
losing our share of all good things? For me,
this will be the contest. Grant me this cherished feat."
So he spoke. Nor did he reach for fruitless
words. The god, exalting him,
gave him a golden chariot and tireless horses with wings.

1.39–101

ἐγὼν δ' ἀείδω
Ἀγιδῶς τὸ φῶς· ὁρῶ
ϝ' ὥτ' ἅλιον, ὅνπερ ἇμιν
Ἀγιδὼ μαρτύρεται
φαίνην· ἐμὲ δ' οὔτ' ἐπαινῆν
οὔτε μωμήσθαι νιν ἁ κλεννὰ χοραγὸς
οὐδ' ἁμῶς ἐῆι· δοκεῖ γὰρ ἤμεν αὔτα
ἐκπρεπὴς τὼς ὥπερ αἴτις
ἐν βοτοῖς στάσειεν ἵππον
παγὸν ἀεθλοφόρον καναχάποδα
τῶν ὑποπετριδίων ὀνείρων·

3 I'M COMING OUT: GIRL / FRIENDS

From the mysterious world of archaic Sparta, we receive bits of poetry on homoerotic rites of passage among young women, which are sometimes interpreted as training grounds for their later, heteronormative sexual lives. In any case, Alcman's choral songs, performed by groups of maidens, allow these young women to express their admiration and desire for one another.

Alcman

I myself sing
the light of Agido.[1] I see
her as the sun, which Agido
summons us to witness
as it shines. But our renowned chorus-leader
forbids me to either praise
or find fault with her. For she seems
to stand out, just as if someone
had placed a horse among cattle,
a strong prize-winner with loudly tramping feet,
one from dreams under the shadows of stones.

ἦ οὐχ ὁρῆις; ὁ μὲν κέλης
Ἐνετικός· ἁ δὲ χαίτα
τᾶς ἐμᾶς ἀνεψιᾶς
Ἁγησιχόρας ἐπανθεῖ
χρυσὸς [ὣ]ς ἀκήρατος·
τό τ’ ἀργύριον πρόσωπον,
διαφάδαν τί τοι λέγω;
Ἁγησιχόρα μὲν αὕτα·
ἁ δὲ δευτέρα πεδ’ Ἀγιδὼ τὸ ϝεῖδος
ἵππος Ἰβηνῶι Κολαξαῖος δραμήται·
ταὶ Πεληάδες γὰρ ἆμιν
ὀρθρίαι φᾶρος φεροίσαις
νύκτα δι’ ἀμβροσίαν ἅτε σήριον
ἄστρον ἀυηρομέναι μάχονται·

οὔτε γάρ τι πορφύρας
τόσσος κόρος ὥστ’ ἀμύναι,
οὔτε ποικίλος δράκων
παγχρύσιος, οὐδὲ μίτρα
Λυδία, νεανίδων
ἰανογ[λ]εφάρων ἄγαλμα,
οὐδὲ ταὶ Ναννῶς κόμαι,
ἀλλ’ οὐ[δ’] Ἀρέτα σιειδής,
οὐδὲ Σύλακίς τε καὶ Κλεησισήρα,
οὐδ’ ἐς Αἰνησιμβρ[ό]τας ἐνθοῖσα φασεῖς·
Ἀσταφίς [τ]έ μοι γένοιτο

I'M COMING OUT

Do you not see her? The racehorse
is Venetic. And the hair
of my cousin
Hagesichora blossoms
like pure gold.
And her silvery face,
why should I speak of it
—isn't it clear to you?
This is Hagesichora.
And the second in beauty after Agido
will run as a Colaxaean horse with an Ibenian steed.
For the Pleiades do battle with us,
as we bring a plough to dawn,
just as Sirius, the dog-star, rises up
through the ambrosial night.

And no surfeit of purple wealth
can protect us at all,
nor can an inlaid serpentine bangle
made all of gold, nor a headband
from Lydia, the delight
of violet-eyed maidens,
nor the hair of Nanno,
and not even Areta, divine in beauty,
nor Sylakis nor Cleasisara, and nor will you go
to the house of Ainesimbrota and say,
let Astaphis be mine

καὶ ποτιγλέποι Φίλυλλα
Δαμαρ[έ]τα τ' ἐρατά τε Fιανθεμίς·
ἀλλ' Ἁγησιχόρα με τείρει.

οὐ γὰρ ἁ κ[α]λλίσφυρος
Ἁγησιχ[ό]ρ[α] πάρ' αὐτεῖ,
Ἀγιδοῖ....αρμένει
θωστήρ[ιά τ'] ἅμ' ἐπαινεῖ.
ἀλλὰ τᾶν [..]...σιοὶ
δέξασθε· [σι]ῶν γὰρ ἄνα
καὶ τέλος· [χο]ροστάτις,
ϝείποιμί δ', [ἐ]γὼν μὲν αὐτὰ
παρσένος μάταν ἀπὸ θράνω λέλακα
γλαύξ· ἐγὼ[ν] δὲ τᾶι μὲν Ἀώτι μάλιστα
ϝανδάνην ἐρῶ· πόνων γὰρ
ἇμιν ἰάτωρ ἔγεντο·
ἐξ Ἁγησιχόρ[ας] δὲ νεάνιδες
ἰρ]ήνας ἐρατ[ᾶ]ς ἐπέβαν·

τῶ]ι τε γὰρ σηραφόρωι
..]τῶς εδ...........
τ[ῶι] κυβερνάται δὲ χρὴ
κ[ὴ]ν νᾶϊ μάλιστ' ἀκούην·
ἁ δὲ τᾶν Σηρην[ί]δων
ἀοιδοτέρα μ[ὲν οὐχί,
σιαὶ γάρ, ἀντ[ὶ δ' ἕνδεκα
παίδων δεκ[ὰς ἅδ' ἀείδ]ει·

and may Philylla look my way
and Damareta and lovely Viathemis.
But Hagesichora wears me down.

For isn't Hagesichora
with the beautiful ankles standing right here?
She remains by Agido
and praises our festival.
But, gods, may you accept
our efforts. For the end and outcome
belong to the gods. Choral leader,
if I may say so, I myself am
just a girl who screeches
in vain from the rafters,
an owl. But I want most of all
to please Aotis. For she was the healer
of our suffering.
And because of Hagesichora, we maidens
walked the way of lovely peace.

For like to a trace horse,
or a helmsman in a ship, it is necessary
most of all to listen.
Though it is not better at singing
than the Sirens—for they are gods—
this chorus of ten sings
in place of a chorus of eleven.

φθέγγεται δ' [ἄρ'] ὤ[τ' ἐπὶ] Ξάνθω ῥοαῖσι
κύκνος· ἁ δ' ἐπιμέρωι ξανθᾶι κομίσκαι

3

Μῶσαι 'Ολ]υμπιάδες περί με φρένας
ἱμέρωι νέα]ς ἀοιδᾶς
πίμπλατ' ἰθύ]ω δ' ἀκούσαι
παρσενηί]ας ὀπός
πρὸς αἰ]θέρα καλὸν ὑμνιοισᾶν μέλος
]. οι
ὕπνον ἀ]πὸ γλεφάρων σκεδ[α]σεῖ γλυκύν
]ς δέ μ' ἄγει πεδ' ἀγῶν' ἴμεν
ἇχι μά]λιστα κόμ[αν ξ]ανθὰν τινάξω·
[ ].σχ [ἁπ]αλοὶ πόδες

. . . . .

λυσιμελεῖ τε πόσωι, τακερώτερα
δ' ὕπνω καὶ σανάτω ποτιδέρκεται·
οὐδέ τι μαψιδίως γλυκ..ήνα·

Ἀ[σ]τυμέλοισα δέ μ' οὐδὲν ἀμείβεται
ἀλλὰ τὸ]ν πυλεῶν' ἔχοισα
[ὥ] τις αἰγλά[ε]ντος ἀστήρ
ὠρανῶ διαιπετής
ἢ χρύσιον ἔρνος ἢ ἁπαλὸ[ν ψίλ]ον

I'M COMING OUT

It calls out by the waters of the river Xanthus
like a swan. And she with the lovely golden hair . . .

. . . . .

Olympian Muses, you have filled my mind[2]
with longing for a new song
and I desire to hear
the maidenly voice
of girls singing a song to heaven,
that will scatter sweet sleep
from my eyes and lead me
to go to the gathering
where I will shake my golden hair.
And tender feet . . .

. . . . .

With longing that loosens limbs, more meltingly
than sleep or death, she looks at me.
Not at all in vain is her sweetness.

Astymeloisa does not answer me at all,
but instead holding the garland,
like a gleaming meteor
flying through heaven
or like a branch of gold or a tender stripling

[.῀.]ν
[ ]. διέβα ταναοῖς πο[σί·]
[—κ]ομος νοτία Κινύρα χ[άρ]ις
[ἐπὶ π]αρσενικᾶν χαίταισιν ἴσδει·
[Ἀ]στυμέλοισα κατὰ στρατόν
[ ] μέλημα δάμωι
[ ]μ̣αν ἑλοῖσα
[ ]λέγω·
[ ]εναβαλ' α[ἰ] γὰρ ἄργυριν
[ ].[.]ία
[ ]α ἴδοιμ' αἴ πως με̣..ο̣ν φιλοι
ἄσ]σ̣ο̣ν [ἰο]ῖ̣σ' ἀπαλᾶς χηρὸς λάβοι,
αἶψά κ' [ἐγὼν ἰ]κ̣έτις κήνας γενοίμαν·
νῦν δ' [ ]δα παίδα βα[.]ύφρονα
παιδι. [ ]μ' ἔχοισαν
[ ].·ε̣ [ ].ν ἀ παίς
[ ] χάριν·

I'M COMING OUT

. . .
. . . she passed on slender feet.
The moist grace of Cinyras rests
upon her maidenly flowing hair.
Astymeloisa moves through the host,
beloved to the people, taking
            I say . . .
for if only a silver vessel
. . .

I would see somehow that she might love me.
If, coming nearer, she were to take my tender hand,
immediately I would become her suppliant.
But now a girl . . . having me, a deep-minded girl,
to a girl . . . grace . . .

4 JUST LIKE A WOMAN: THE FEMALE GAZE

Sappho, of the seventh to sixth centuries BCE, is critical to our modern conceptions of same-sex female eroticism, so much so that the word "lesbian" derives from her origin, the island of Lesbos, and the term "Sapphic love" refers to eroticism between women. Here we see how Sappho presents the piercing female gaze and constructs a supple flow of desire between lover and beloved, with the lover usually represented as "Sappho" herself, and a female beloved who is either unnamed (1, 31, 94) or given an otherwise unattested name, like Anactoria (16) and Atthis (96 and 131). This section ends with a short poem by Anacreon, a sixth-century Ionic poet, whom we meet again in chapter 6. This poem offers the triangulated view of a woman's desire for another woman from a male perspective that is portrayed as excluded from the game of eros.

1

πο]ικιλόθρο[ν' ἀθανάτ' Ἀφρόδιτα,
παῖ] Δ[ί]ος δολ[όπλοκε, λίσσομαί σε,
μή μ'] ἄσαισι [μηδ' ὀνίαισι δάμνα,
πότν]ια, θῦ[μον,

ἀλλ]ὰ τυίδ' ἔλ[θ', αἴ ποτα κἀτέρωτα
τὰ]ς ἔμας αὔ[δας ἀίοισα πήλοι
ἔκ]λυες, πάτρο[ς δὲ δόμον λίποισα
χ]ρύσιον ἦλθ[ες

ἄρ]μ' ὐπασδε[ύξαισα· κάλοι δέ σ' ἆγον
ὤ]κεες στροῦ[θοι περὶ γᾶς μελαίνας
πύ]κνα δίν[νεντες πτέρ' ἀπ' ὠράνωἴθε-
ρο]ς διὰ μέσσω·

αἶ]ψα δ' ἐξίκο[ντο· σὺ δ', ὦ μάκαιρα,
μειδιαί[σαισ' ἀθανάτωι προσώπωι
ἤ]ρε' ὄττ[ι δηὖτε πέπονθα κὤττι
δη]ὖτε κ[άλ]η[μμι

κ]ὤττι [μοι μάλιστα θέλω γένεσθαι
μ]αινόλαι [θύμωι· τίνα δηὖτε πείθω
.].σάγην [ἐς σὰν φιλότατα; τίς σ', ὦ
Ψά]πφ', [ἀδικήει;

Sappho

On the throne of many hues, immortal Aphrodite,
child of Zeus, weaving wiles: I beg you,
do not break my spirit, o queen,
with pain or sorrow

but come—if ever before from far away
you heard my voice and listened,
and leaving your father's
golden home you came,

your chariot yoked with lovely sparrows
drawing you quickly over the dark earth
in a whirling cloud of wings, down
from the sky through midair,

and suddenly they were here. O blessed one, with a smile
on your deathless face, you asked
what again have I suffered
and why again do I call

and what in my wild heart do I most wish
would happen: "Once again who must I
persuade to turn back to your love?
Sappho, who wrongs you?

κα]ὶ γ[ὰρ αἰ φεύγει, ταχέως διώξει,
⟨αἰ δὲ δῶρα μὴ δέκετ’, ἀλλὰ δώσει,⟨
⟨αἰ δὲ μὴ φίλει, ταχέως φιλήσει⟨
⟨ κωὐκ ἐθέλοισα.⟨

⟨ἔλθε μοι καὶ νῦν, χαλέπαν δὲ λῦσον⟨
⟨ἐκ μερίμναν, ὄσσα δέ μοι τέλεσσαι⟨
⟨θῦμος ἰμέρρει, τέλεσον, σὺ δ’ αὔτα⟨
⟨σύμμαχος ἔσσο.⟨

16

ο]ἰ μὲν ἰππήων στρότον οἰ δὲ πέσδων
οἰ δὲ νάων φαῖσ’ ἐπ[ὶ] γᾶν μέλαι[ν]αν
ἔ]μμεναι κάλλιστον, ἔγω δὲ κῆν’ ὄτ-
τω τις ἔραται·

πά]γχυ δ’ εὔμαρες σύνετον πόησαι
π]άντι τ[ο]ῦ̣τ’, ἀ γὰρ πόλυ περσκέ̣θ̣ο̣ι̣σ̣α
κ̣άλ̣λο̣ς̣ [ἀνθ]ρ̣ώπων ’Ελένα [τὸ]ν ἄνδρα
τ̣ὸν̣ [ ].στον

κ̣αλλ[ίποι]σ̣’ ἔβα ’ς Τροΐαν πλέοι̣[σα
κωὐδ[ὲ πα]ῖδος οὐδὲ φίλων το[κ]ήων
π̣ά[μπαν] ἐμνάσθη, ἀλλὰ παράγ̣α̣γ’ α̣ὔταν
]σαν

If now she flees, soon she will chase.
If now she does not accept gifts, rather she will give.
If she does not love, soon she will love
even against her will."

Come to me now—release me from these hard
troubles, and everything my heart longs
to have fulfilled, fulfill, and you yourself
be my ally.

. . . . .

Some say a host of horsemen, others
say a host of foot soldiers, and still others say one
    of ships
is the finest thing on the dark earth.
I say it is whatever one desires.

Everyone can understand this. Consider
how Helen, far surpassing the beauty
of mortals, left behind
the best man of all

to sail away to Troy. She remembered
neither daughter nor dear parents,
as [Aphrodite] led her away

]αμπτον γὰρ [
]. . . κούφως τ [ ]οη.[.]ν̣
..]μ̣ε̣ νῦν Ἀνακτορί[ας ὀ]ν̣έ̣μναι-
σ’ οὐ] παρεοίσας,

τᾶ]ς ‹κ‹ε βολλοίμαν ἔρατόν τε βᾶμα
κἀμάρυχμα λάμπρον ἴδην προσώπω
ἢ τὰ Λύδων ἄρματα †κανοπλοισι
μ]άχεντας.

].μεν οὐ δύνατον γένεσθαι
].ν ἀνθρωπ[..(.) π]εδέχην δ’ ἄρασθαι

358

σφαίρηι δηὖτέ με πορφυρῆι
βάλλων χρυσοκόμης Ἔρως
νήνι ποικιλοσαμβάλωι
συμπαίζειν προκαλεῖται·

ἡ δ’, ἐστὶν γὰρ ἀπ’ εὐκτίτου
Λέσβου, τὴν μὲν ἐμὴν κόμην,
λευκὴ γάρ, καταμέμφεται,
πρὸς δ’ ἄλλην τινὰ χάσκει.

. . . [un]bending . . . mind
. . . lightly . . . thinks.
. . . reminding me now
of Anactoria gone.

I would rather see her lovely step
and the radiant sparkle of her face
than all the war chariots in Lydia
and soldiers battling in arms.

Impossible . . . to happen
. . . human, but to pray for a share . . .

Anacreon

Tossing a purple ball at me again,
golden-haired Eros invites me
to come hither and play
   with the girl in embroidered sandals.

But since she is from well built
Lesbos, she grimaces at my hair,
for it is white, and gapes
   instead at a certain other girl.

31

φαίνεταί μοι κῆνος ἴσος θέοισιν
ἔμμεν' ὤνηρ, ὄττις ἐνάντιός τοι
ἰσδάνει καὶ πλάσιον ἆδυ φωνεί-
σας ὐπακούει

καὶ γελαίσας ἰμέροεν, τό μ' ἦ μὰν
καρδίαν ἐν στήθεσιν ἐπτόαισεν,
ὠς γὰρ ἔς σ' ἴδω βρόχε' ὤς με φώναι-
σ' οὐδ' ἒν ἔτ' εἴκει,

ἀλλ' ἄκαν μὲν γλῶσσα †ἔαγε λέπτον
δ' αὔτικα χρῶι πῦρ ὐπαδεδρόμηκεν,
ὀππάτεσσι δ' οὐδ' ἒν ὄρημμ', ἐπιρρόμ-
βεισι δ' ἄκουαι,

5 CRASH INTO ME: THE SCORCH OF LUST

Here we see Sappho explore the experience and depth of erotic experience, showing how it burns, tortures, and unravels the self, while she ruminates on longing and memories of sexual fulfillment.

Sappho

To me that man seems equal
to the gods, whoever sits beside you
closely and listens to you
sweetly speaking

and laughing temptingly. My heart
flutters in my breast whenever
I quickly glance at you—
I can say nothing,

for my tongue is broken. A delicate fire
runs under my skin, my eyes
see nothing, my ears
roar,

†έκαδε μ' ἴδρως ψῦχρος κακχέεται† τρόμος δὲ
παῖσαν ἄγρει, χλωροτέρα δὲ ποίας
ἔμμι, τεθνάκην δ' ὀλίγω 'πιδεύης
φαίνομ' ἔμ' αὔται·

ἀλλὰ πὰν τόλματον ἐπεὶ †καὶ πένητα†

94

τεθνάκην δ' ἀδόλως θέλω·
ἄ με ψισδομένα κατελίμπανεν

πόλλα καὶ τόδ' ἔειπ.[
ὤιμ' ὡς δεῖνα πεπ[όνθ]αμεν,
Ψάπφ', ἦ μάν σ' ἀέκοισ' ἀπυλιμπάνω.

τὰν δ' ἔγω τάδ' ἀμειβόμαν·
χαίροισ' ἔρχεο κἄμεθεν
μέμναισ', οἶσθα γὰρ ὤς σε πεδήπομεν·

αἰ δὲ μή, ἀλλά σ' ἔγω θέλω
ὄμναισαι [. . . (.)].[..(.)]..αι
.. [ ] καὶ κάλ' ἐπάσχομεν·

πὸ̣[λλοις γὰρ στεφάν]οις ἴων
βρ[όδων κρο]κ̣ίων τ' ὔμοι
κα.. [ ] πὰρ ἔμοι περεθήκαο,

cold sweat pours down me, and trembling
seizes me all over, and I am greener than grass.
I need but little just to die,
it seems to me.

Yet all must be endured, since even poverty . . .

▪ ▪ ▪ ▪ ▪

I simply wish to die.[1]
Weeping she left me

and told me this too:
We've suffered terribly, Sappho.
I leave you against my will.

I answered: Go happily
and remember me—
you know how I cared for you.

If not, let me remind you
. . .
. . . and the lovely times we shared

Many crowns of violets,
roses, and crocuses together
. . . you put on by my side

καὶ πό̣[λλαις ὐπα]θύμιδας
πλέκ[ταις ἀμφ᾽ ἀ]πάλαι δέραι
ἀνθέων . [ ] πεποημμέναις

καὶ π. . . . . [ ]. μύρωι
βρενθείωι̣. [ ]ρυ̣[..]ν
ἐξαλείψαο κα̣[ὶ βασ]ι̣ληΐωι

καὶ στρώμν[αν ἐ]πὶ μολθάκαν
ἀπάλαν πα. [ ] . . . ων
ἐξίης πόθο̣ [ ].νίδων

κωὔτε τισ [ ]..τι
ἶρον οὐδυ [ ]
ἔπλετ᾽ ὄππ̣[οθεν ἄμ]μες ἀπέσκομεν,

οὐκ ἄλσος . [ ].ρος
[ ]ψοφος

96

[ ]σαρδ. [. .]
[πόλ]λακι τυίδε̣ [ν]ῶν ἔχοισα

ὠσπ . [. . .] . ώομεν, . [. . .] . . χ[. .]
σε θέαι σ᾽ ἰκέλαν ἀρι-
γνώται, σᾶι δὲ μάλιστ᾽ ἔχαιρε μόλπαι̣·

and many scented wreaths
woven from blossoms
around your delicate throat.

And . . . with pure, sweet oil
[for a queen] . . .
you anointed . . .

and on soft beds
. . . delicate . . .
you quenched your desire.

Not any . . .
no holy site . . .
we left uncovered,

no grove . . . dance
. . . sound.

▪ ▪ ▪ ▪ ▪

Often turning her mind that way

she [thought of] you
and saw you as like to a goddess,
and felt delight most of all in your song.

νῦν δὲ Λύδαισιν ἐμπρέπεται γυναί-
κεσσιν ὤς ποτ᾽ ἀελίω
δύντος ἀ βροδοδάκτυλος σελάννα

πάντα περρέχοισ᾽ ἄστρα· φάος δ᾽ ἐπί-
σχει θάλασσαν ἐπ᾽ ἀλμύραν
ἴσως καὶ πολυανθέμοις ἀρούραις·

ἀ δ᾽ ἐέρσα κάλα κέχυται τεθά-
λαισι δὲ βρόδα κἄπαλ᾽ ἄν-
θρυσκα καὶ μελίλωτος ἀνθεμώδης·

πόλλα δὲ ζαφοίταισ᾽ ἀγάνας ἐπι-
μνάσθεισ᾽ Ἄτθιδος ἰμέρωι
λέπταν ποι φρένα κ[ᾶ]ρ̣[ι σᾶι] βόρηται·

κῆθι δ᾽ ἔλθην ἀμμ . [. .] . . ισα τọδ᾽ οὐ
νῶντ᾽ ἀ [. .] υστονυμ̣ [. . .] πόλυς
γαρύει̣ [. . .]αλον̣[. . . . . .] . ọ μέσσον·

130

Ἔρος δηὖτέ μ᾽ ὀ λυσιμέλης δόνει,
γλυκύπικρον ἀμάχανον ὄρπετον

131

Ἄτθι, σοὶ δ᾽ ἔμεθεν μὲν ἀπήχθετο
φροντίσδην, ἐπὶ δ᾽ Ἀνδομέδαν πότη̣

CRASH INTO ME

But now she stands out among
the Lydian women just as when the sun
sets and the rosy-fingered moon

outshines all the stars, and light
spreads over the salty sea
and on the flowery fields alike.

And the lovely dew pours down,
and roses bloom, along with mild herbs
and flowering clover.

Often as she wanders, she remembers
gentle Atthis with desire and, I know,
her delicate heart is devoured by your death.

To go there for me . . . where
my mind . . . much
sings . . . between . . .

. . . . .

Eros, limb-loosening, whirls me about again,
that bittersweet, implacable creature.

. . . . .

Atthis, since the thought of me has become repulsive
to you, you are flying to Andromeda.

357

ὦναξ, ὧι δαμάλης Ἔρως
καὶ Νύμφαι κυανώπιδες
πορφυρῆ τ' Ἀφροδίτη
συμπαίζουσιν, ἐπιστρέφεαι
δ' ὑψηλὰς ὀρέων κορυφάς·
γουνοῦμαί σε, σὺ δ' εὐμενὴς
ἔλθ' ἡμίν, κεχαρισμένης
δ' εὐχωλῆς ἐπακούειν·

6 BOY'S GONE CRAZY: THE DEPTHS OF DESIRE

Anacreon, of the sixth century BCE, is the earliest lyric poet on record to express the pleasures and pains of queer, male lust, though the archaic poets Alcaeus and Ibycus are known in antiquity to have expressed these passions too in poems that are now lost. Such passion is by turns joyous and heated, pleasing and torturous. In a later epigram about Anacreon, the third-century BCE poet Theocritus reminds the reader that Anacreon must be known by his erotic delight. Pindar also expounds upon the pleasures of adoring a young man, as do the banqueters in Xenophon's Symposium.

Anacreon

Lord, with whom Eros
and the dark-eyed Nymphs
and glowing Aphrodite
play, you hang around
the highest mountain peaks.
I beg you, be kind
and come to me, and hear
my prayer as pleasing:

Κλεοβούλωι δ' ἀγαθὸς γένεο
σύμβουλος, τὸν ἐμόν γ' ἔρω-
τ', ὦ Δεόνυσε, δέχεσθαι.

359

Κλεοβούλου μὲν ἔγωγ' ἐρέω,
Κλεοβούλωι δ' ἐπιμαίνομαι,
Κλεόβουλον δὲ διοσκέω.

360

ὦ παῖ παρθένιον βλέπων
δίζημαί σε, σὺ δ' οὐ κλύεις,
οὐκ εἰδὼς ὅτι τῆς ἐμῆς
ψυχῆς ἡνιοχεύεις.

378

ἀναπέτομαι δὴ πρὸς Ὄλυμπον πτερύγεσσι κούφηις
διὰ τὸν Ἔρωτ'· οὐ γὰρ ἐμοὶ <–⏑> θέλει συνηβᾶν.

398

ἀστραγάλαι δ' Ἔρωτός εἰσιν
μανίαι τε καὶ κυδοιμοί

be a good guide
to Cleoboulus, o Dionysus,
tell him to consent
to my desire.

. . . . . .

Cleoboulus is the one I love,[1]
Cleoboulus who drives me mad,
Cleoboulus whom I pursue.

. . . . . .

O maidenly boy, I look
at you and look for you, but you do not heed,
no, you do not know that you hold
the reins of my soul.

. . . . . .

I fly up to Olympus on lightweight wings,
thanks to Eros. For my love does not wish to pass his
youth with me.

. . . . . .

The dice of Eros
are madness and tumult.

407

ἀλλὰ πρόπινε
ῥαδινοὺς ὦ φίλε μηρούς

413

μεγάλωι δηὖτέ μ' Ἔρως ἔκοψεν ὥστε χαλκεὺς
πελέκει, χειμερίηι δ' ἔλουσεν ἐν χαράδρηι.

Epigram 17

Θᾶσαι τὸν ἀνδριάντα τοῦτον, ὦ ξένε,
σπουδᾷ, καὶ λέγ' ἐπὴν ἐς οἶκον ἔνθῃς·
Ἀνακρέοντος εἰκόν' εἶδον ἐν Τέῳ
τῶν πρόσθ' εἴ τι περισσὸν ᾠδοποιῶν.
προσθεὶς δὲ χὤτι τοῖς νέοισιν ἅδετο,
ἐρεῖς ἀτρεκέως ὅλον τὸν ἄνδρα.

Fr. 108

Χρῆν μὲν κατὰ καιρὸν ἐρώτων δρέπεσθαι,
θυμέ, σὺν ἁλικίᾳ·
τὰς δὲ Θεοξένου ἀκτῖνας πρὸς ὄσσων
μαρμαρυζοίσας δρακείς
ὃς μὴ πόθῳ κυμαίνεται, ἐξ ἀδάμαντος
ἢ σιδάρου κεχάλκευται μέλαιναν καρδίαν

ψυχρᾷ φλογί, πρὸς δ' Ἀφροδίτας ἀτιμα-
σθεὶς ἑλικογλεφάρου

. . . . .

But pledge,
my love, your tender thighs.

. . . . .

Once again, like a blacksmith, Eros slams me
with a great axe, and plunges me in a wintry torrent.

Theocritus

Gaze upon this statue, stranger,
  carefully, and when you come home say,
"I saw an image of Anacreon in Teos,
  outstanding among the poets of old."
And if you add that he delighted in young men,
  you will explain the whole man exactly.

Pindar, "For Theoxenus of Tenedos"

It is right to gather one's loves in due season,
  my heart, in the prime of life.
But the rays from the eyes of Theoxenus—
whoever has seen them flashing
and does not surge with desire has a black heart
forged from adamantine or iron

in a cool fire, and is dishonored
  by spiral-eyed Aphrodite,

ἢ περὶ χρήμασι μοχθίζει βιαίως
ἢ γυναικείῳ θράσει
ψυχρὰν† φορεῖται πᾶσαν ὁδὸν θεραπεύων.
ἀλλ' ἐγὼ τᾶς ἕκατι κηρὸς ὣς δαχθεὶς ἕλᾳ

ἱρᾶν μελισσᾶν τάκομαι, εὖτ' ἂν ἴδω
παίδων νεόγυιον ἐς ἥβαν· ἐν δ' ἄρα καὶ Τενέδῳ
Πειθώ τ' ἔναιεν καὶ Χάρις
υἱὸν Ἁγησίλα.

1.1–10

Ἀλλ' ἐμοὶ δοκεῖ τῶν καλῶν κἀγαθῶν ἀνδρῶν ἔργα οὐ μόνον τὰ μετὰ σπουδῆς πραττόμενα ἀξιομνημόνευτα εἶναι, ἀλλὰ καὶ τὰ ἐν ταῖς παιδιαῖς. οἷς δὲ παραγενόμενος ταῦτα γιγνώσκω δηλῶσαι βούλομαι.

or labors violently for money,
or for womanly boldness
is borne on a road that is all cold.
But I on account of the goddess, like wax bitten

by the sun of holy honey-bees, melt whenever I see
the fresh-limbed youth of boys. And indeed in Tenedos
Persuasion and Grace dwell
in the son of Hegisilas.

Xenophon, *Symposium*

Xenophon composed his Symposium *in the late 360s BCE. Unlike Plato's* Symposium, *written about twenty years earlier, Xenophon portrays a lighthearted gathering, in which discussion touches on a range of topics, including the desire of guests at the party for one another: Callias for Autolycus, and Critoboulus for Cleinias. The opening part of the* Symposium *is given here, which describes how the gathering came together. Then comes Critoboulus's speech, from later in the text, on the value of his own beauty, followed by some teasing about the dangers of desire.*

Now to me it seems that when it comes to noble men, it is not only their serious deeds that are worth telling, but also the things they do for fun. I want to reveal how I know this.

ἦν μὲν γὰρ Παναθηναίων τῶν μεγάλων ἱπποδρομία, Καλλίας δὲ ὁ Ἱππονίκου ἐρῶν ἐτύγχανεν Αὐτολύκου παιδὸς ὄντος, καὶ νενικηκότα αὐτὸν παγκράτιον ἧκεν ἄγων ἐπὶ τὴν θέαν. ὡς δὲ ἡ ἱπποδρομία ἔληξεν, ἔχων τόν τε Αὐτόλυκον καὶ τὸν πατέρα αὐτοῦ ἀπῄει εἰς τὴν ἐν Πειραιεῖ οἰκίαν· συνείπετο δὲ αὐτῷ καὶ Νικήρατος. ἰδὼν δὲ ὁμοῦ ὄντας Σωκράτην τε καὶ Κριτόβουλον καὶ Ἑρμογένην καὶ Ἀντισθένην καὶ Χαρμίδην, τοῖς μὲν ἀμφ᾽ Αὐτόλυκον ἡγεῖσθαί τινα ἔταξεν, αὐτὸς δὲ προσῆλθε τοῖς ἀμφὶ Σωκράτην, καὶ εἶπεν· Εἰς καλόν γε ὑμῖν συντετύχηκα· ἑστιᾶν γὰρ μέλλω Αὐτόλυκον καὶ τὸν πατέρα αὐτοῦ. οἶμαι οὖν πολὺ ἂν τὴν κατασκευήν μοι λαμπροτέραν φανῆναι εἰ ἀνδράσιν ἐκκεκαθαρμένοις τὰς ψυχὰς ὥσπερ ὑμῖν ὁ ἀνδρὼν κεκοσμημένος εἴη μᾶλλον ἢ εἰ στρατηγοῖς καὶ ἱππάρχοις καὶ σπουδαρχίαις.

καὶ ὁ Σωκράτης εἶπεν· Ἀεὶ σὺ ἐπισκώπτεις ἡμᾶς καταφρονῶν, ὅτι σὺ μὲν Πρωταγόρᾳ τε πολὺ ἀργύριον δέδωκας ἐπὶ σοφίᾳ καὶ Γοργίᾳ καὶ Προδίκῳ καὶ ἄλλοις πολλοῖς, ἡμᾶς δ᾽ ὁρᾷς αὐτουργούς τινας τῆς φιλοσοφίας ὄντας.

καὶ ὁ Καλλίας, Καὶ πρόσθεν μέν γε, ἔφη, ἀπεκρυπτόμην ὑμᾶς ἔχων πολλὰ καὶ σοφὰ λέγειν, νῦν δέ, ἐὰν παρ᾽ ἐμοὶ ἦτε, ἐπιδείξω ὑμῖν ἐμαυτὸν πάνυ πολλῆς σπουδῆς ἄξιον ὄντα.

οἱ οὖν ἀμφὶ τὸν Σωκράτην πρῶτον μέν, ὥσπερ εἰκὸς ἦν, ἐπαινοῦντες τὴν κλῆσιν οὐχ ὑπισχνοῦντο συνδειπνήσειν· ὡς

It was the time of the horse races of the Panathenaea.[2] Callias son of Hipponicus was then in love with Autolycus, who was still a young man. Having won the pankration,[3] he brought him along to the show. When the race was done, Callias took Autolycus and his father, and made his way to his house in the Peiraeus. Niceratos was with him too. But when he saw Socrates, Critoboulus, Hermogenes, Antisthenes, and Charmides all together, Callias bid one of his men to bring Autolycus and the others. He then approached the group around Socrates and said, "How lucky I am to run into you! For I am about to have a dinner for Autolycus and his father. Think how much more brilliant my surroundings will appear in the presence of such men as you, whose souls are purified, than were it to be decorated merely by men who are generals or commanders of the cavalry or candidates for office."

And Socrates replied, "You are always poking fun at us, looking down at us as you do, since you have paid a lot of money to Protagoras for his wisdom, as well as to Gorgias and Prodicus, and many others, but you see us as mere simpletons at philosophy."

"Yes," answered Callias. "So far I have kept you in the dark regarding how long and wisely I can speak, but now if you come to my place, I will display for you how very worthy of serious pursuits am I."

At first, Socrates and his friends, as one would expect, expressed appreciation for the invitation but did not commit

δὲ πάνυ ἀχθόμενος φανερὸς ἦν, εἰ μὴ ἕψοιντο, συνηκολούθησαν. ἔπειτα δὲ αὐτῷ οἱ μὲν γυμνασάμενοι καὶ χρισάμενοι, οἱ δὲ καὶ λουσάμενοι παρῆλθον. Αὐτόλυκος μὲν οὖν παρὰ τὸν πατέρα ἐκαθέζετο, οἱ δ' ἄλλοι, ὥσπερ εἰκός, κατεκλίθησαν.

εὐθὺς μὲν οὖν ἐννοήσας τις τὰ γιγνόμενα ἡγήσατ' ἂν φύσει βασιλικόν τι κάλλος εἶναι, ἄλλως τε καὶ ἂν μετ' αἰδοῦς καὶ σωφροσύνης, καθάπερ Αὐτόλυκος τότε, κεκτῆταί τις αὐτό. πρῶτον μὲν γάρ, ὥσπερ ὅταν φέγγος τι ἐν νυκτὶ φανῇ, πάντων προσάγεται τὰ ὄμματα, οὕτω καὶ τότε τοῦ Αὐτολύκου τὸ κάλλος πάντων εἷλκε τὰς ὄψεις πρὸς αὐτόν· ἔπειτα τῶν ὁρώντων οὐδεὶς οὐκ ἔπασχέ τι τὴν ψυχὴν ὑπ' ἐκείνου. οἱ μέν γε σιωπηρότεροι ἐγίγνοντο, οἱ δὲ καὶ ἐσχηματίζοντό πως.

πάντες μὲν οὖν οἱ ἐκ θεῶν του κατεχόμενοι ἀξιοθέατοι δοκοῦσιν εἶναι· ἀλλ' οἱ μὲν ἐξ ἄλλων πρὸς τὸ γοργότεροί τε ὁρᾶσθαι καὶ φοβερώτερον φθέγγεσθαι καὶ σφοδρότεροι εἶναι φέρονται, οἱ δ' ὑπὸ τοῦ σώφρονος ἔρωτος ἔνθεοι τά τε ὄμματα φιλοφρονεστέρως ἔχουσι καὶ τὴν φωνὴν πρᾳοτέραν ποιοῦνται καὶ τὰ σχήματα εἰς τὸ ἐλευθεριώτερον ἄγουσιν. ἃ δὴ καὶ Καλλίας τότε διὰ τὸν ἔρωτα πράττων ἀξιοθέατος ἦν τοῖς τετελεσμένοις τούτῳ τῷ θεῷ.

4.10–29

ὁ δὲ Κριτόβουλος, Οὐκοῦν αὖ ἐγὼ λέξω, ἔφη, ἐξ ὧν ἐπὶ τῷ κάλλει μέγα φρονῶ.

Λέγε, ἔφασαν.

to dinner. But Callias was clearly so very pained that they would not come that they relented and went after all. Soon, his guests arrived, some from their exercise and anointing, and others after a bath. Autolycus sat down by his father, and the others as usual reclined.

Someone observing all of this would surmise that beauty is by nature a regal thing, and most of all when it is joined with modesty and temperance,[4] even as it was in Autolycus. For, first of all, just as light in the darkness of night shines out, and draws to it the gaze of all men, so then did the beauty of Autolycus draw the eyes of everyone to him. Indeed, there was no one of those who gazed at him who did not feel something stirring in his soul. Some of them fell silent, and others struck an alluring pose.

Indeed, anyone possessed by the gods seems worthy of our gaze, but those who are possessed by other gods are more terrifying to look upon or frightful in their tone, or more zealous, while those who are inspired by this temperate Eros have a more kindly look in their eyes and a more gentle voice, and hold themselves with a more casual grace. This is just what Callias was like then, acting in the power of Eros, and worthy of the gaze of those initiated in the rites of this god.

▪ ▪ ▪ ▪ ▪

"Well then," said Critoboulus. "Shall I tell you for what reasons I take great pride in my beauty?"

"Speak!" said the others.

Εἰ μὲν τοίνυν μὴ καλός εἰμι, ὡς οἴομαι, ὑμεῖς ἂν δικαίως ἀπάτης δίκην ὑπέχοιτε· οὐδενὸς γὰρ ὁρκίζοντος ἀεὶ ὀμνύοντες καλόν μέ φατε εἶναι. κἀγὼ μέντοι πιστεύω. καλοὺς γὰρ καὶ ἀγαθοὺς ὑμᾶς ἄνδρας νομίζω. εἰ δ' εἰμί τε τῷ ὄντι καλὸς καὶ ὑμεῖς τὰ αὐτὰ πρὸς ἐμὲ πάσχετε οἷάπερ ἐγὼ πρὸς τὸν ἐμοὶ δοκοῦντα καλὸν εἶναι, ὄμνυμι πάντας θεοὺς μὴ ἑλέσθαι ἂν τὴν βασιλέως ἀρχὴν ἀντὶ τοῦ καλὸς εἶναι. νῦν γὰρ ἐγὼ Κλεινίαν ἥδιον μὲν θεῶμαι ἢ τἆλλα πάντα τὰ ἐν ἀνθρώποις καλά· τυφλὸς δὲ τῶν ἄλλων ἁπάντων μᾶλλον δεξαίμην ἂν εἶναι ἢ Κλεινίου ἑνὸς ὄντος· ἄχθομαι δὲ καὶ νυκτὶ καὶ ὕπνῳ ὅτι ἐκεῖνον οὐχ ὁρῶ, ἡμέρᾳ δὲ καὶ ἡλίῳ τὴν μεγίστην χάριν οἶδα ὅτι μοι Κλεινίαν ἀναφαίνουσιν.

ἄξιόν γε μὴν ἡμῖν τοῖς καλοῖς καὶ ἐπὶ τοῖσδε μέγα φρονεῖν, ὅτι τὸν μὲν ἰσχυρὸν πονοῦντα δεῖ κτᾶσθαι τἀγαθὰ καὶ τὸν ἀνδρεῖον κινδυνεύοντα, τὸν δέ γε σοφὸν λέγοντα· ὁ δὲ καλὸς καὶ ἡσυχίαν ἔχων πάντ' ἂν διαπράξαιτο. ἐγὼ γοῦν καίπερ εἰδὼς ὅτι χρήματα ἡδὺ κτῆμα ἥδιον μὲν ἂν Κλεινίᾳ τὰ ὄντα διδοίην ἢ ἕτερα παρ' ἄλλου λαμβάνοιμι, ἥδιον δ' ἂν δουλεύοιμι ἢ ἐλεύθερος εἴην, εἴ μου Κλεινίας ἄρχειν ἐθέλοι. καὶ γὰρ πονοίην ἂν ῥᾷον ἐκείνῳ ἢ ἀναπαυοίμην, καὶ κινδυνεύοιμ' ἂν πρὸ ἐκείνου ἥδιον ἢ ἀκίνδυνος ζῴην.

ὥστε εἰ σύ, ὦ Καλλία, μέγα φρονεῖς ὅτι δικαιοτέρους δύνασαι ποιεῖν, ἐγὼ πρὸς πᾶσαν ἀρετὴν δικαιότερος σοῦ

"If, then, I am not as good-looking as I think, you would justly be held accountable for deceit. For, though no one makes you swear to it, you always vow nonetheless that I am handsome. And indeed I believe you, for I consider you to be noble men. And if I am truly handsome, and you feel toward me the same things that I feel toward someone who seems handsome to me, then I swear by all the gods that I would not choose the power of the king of Persia over being beautiful. For now I would be happier to gaze upon Cleinias than at any other beautiful thing among men. And I would rather be blind to all other things than be blind to Cleinias alone. I ache both at night and in sleep since I cannot see him, and in the day and sunlight I know the greatest joy when they display Cleinias to me.

"It is right for us good-looking people to be proud of this, since a strong man needs to work to get good things, and a brave man needs to take risks, and a wise man needs to talk. But a good-looking man can take it easy and get anything. Thus, though I know that money is a sweet thing to have, I would find it sweeter to give however much I have to Cleinias than to take more money for myself from another man. And I would find it sweeter to be enslaved than to be free, if Cleinias were willing to rule over me. For it would be easier to work for him than to rest, and to be in danger for his sake would be sweeter than living without risk.

"So if you, Callias, are proud that you can make people more just, I am more just than you in respect to every

εἰμι ἄγων ἀνθρώπους. διὰ γὰρ τὸ ἐμπνεῖν τι ἡμᾶς τοὺς καλοὺς τοῖς ἐρωτικοῖς ἐλευθεριωτέρους μὲν αὐτοὺς ποιοῦμεν εἰς χρήματα, φιλοπονωτέρους δὲ καὶ φιλοκαλωτέρους ἐν τοῖς κινδύνοις, καὶ μὴν αἰδημονεστέρους τε καὶ ἐγκρατεστέρους, οἵ γε καὶ ὧν δέονται μάλιστα ταῦτ᾽ αἰσχύνονται. μαίνονται δὲ καὶ οἱ μὴ τοὺς καλοὺς στρατηγοὺς αἱρούμενοι. ἐγὼ γοῦν μετὰ Κλεινίου κἂν διὰ πυρὸς ἰοίην· οἶδα δ᾽ ὅτι καὶ ὑμεῖς μετ᾽ ἐμοῦ. ὥστε μηκέτι ἀπόρει, ὦ Σώκρατες, εἴ τι τοὐμὸν κάλλος ἀνθρώπους ὠφελήσει.

ἀλλ᾽ οὐδὲ μέντοι ταύτῃ γε ἀτιμαστέον τὸ κάλλος ὡς ταχὺ παρακμάζον, ἐπεὶ ὥσπερ γε παῖς γίγνεται καλός, οὕτω καὶ μειράκιον καὶ ἀνὴρ καὶ πρεσβύτης. τεκμήριον δέ· θαλλοφόρους γὰρ τῇ Ἀθηνᾷ τοὺς καλοὺς γέροντας ἐκλέγονται, ὡς συμπαρομαρτοῦντος πάσῃ ἡλικίᾳ τοῦ κάλλους.

εἰ δὲ ἡδὺ τὸ παρ᾽ ἑκόντων διαπράττεσθαι ὧν τις δέοιτο, εὖ οἶδ᾽ ὅτι καὶ νυνὶ θᾶττον ἂν ἐγὼ καὶ σιωπῶν πείσαιμι τὸν παῖδα τόνδε καὶ τὴν παῖδα φιλῆσαί με ἢ σύ, ὦ Σώκρατες, εἰ καὶ πάνυ πολλὰ καὶ σοφὰ λέγοις.

Τί τοῦτο; ἔφη ὁ Σωκράτης· ὡς γὰρ καὶ ἐμοῦ καλλίων ὢν ταῦτα κομπάζεις.

Νὴ Δί᾽, ἔφη ὁ Κριτόβουλος, ἢ πάντων Σειληνῶν τῶν ἐν τοῖς σατυρικοῖς αἴσχιστος ἂν εἴην.

[ὁ δὲ Σωκράτης καὶ ἐτύγχανε προσεμφερὴς τούτοις ὤν.]

Ἄγε νυν, ἔφη ὁ Σωκράτης, ὅπως μεμνήσῃ διακριθῆναι περὶ τοῦ κάλλους, ἐπειδὰν οἱ προκείμενοι λόγοι περιέλθωσι.

virtue as a leader of men. For since we good-looking men have a rather inspirational effect on our lovers, we make them more free with their money, more willing to work, more willing to seek honor in danger, and even more modest and controlled, since they feel ashamed about that which they want most of all. Whoever does not choose handsome men to be generals is crazy. I at least would walk through fire with Cleinias, and I know that you would too. Therefore, Socrates, you should no longer be in doubt as to whether my beauty will benefit men.

"But, moreover, beauty should not be dishonored for this point either, that quickly its prime is passed, since even as a boy is beautiful, so too is a lad and a fully grown man and an elderly man. Here is proof: in Athens, they select handsome old men to be the bearers of olive branches, thus bearing witness to beauty at every stage of life.

"And if it is sweet to get what one wants from those willing to give it, I know that even now I could more quickly, and in complete silence, persuade this boy or girl to kiss me than could you, Socrates, even if you were to say a great many wise things."

"What is this?" said Socrates. "You brag as if you were more handsome than I!"

"By Zeus," said Critoboulus. "Or I would be the ugliest of all the sileni in a satyr play!"

(Socrates really did resemble them.)[5]

"Come now," said Socrates. "Remember to be judged against me in beauty when the present conversation has

κρινάτω δ' ἡμᾶς μὴ Ἀλέξανδρος ὁ Πριάμου, ἀλλ' αὐτοὶ οὗτοι οὕσπερ σὺ οἴει ἐπιθυμεῖν σε φιλῆσαι.

Κλεινίᾳ δ', ἔφη, ὦ Σώκρατες, οὐκ ἂν ἐπιτρέψαις;

Καὶ ὃς εἶπεν· Οὐ γὰρ παύσῃ σὺ Κλεινίου μεμνημένος;

Ἢν δὲ μὴ ὀνομάζω, ἧττόν τί με οἴει μεμνῆσθαι αὐτοῦ; οὐκ οἶσθα ὅτι οὕτω σαφὲς ἔχω εἴδωλον αὐτοῦ ἐν τῇ ψυχῇ ὡς εἰ πλαστικὸς ἢ ζωγραφικὸς ἦν, οὐδὲν ἂν ἧττον ἐκ τοῦ εἰδώλου ἢ πρὸς αὐτὸν ὁρῶν ὅμοιον αὐτῷ ἀπειργασάμην;

Καὶ ὁ Σωκράτης ὑπέλαβε· Τί δῆτα οὕτως ὅμοιον εἴδωλον ἔχων πράγματά μοι παρέχεις ἄγεις τε αὐτὸν ὅπου ὄψει;

Ὅτι, ὦ Σώκρατες, ἡ μὲν αὐτοῦ ὄψις εὐφραίνειν δύναται, ἡ δὲ τοῦ εἰδώλου τέρψιν μὲν οὐ παρέχει, πόθον δὲ ἐμποιεῖ.

Καὶ ὁ Ἑρμογένης εἶπεν· Ἀλλ' ἐγώ, ὦ Σώκρατες, οὐδὲ πρὸς σοῦ ποιῶ τὸ περιιδεῖν Κριτόβουλον οὕτως ὑπὸ τοῦ ἔρωτος ἐκπλαγέντα.

Δοκεῖς γάρ, ἔφη ὁ Σωκράτης, ἐξ οὗ ἐμοὶ σύνεστιν οὕτω διατεθῆναι αὐτόν;

Ἀλλὰ πότε μήν;

Οὐχ ὁρᾷς ὅτι τούτῳ μὲν παρὰ τὰ ὦτα ἄρτι ἴουλος καθέρπει, Κλεινίᾳ δὲ πρὸς τὸ ὄπισθεν ἤδη ἀναβαίνει; οὗτος οὖν συμφοιτῶν εἰς ταὐτὸ διδασκαλεῖον ἐκείνῳ τότε ἰσχυρῶς

gone its rounds. And let us not have Alexander, son of Priam,[6] judge us, but these very ones whom you think are lusting to kiss you."

"Would you not entrust this to Cleinias, Socrates?" he replied.

"So you cannot take a break from thinking of Cleinias?" Socrates answered in turn.

"Were I not to mention his name, do you think I would be thinking of him any less? Don't you know that I have so clear an image of him in my soul that, if I were a sculptor or a painter, I could produce a likeness of him from this image no less than if I were doing so while looking upon him in the flesh?"

"Why then," retorted Socrates, "if you hold so like an image in your mind do you hassle me to take you to where you will see him?"

"Because, Socrates, the sight of him can fill me with me joy, while the sight of his image does not bring delight, but causes desire."

Then Hermogenes spoke, "But I, Socrates, do not think it is like you to allow Critoboulus to be so stricken by desire."

"Do you suppose, said Socrates, "that it is since he has been with me that he became so disposed?"

"But since when then?"

"Do you not see that the down is just starting to creep up by his ears, while on Cleinias it has already grown all the way up behind them? It was from when he used to go

προσεκαύθη. ἃ δὴ αἰσθόμενος ὁ πατὴρ παρέδωκέ μοι αὐτόν, εἴ τι δυναίμην ὠφελῆσαι. καὶ μέντοι πολὺ βέλτιον ἤδη ἔχει. πρόσθεν μὲν γάρ, ὥσπερ οἱ τὰς Γοργόνας θεώμενοι, λιθίνως ἔβλεπε πρὸς αὐτὸν καὶ [λιθίνως] οὐδαμοῦ ἀπῄει ἀπ' αὐτοῦ· νῦν δὲ ἤδη εἶδον αὐτὸν καὶ σκαρδαμύξαντα. καίτοι νὴ τοὺς θεούς, ὦ ἄνδρες, δοκεῖ μοί γ', ἔφη, ὡς ἐν ἡμῖν αὐτοῖς εἰρῆσθαι, οὗτος καὶ πεφιληκέναι τὸν Κλεινίαν· οὗ ἔρωτος οὐδέν ἐστι δεινότερον ὑπέκκαυμα. καὶ γὰρ ἄπληστον καὶ ἐλπίδας τινὰς γλυκείας παρέχει. οὗ ἕνεκα ἀφεκτέον ἐγώ φημι εἶναι φιλημάτων <τῶν> ὡραίων τῷ σωφρονεῖν δυνησομένῳ.

Καὶ ὁ Χαρμίδης εἶπεν· Ἀλλὰ τί δή ποτε, ὦ Σώκρατες, ἡμᾶς μὲν οὕτω τοὺς φίλους μορμολύττῃ ἀπὸ τῶν καλῶν, αὐτὸν δέ σε, ἔφη, ἐγὼ εἶδον ναὶ μὰ τὸν Ἀπόλλω, ὅτε παρὰ τῷ γραμματιστῇ ἐν τῷ αὐτῷ βιβλίῳ ἀμφότεροι ἐμαστεύετέ τι, τὴν κεφαλὴν πρὸς τῇ κεφαλῇ καὶ τὸν ὦμον γυμνὸν πρὸς γυμνῷ τῷ Κριτοβούλου ὤμῳ ἔχοντα.

Καὶ ὁ Σωκράτης, Φεῦ, ἔφη, ταῦτ' ἄρα, ἐγὼ ὥσπερ ὑπὸ θηρίου τινὸς δεδηγμένος τόν τε ὦμον πλεῖν ἢ πέντε ἡμέρας ὤδαξον καὶ ἐν τῇ καρδίᾳ ὥσπερ κνῆσμά τι ἐδόκουν ἔχειν. ἀλλὰ νῦν τοί σοι, ἔφη, ὦ Κριτόβουλε, ἐναντίον τοσούτων μαρτύρων προαγορεύω μὴ ἅπτεσθαί μου πρὶν ἂν τὸ γένειον τῇ κεφαλῇ ὁμοίως κομήσῃς.

Καὶ οὗτοι μὲν δὴ οὕτως ἀναμὶξ ἔσκωψάν τε καὶ ἐσπούδασαν.

to the same school as him that he became so mightily inflamed. His father, perceiving this, handed him over to me, in case I might be able to help somehow. And indeed he is already much better. For before, like men who gaze upon the Gorgons, he would stare at him as if he were made of stone, and would never be away from him. But now I have even seen him blink! And yet, by the gods, dear men, it seems to me," continued Socrates, "to speak amongst ourselves, that he has even kissed Cleinias. There is nothing more fearsome than this for fueling desire. For it is insatiate and holds out certain sweet hopes. For this reason, I maintain that it is necessary for whomever wants to have self-control to abstain from kissing someone at his most beautiful."

"But why in the world, Socrates," said Charmides, "do you seek to scare off your friends like this from good-looking men, when by Apollo I have seen you yourself at the school, when both of you were seeking something in the same book, holding your head to his head and your naked shoulder to the naked shoulder of Critoboulus!"

"Ah!" said Socrates. "It is so! As if bitten by some wild beast, I have felt pain for more than five days on my shoulder and it is as if I had some sting in my heart. But now, as for you, Critoboulus," he added, "I declare in the presence of all these witnesses that you are not to touch me before you can comb as much of a beard as you have hair on your head!"

In this way they talked, mixing serious conversation with mockery.

237–54

Σοὶ μὲν ἐγὼ πτέρ᾽ ἔδωκα, σὺν οἷσ᾽ ἐπ᾽ ἀπείρονα πόντον
πωτήσηι, κατὰ γῆν πᾶσαν ἀειρόμενος
ῥηϊδίως· θοίνηις δὲ καὶ εἰλαπίνηισι παρέσσηισ
ἐν πάσαις πολλῶν κείμενος ἐν στόμασιν,
καί σε σὺν αὐλίσκοισι λιγυφθόγγοις νέοι ἄνδρες
εὐκόσμως ἐρατοὶ καλά τε καὶ λιγέα
ἄισονται. καὶ ὅταν δνοφερῆς ὑπὸ κεύθεσι γαίης

7 DON'T DO ME LIKE THAT: GETTING PLAYED

The course of love, and lust, never did run smooth, or straight. In a series of elegiac couplets, sixth-century BCE poet Theognis of Megara cajoles his beloved as inconstant, often addressing the beloved just as "boy," and sometimes using the name "Cyrnus." He laments the pains of love unevenly requited, or gone for good, presenting a guide on the bittersweet experiences of love and loss.

Theognis

To you I have given wings with which over the
    boundless sea
  you may fly, soaring above the entire earth
easily. And you will be present too at every party and
    feast,
  sitting in the mouths of many,
and handsome young men with their shrill-voiced little
    flutes
  will sing beautiful, high-pitched songs in harmony,
songs of you. Even when beneath the depths of the
    dark earth

βῆις πολυκωκύτους εἰς Ἀίδαο δόμους,
οὐδέποτ᾽ οὐδὲ θανὼν ἀπολεῖς κλέος, ἀλλὰ μελήσεις
ἄφθιτον ἀνθρώποισ᾽ αἰὲν ἔχων ὄνομα,
Κύρνε, καθ᾽ Ἑλλάδα γῆν στρωφώμενος, ἠδ᾽ ἀνὰ νήσους
ἰχθυόεντα περῶν πόντον ἐπ᾽ ἀτρύγετον,
οὐχ ἵππων νώτοισιν ἐφήμενος· ἀλλά σε πέμψει
ἀγλαὰ Μουσάων δῶρα ἰοστεφάνων.
πᾶσι δ᾽, ὅσοισι μέμηλε, καὶ ἐσσομένοισιν ἀοιδή
ἔσσηι ὁμῶς, ὄφρ᾽ ἂν γῆ τε καὶ ἠέλιος.
αὐτὰρ ἐγὼν ὀλίγης παρὰ σεῦ οὐ τυγχάνω αἰδοῦς,
ἀλλ᾽ ὥσπερ μικρὸν παῖδα λόγοις μ᾽ ἀπατᾶις.

1235–38

Ὦ παῖ, ἄκουσον ἐμεῦ δαμάσας φρένας· οὔ τοι ἀπειθῆ
μῦθον ἐρῶ τῆι σῆι καρδίηι οὐδ᾽ ἄχαριν.
ἀλλὰ τλῆθι νόωι συνιδεῖν ἔπος· οὔ τοι ἀνάγκη
τοῦθ᾽ ἔρδειν, ὅ τι σοὶ μὴ καταθύμιον ἦι.

you have gone, and into the much mourned house of
Hades,
never, though you are dead, will your glory die, but you
will matter
to people always. You will have an undying name,
Cyrnus, whirling through the Greek land, and
throughout the islands,
crossing over the fish-filled and barren sea,
not needing to sit on the backs of horses. The glorious
gifts
of the violet-crowned Muses will convey you.
For everyone to whom song matters, even for people in
the future,
you will exist, so long as there is an earth and sun.
Yet I do not receive from you even a micron of respect,
but, as if I were a small child, you use your words to
deceive me.

. . . . .

O boy, listen, for you have subdued my thoughts.
I won't say
any unconvincing word, nothing that is graceless to
your heart.
But take the time to understand this statement in your
mind: "there is no need
to do a thing that is not pleasing to your soul."

1249–52

Παῖ, σὺ μὲν αὔτως ἵππος, ἐπεὶ κριθῶν ἐκορέσθης,
  αὖθις ἐπὶ σταθμοὺς ἤλυθες ἡμετέρους
ἡνίοχόν τε ποθῶν ἀγαθὸν λειμῶνά τε καλόν
  κρήνην τε ψυχρὴν ἄλσεά τε σκιερά.

1259–62

Ὦ παῖ, τὴν μορφὴν μὲν ἔφυς καλός, ἀλλ' ἐπίκειται
  καρτερὸς ἀγνώμων σῆι κεφαλῆι στέφανος·
ἰκτίνου γὰρ ἔχεις ἀγχιστρόφου ἐν φρεσὶν ἦθος
  ἄλλων ἀνθρώπων ῥήμασι πειθόμενος.

1263–66

Ὦ παῖ, ὅς εὖ ἔρδοντι κακὴν ἀπέδωκας ἀμοιβήν,
  οὐδέ τις ἀντ' ἀγαθῶν ἐστὶ χάρις παρὰ σοί·
οὐδέν πώ μ' ὤνησας· ἐγὼ δέ σε πολλάκις ἤδη
  εὖ ἔρδων αἰδοῦς οὐδεμιῆς ἔτυχον.

1267–70

Παῖς τε καὶ ἵππος ὁμοῖον ἔχει νόον· οὔτε γὰρ ἵππος
  ἡνίοχον κλαίει κείμενον ἐν κονίηι,
ἀλλὰ τὸν ὕστερον ἄνδρα φέρει κριθαῖσι κορεσθείς·
  ὣς δ' αὔτως καὶ παῖς τὸν παρεόντα φιλεῖ.

DON'T DO ME LIKE THAT

. . . . .

Boy, you are like a horse who, once glutted on feed,
  comes back again to my stables,
longing for his skillful rider, a lovely meadow,
  the cool spring, and the shaded groves.

. . . . .

O boy, you have a fine body, but there sits
  on your head a strong but thoughtless crown.
For you have the temper in your mind of a quickly
    wheeling kite,
  pushed about by the words of other men.

. . . . .

O boy, you who have given a poor return to one who did
    you right,
  there is no gratitude for good things from you.
Never yet have you treated me well. And though often
    I have
  done you right, I have gained no respect at all.

. . . . .

A boy and a horse have a similar mind. For a horse
  does not weep when his rider lies in the dust,
but just carries another man, once glutted on fodder.
  In such a way does a boy love the one he's with.

1271–74

Ὦ παῖ, μαργοσύνης ἄπο μευ νόον ὤλεσας ἐσθλόν,
  αἰσχύνη δὲ φίλοισ᾽ ἡμετέροισ᾽ ἐγένου·
ἄμμε δ᾽ ἀνέψυξας μικρὸν χρόνον· ἐκ δὲ θυελλῶν
  ἧκά γ᾽ ἐνωρμίσθην νυκτὸς ἐπειγόμενος.

1283–1394

Ὦ παῖ, μή μ᾽ ἀδίκει—ἔτι σοι καταθύμιος εἶναι
  βούλομαι—εὐφροσύνηι τοῦτο συνεὶς ἀγαθῆι·
<οὐ γάρ τοί με δόλωι> παρελεύσεαι οὐδ᾽ ἀπατήσεις·
  νικήσας γὰρ ἔχεις τὸ πλέον ἐξοπίσω.
ἀλλά σ᾽ ἐγὼ τρώσω φεύγοντά με, ὥς ποτέ φασιν
  Ἰασίου κούρην, παρθένον Ἰασίην,
ὡραίην περ ἐοῦσαν ἀναινομένην γάμον ἀνδρῶν
  φεύγειν ζωσαμένην. ἔργ᾽ ἀτέλεστα τέλει
πατρὸς νοσφισθεῖσα δόμων ξανθὴ Ἀταλάντη·
  ὤιχετο δ᾽ ὑψηλὰς εἰς κορυφὰς ὀρέων
φεύγουσ᾽ ἱμερόεντα γάμον, χρυσῆς Ἀφροδίτης
  δῶρα· τέλος δ᾽ ἔγνω καὶ μάλ᾽ ἀναινομένη.

DON'T DO ME LIKE THAT

. . . . .

O boy, thanks to your lust you have lost your fine mind.
  You disgrace me before my friends.
But how you did refresh me, for a short time, when from
    storms
  in quiet I took shelter in you, pressing on in the night.

. . . . .

O boy, don't do me wrong—I still want to be pleasing
  to your soul—and offer this with an open heart:
not by tricks can you outwit me nor will you deceive me.
  For having won, you would have more of me thereafter.
But I will wound you as you flee from me, even as they say
  that the daughter of Iasion, the maiden Iasiē,
though ripe for marriage, refused it and fled from men,
  girding herself. Golden-haired Atalanta thus
      accomplished deeds
not meant to be accomplished, having forsaken her
    father's house.
  She headed for the highest peaks of the mountains,
fleeing the charms of marriage, the gifts of golden
    Aphrodite.
  But in the end she came to know them, even though she
      had once refused.

1295–98

Ὦ παῖ, μή με κακοῖσιν ἐν ἄλγεσι θυμὸν ὀρίναις,
 μηδέ με σὴ φιλότης δώματα Περσεφόνης
οἴχηται προφέρουσα· θεῶν δ' ἐποπίζεο μῆνιν
 βάξιν τ' ἀνθρώπων, ἤπια νωσάμενος.

1299–1304

Ὦ παῖ, μέχρι τίνος με προφεύξεαι; ὥς σε διώκων
 δίζημ'· ἀλλά τί μοι τέρμα γένοιτο κιχεῖν.
σὴ σοὶ γῆ. σὺ δὲ μάργον ἔχων καὶ ἀγήνορα θυμόν
 φεύγεις, ἰκτίνου σχέτλιον ἦθος ἔχων.
ἀλλ' ἐπίμεινον, ἐμοὶ δὲ δίδου χάριν· οὐκέτι δηρόν
 ἕξεις Κυπρογενοῦς δῶρον ἰοστεφάνου.

1305–10

Θυμῶι γνούς, ὅτι παιδείας πολυηράτου ἄνθος
 ὠκύτερον σταδίου, τοῦτο συνεὶς χάλασον
δεσμοῦ, μή ποτε καὶ σὺ βιήσεαι, ὄβριμε παίδων,
 Κυπρογενοῦς δ' ἔργων ἀντιάσεις χαλεπῶν,
ὥσπερ ἐγὼ νῦν οἶδ' ἐπὶ σοί. σὺ δὲ ταῦτα φύλαξαι,
 μηδέ σε νικήσηι †παιδαΐδη† κακότης.

DON'T DO ME LIKE THAT

▪ ▪ ▪ ▪ ▪

O boy, do not stir my soul to frightful agonies,
and may my love for you not bring me to the house
of Persephone.[1] Respect the rage of the gods
and the talk of men, and think gentle thoughts.

▪ ▪ ▪ ▪ ▪

O boy, for how long will you flee from me? For I am in pursuit,
I seek you out. May there be some end for me.
For the earth is yours, and you with your lustful and proud soul
flee, with the cruel character of a flighty kite.
But abide, and give me grace. Not much longer
will you have the gift of the violet-crowned Cyprus-born.[2]

▪ ▪ ▪ ▪ ▪

In your soul know this: the bloom of lovely youth
goes faster than a sprint. Understanding that, slacken
my chains, lest someday even you be overpowered, strong boy,
and meet with the hard deeds of the Cyprus-born,
even as I know her now, thanks to you. Be on guard for these things,
and do not be overcome by childish malice.

1311–18

Οὐκ ἔλαθες κλέψας, ὦ παῖ· καὶ γάρ σε διῶμμαι·
τούτοισ', οἷσπερ νῦν ἄρθμιος ἠδὲ φίλος
ἔπλευ—ἐμὴν δὲ μεθῆκας ἀτίμητον φιλότητα—
οὐ μὲν δὴ τούτοις γ' ἦσθα φίλος πρότερον.
ἀλλ' ἐγὼ ἐκ πάντων σ' ἐδόκουν θήσεσθαι ἑταῖρον
πιστόν· καὶ δὴ νῦν ἄλλον ἔχοισθα φίλον.
ἀλλ' ὁ μὲν εὖ ἕρδων κεῖμαι· σὲ δὲ μήτις ἁπάντων
ἀνθρώπων ἐσορῶν †παιδοφιλειν† ἐθέλοι.

1318a–b

Ὤιμοι ἐγὼ δειλός· καὶ δὴ κατάχαρμα μὲν ἐχθροῖς,
τοῖσι φίλοις δὲ πόνος δεινὰ παθὼν γενόμην.

1319–22

Ὦ παῖ, ἐπεί τοι δῶκε θεὰ χάριν ἱμερόεσσαν
Κύπρις, σὸν δ' εἶδος πᾶσι νέοισι μέλει,
τῶνδ' ἐπάκουσον ἐπῶν καὶ ἐμὴν χάριν ἔνθεο θυμῶι,
γνοὺς ἔρος ὡς χαλεπὸν γίνεται ἀνδρὶ φέρειν.

▪ ▪ ▪ ▪ ▪

Your cheating has not escaped me, o boy. Even so
    I pursue you.
  These men, with whom you are now joined in friendship—
having cast aside my own affection as unworthy—
  were certainly not your friends before.
But I thought that of everyone, you would become the
    companion
  most loyal. Well then, may have you have another now.
For though I treated you well, I am neglected. May no
    one of all
  men, seeing you, wish to love a youth.

▪ ▪ ▪ ▪ ▪

Alas, I am wretched! Indeed I am a cause of joy for my
    enemies,
  and a burden to my friends, for I have suffered terribly.

▪ ▪ ▪ ▪ ▪

O boy, since the goddess Cypris granted you the grace
    of beauty,
  and your body is wanted by all young men,
hear these words and place some grace for me in
    your soul,
  knowing that desire is hard for a man to bear.

1323–26

Κυπρογένη, παῦσόν με πόνων, σκέδασον δὲ μερίμνας
  θυμοβόρους, στρέψον δ' αὖθις ἐς εὐφροσύνας·
μερμήρας δ' ἀπόπαυε κακάς, δὸς δ' εὔφρονι θυμῶι
  μέτρ' ἥβης τελέσαντ' ἔργματα σωφροσύνης.

1327–34

Ὦ παῖ, ἕως ἂν ἔχηις λείαν γένυν, οὔποτε σαίνων
  παύσομαι, οὐδ' εἴ μοι μόρσιμόν ἐστι θανεῖν.
σοί τε διδόντ' ἔτι καλόν, ἐμοί τ' οὐκ αἰσχρὸν ἐρῶντι
  αἰτεῖν· ἀλλὰ γονέων λίσσομαι ἡμετέρων·
αἰδέο μ', ὦ παῖ <δῖε>, διδοὺς χάριν, εἴ ποτε καὶ σύ
  ἕξεις Κυπρογενοῦς δῶρον ἰοστεφάνου,
χρηΐζων καὶ ἐπ' ἄλλον ἐλεύσεαι· ἀλλὰ σὲ δαίμων
  δοίη τῶν αὐτῶν ἀντιτυχεῖν ἐπέων.

1335–36

Ὄλβιος ὅστις ἐρῶν γυμνάζεται οἴκαδε ἐλθών
  εὕδειν σὺν καλῶι παιδὶ πανημέριος.

DON'T DO ME LIKE THAT

. . . . .

Cyprus-born, ease my burdens and scatter the cares
that eat at my soul, and turn me back toward good cheer.
End these evil troubles, and grant me with a cheery soul
the art of self-control, for I have completed my measure of youth.

. . . . .

O boy, so long as you have a smooth chin, I will never stop
fawning, not even if death is destined for me.
For you it is still noble to give, and for me in love it is not shameful
to beg. But I beseech you by our forebears,
respect me, o divine boy, and give me favor. If someday even you
have the gift of the violet-crowned Cyprus-born goddess,
and, filled with longing, approach someone else, then may the gods
grant that you meet in return with these same words.

. . . . .

Blessed is he who, in love, does his training and, when he goes home,
sleeps with a lovely young man for the rest of the day.

1337–40

Οὐκέτ' ἐρῶ παιδός, χαλεπὰς δ' ἀπελάκτισ' ἀνίας
  μόχθους τ' ἀργαλέους ἄσμενος ἐξέφυγον,
ἐκλέλυμαι δὲ πόθου πρὸς ἐυστεφάνου Κυθερείης·
  σοὶ δ', ὦ παῖ, χάρις ἔστ' οὐδεμία πρὸς ἐμοῦ.

1341–50

Αἰαῖ, παιδὸς ἐρῶ ἁπαλόχροος, ὅς με φίλοισιν
  πᾶσι μάλ' ἐκφαίνει κοὐκ ἐθέλοντος ἐμοῦ.
τλήσομαι οὐ κρύψας ἀεκούσι<α> πολλὰ βίαια·
  οὐ γὰρ ἐπ' αἰκελίωι παιδὶ δαμεὶς ἐφάνην.
παιδοφιλεῖν δέ τι τερπνόν, ἐπεί ποτε καὶ Γανυμήδους
  ἤρατο καὶ Κρονίδης, ἀθανάτων βασιλεύς,
ἁρπάξας δ' ἐς Ὄλυμπον ἀνήγαγε καί μιν ἔθηκεν
  δαίμονα, παιδείης ἄνθος ἔχοντ' ἐρατόν.
οὕτω μὴ θαύμαζε, Σιμωνίδη, οὕνεκα κἀγὼ
  ἐξεφάνην καλοῦ παιδὸς ἔρωτι δαμείς.

1351–52

Ὦ παῖ, μὴ κώμαζε, γέροντι δὲ πείθεο ἀνδρί·
  οὔ τοι κωμάζειν σύμφορον ἀνδρὶ νέωι.

. . . . .

No longer am I in love with the boy. I kicked aside those harsh sorrows
and grievous toils, glad to escape.
I am free from longing thanks to Cytherea of the lovely crown.
And for you, o boy, there is no more favor from me.

. . . . .

Alas, I desire a soft-skinned boy, who shows me off before all
of his friends, though I wish he wouldn't.
I will endure it, not hiding these many things I am forced to do against my will.
For by no unseemly boy am I paraded as a prize.
To love a boy is a delightful thing, ever since even Ganymede
was desired by the son of Cronos, king of the gods,
who snatched him up and carried him to Olympus and made him
a god, bearing forever the lovely bloom of youth.[3]
Do not then wonder so, Simonides, that I too
am revealed to have been conquered by love.

. . . . .

O boy, do not go out partying, but obey an old man.
For it is not proper for a young man to party.

1353–56

Πικρὸς καὶ γλυκύς ἐστι καὶ ἁρπαλέος καὶ ἀπηνής,
  ὄφρα τέλειος ἔηι, Κύρνε, νέοισιν ἔρως.
ἢν μὲν γὰρ τελέσηι, γλυκὺ γίνεται· ἢν δὲ διώκων
  μὴ τελέσηι, πάντων τοῦτ᾽ ἀνιηρότατον.

1357–60

Αἰεὶ παιδοφίλησιν ἐπὶ ζυγὸν αὐχένι κεῖται
  δύσμορον, ἀργαλέον μνῆμα φιλοξενίης.
χρὴ γάρ τοι περὶ παῖδα πονούμενον εἰς φιλότητα
  ὥσπερ κληματίνωι χεῖρα πυρὶ προσάγειν.

1361–62

Ναῦς πέτρηι προσέκυρσας ἐμῆς φιλότητος ἁμαρτών,
  ὦ παῖ, καὶ σαπροῦ πείσματος ἀντελάβου.

1363–64

Οὐδαμά σ᾽ οὐδ᾽ ἀπεὼν δηλήσομαι· οὐδέ με πείσει
  οὐδεὶς ἀνθρώπων ὥστε με μή σε φιλεῖν.

1365–66

Ὦ παίδων κάλλιστε καὶ ἱμεροέστατε πάντων,
  στῆθ᾽ αὐτοῦ καί μου παῦρ᾽ ἐπάκουσον ἔπη.

. . . . .

It is bitter and sweet and pleasant and rough,
until it is fulfilled, Cyrnus—desire for the young.
For if you fulfill it, it is sweet. But if you pursue it
and do not find fulfillment, it is the most painful thing of all.

. . . . .

Always for anyone in love with a boy there is a yoke lying on his neck
ill-starred, a harsh reminder of such hospitality.
For whoever labors for the love of a boy must, in essence,
put his hand over a quickly burning flame.

. . . . .

Like a ship you hit a rock and lost my love,
o boy, and grasped a rotten rope.

. . . . .

Never will I do you harm, even when I'm gone. And no one of men
will ever persuade me not to love you.

. . . . .

O most beautiful and most desirable of all boys,
stay here and do not stop hearing my words.

1367–68

Παιδός τοι χάρις ἐστί· γυναικὶ δὲ πιστὸς ἑταῖρος
οὐδείς, ἀλλ' αἰεὶ τὸν παρεόντα φιλεῖ.

1369–72

Παιδὸς ἔρως καλὸς μὲν ἔχειν, καλὸς δ' ἀποθέσθαι·
πολλὸν δ' εὑρέσθαι ῥήιτερον ἢ τελέσαι.
μυρία δ' ἐξ αὐτοῦ κρέμαται κακά, μυρία δ' ἐσθλά·
ἀλλ' ἔν τοι ταύτηι καί τις ἔνεστι χάρις.

1373–74

Οὐδαμά πω κατέμεινας ἐμὴν χάριν, ἀλλ' ὑπὸ πᾶσαν
αἰεὶ σπουδαίην ἔρχεαι ἀγγελίην.

1375–76

Ὄλβιος ὅστις παιδὸς ἐρῶν οὐκ οἶδε θάλασσαν,
οὐδέ οἱ ἐν πόντωι νὺξ ἐπιοῦσα μέλει.

1377–80

Καλὸς ἐὼν κακότητι φίλων δειλοῖσιν ὁμιλεῖς
ἀνδράσι, καὶ διὰ τοῦτ' αἰσχρὸν ὄνειδος ἔχεις,

DON'T DO ME LIKE THAT

▪ ▪ ▪ ▪ ▪

In a boy there is grace, but in a woman there is no
trustworthy
companion to be had. She always loves the one she's
with.

▪ ▪ ▪ ▪ ▪

Desire for a boy is fine to feel, and fine to lay aside.
It is much easier to find than to fulfill.
Myriad are the evils that hang on it, and myriad the
blessings.
But in this, at least, there is some favor.

▪ ▪ ▪ ▪ ▪

You have never ever waited for my favor, but for every
earnest message you always come.

▪ ▪ ▪ ▪ ▪

Blessed is he who, in love with a boy, does not know
the sea,
and for whom night coming over the ocean is not a care.

▪ ▪ ▪ ▪ ▪

You are good, but hang around with a bad crowd of
vile men,
and for this reason have a shameful reputation,

ὦ παῖ· ἐγὼ δ’ ἀέκων τῆς σῆς φιλότητος ἁμαρτών
ὠνήμην ἔρδων οἷά τ’ ἐλεύθερος ὤν.

1381–85

Ἄνθρωποί σ’ ἐδόκουν χρυσῆς παρὰ δῶρον ἔχοντα
ἐλθεῖν Κυπρογενοῦς. δῶρον ἰοστεφάνου
γίνεται ἀνθρώποισιν ἔχειν χαλεπώτατον ἄχθος,
ἂν μὴ Κυπρογενὴς δῶι λύσιν ἐκ χαλεπῶν.

1386–89

Κυπρογενὲς Κυθέρεια δολοπλόκε, σοὶ τί περισσόν
Ζεὺς τόδε τιμήσας δῶρον ἔδωκεν ἔχειν;
δαμνᾶις δ’ ἀνθρώπων πυκινὰς φρένας, οὐδέ τίς ἐστιν
οὕτως ἴφθιμος καὶ σοφὸς ὥστε φυγεῖν.

boy. Though I was unhappy to lose your love,
I profited by doing what a free man does.

. . . . .

Men thought that you had a gift that came from the golden
Cyprus-born, but the gift of the violet-crowned one
becomes a very harsh grief for men to bear,
if the Cyprus-born does not grant relief from griefs.

. . . . .

Cyprus-born Cytherean weaver of wiles, why did Zeus honor you
so exceedingly, granting it to you to hold this gift?
For you conquer the quick wits of men, and there is no one
strong or wise enough to flee.

8 THE WILD SIDE: GENDER BENDING

From the Greek stage come two scenes of men putting on women's clothing, scenes that can be seen as standing in for the whole theatrical enterprise of men dressing up as women, inasmuch as all the parts in Greek drama, including female ones, were played by men. These scenes compel us to wonder whether the donning of women's clothes for the stage made men consider the stability of their gender off the stage as well. In the late fifth-century play, Women at the Thesmophoria, *comic playwright Aristophanes portrays the tragedian Agathon trying out the clothes, gestures, and voices of women; he appears on stage singing both the parts of a female chorus and a female choral leader, and is soon questioned about his methods by a character known as Euripides' "Kinsman," as we see here. While Agathon announces that this cross-dressing works toward the goal of portraying women and writing refined poetry, the play suggests slyly that Agathon's real-life practices included this form of self-expression too.*

Euripides' Bacchae *gives us both Dionysus and Pentheus looking like or dressing as women: first Dionysus in his human manifestation as a "stranger," whom we watch being questioned by Pentheus after Dionysus has allowed*

130–67

Κη. ὡς ἡδὺ τὸ μέλος, ὦ πότνιαι Γενετυλλίδες,
καὶ θηλυδριῶδες καὶ κατεγλωττισμένον
καὶ μανδαλωτόν, ὥστ᾽ ἐμοῦ γ᾽ ἀκροωμένου
ὑπὸ τὴν ἕδραν αὐτὴν ὑπῆλθε γάργαλος.
καί σ᾽, ὦ νεανίσχ᾽, ἥτις εἶ, κατ᾽ Αἰσχύλον
ἐκ τῆς Λυκουργείας ἐρέσθαι βούλομαι.
ποδαπὸς ὁ γύννις; τίς πάτρα; τίς ἡ στολή;
τίς ἡ τάραξις τοῦ βίου; τί βάρβιτος
λαλεῖ κροκωτῷ; τί δὲ λύρα κεκρυφάλῳ;
τί λήκυθος καὶ στρόφιον; ὡς οὐ ξύμφορον.
τίς δαὶ κατρόπτου καὶ ξίφους κοινωνία;
σύ τ᾽ αὐτός, ὦ παῖ, πότερον ὡς ἀνὴρ τρέφει;
καὶ ποῦ πέος; ποῦ χλαῖνα; ποῦ Λακωνικαί;

himself to be caught by Pentheus's men; then Pentheus when he has been driven mad by Dionysus and convinced to dress up as a Bacchante, or maenad (a woman who worships Dionysus), so as to go spy upon his mother Agauē and the other women of Thebes, who have likewise been driven mad. While the results of this latter crossing of gendered boundaries are violent, the question of what sorts of truths of the self were on display in the play remains hotly debated to this day.

Aristophanes, *Women at the Thesmophoria*

Kinsman: What a sweet song, o royal Genetyllides,[1]
so womanly, so sensuous a kiss,
with so much tongue that, as I listened, a tickle
moved right up through me from my very foundation.
And you, young man, whatever you are, I wish
to ask you something from Aeschylus's *Lycurgeia*.[2]
Whence comes a female man?[3] What is her fatherland?
What is her dress?
What is the disorder of her life? What instrument
sings with her saffron-dyed dress? What lyre with her
head-scarf?
What oil-flask and what hairband? For they do not fit
together.
What does a mirror have in common with a sword?
You yourself, boy, weren't you raised as a man?
Where is your dick? Where is your overcoat? Where are
your boots?

ἀλλ’ ὡς γυνὴ δῆτ’; εἶτα ποῦ τὰ τιτθία;
τί φῄς; τί σιγᾷς; ἀλλὰ δῆτ’ ἐκ τοῦ μέλους
ζητῶ σ’, ἐπειδή γ’ αὐτὸς οὐ βούλει φράσαι;

Αγ. ὦ πρέσβυ πρέσβυ, τοῦ φθόνου μὲν τὸν ψόγον
ἤκουσα, τὴν δ’ ἄλγησιν οὐ παρεσχόμην·
ἐγὼ δὲ τὴν ἐσθῆθ’ ἅμα γνώμῃ φορῶ.
χρὴ γὰρ ποιητὴν ἄνδρα πρὸς τὰ δράματα
ἃ δεῖ ποιεῖν, πρὸς ταῦτα τοὺς τρόπους ἔχειν.
αὐτίκα γυναικεῖ’ ἢν ποιῇ τις δράματα,
μετουσίαν δεῖ τῶν τρόπων τὸ σῶμ’ ἔχειν.

Κη. οὐκοῦν κελητίζεις, ὅταν Φαίδραν ποιῇς;

Αγ. ἀνδρεῖα δ’ ἢν ποιῇ τις, ἐν τῷ σώματι
ἔνεσθ’ ὑπάρχον τοῦθ’. ἃ δ’ οὐ κεκτήμεθα,
μίμησις ἤδη ταῦτα συνθηρεύεται.

Κη. ὅταν σατύρους τοίνυν ποιῇς, καλεῖν ἐμέ,
ἵνα συμποιῶ σοὔπισθεν ἐστυκὼς ἐγώ.

Αγ. ἄλλως τ’ ἄμουσόν ἐστι ποιητὴν ἰδεῖν
ἀγρεῖον ὄντα καὶ δασύν. σκέψαι δ’ ὅτι
Ἴβυκος ἐκεῖνος κἀνακρέων ὁ Τήιος
κἀλκαῖος, οἵπερ ἁρμονίαν ἐχύμισαν,

Or are you a woman then? Then where are your tits?
What do you say? Why are you silent? In your song
must I seek you, since you refuse to speak?

Agathon: Old man, old man, I hear your attack
of envy, but it does not hurt me.
I wear the outfit that is fitting to my thoughts.
For a man who is a poet of the stage must do
what is needed to take on the ways of his characters.
For example, if someone is staging the deeds of women,
his body must commune with their ways.

Kinsman: Then do you ride cow-girl style when you're
staging *Phaedra*?[4]

Agathon: If one is staging manliness, one has all that's
needed
in his own body. But whatever we don't actually possess,
imitation[5] then tracks it down.

Kinsman: Ah well, whenever you write satyr plays,[6]
call me,
so that I may help you by getting stiff just behind you!

Agathon: Anyway, it is discordant for a poet to seem
coarse and shaggy. Look at how Ibycus
and Anacreon of Teos and Alcaeus, who made such sweet
harmonies,

ἐμιτροφόρουν τε καὶ διεκλῶντ' Ἰωνικῶς.
καὶ Φρύνιχος—τοῦτον γὰρ οὖν ἀκήκοας—
αὐτός τε καλὸς ἦν καὶ καλῶς ἠμπίσχετο·
διὰ τοῦτ' ἄρ' αὐτοῦ καὶ κάλ' ἦν τὰ δράματα.
ὅμοια γὰρ ποιεῖν ἀνάγκη τῇ φύσει.

451–59

Πε. μέθεσθε χειρῶν τοῦδ'· ἐν ἄρκυσιν γὰρ ὢν
οὐκ ἔστιν οὕτως ὠκὺς ὥστε μ' ἐκφυγεῖν.
ἀτὰρ τὸ μὲν σῶμ' οὐκ ἄμορφος εἶ, ξένε,
ὡς ἐς γυναῖκας, ἐφ' ὅπερ ἐς Θήβας πάρει·
πλόκαμός τε γάρ σου ταναὸς οὐ πάλης ὕπο,
γένυν παρ' αὐτὴν κεχυμένος, πόθου πλέως·
λευκὴν δὲ χροιὰν ἐκ παρασκευῆς ἔχεις,
οὐχ ἡλίου βολαῖσιν ἀλλ' ὑπὸ σκιᾶς
τὴν Ἀφροδίτην καλλονῆι θηρώμενος.

912–44

Δι. σὲ τὸν πρόθυμον ὄνθ' ἃ μὴ χρεὼν ὁρᾶν
σπεύδοντά τ' ἀσπούδαστα, Πενθέα λέγω,
ἔξιθι πάροιθε δωμάτων, ὄφθητί μοι,
σκευὴν γυναικὸς μαινάδος βάκχης ἔχων,
μητρός τε τῆς σῆς καὶ λόχου κατάσκοπος·
πρέπεις δὲ Κάδμου θυγατέρων μορφὴν μιᾶι.

wore headbands and lived the pampered, Ionic lifestyle.
Even Phrynicus—for surely you have heard of him—
was himself handsome and dressed handsomely as well.[7]
Thanks to this, his dramas were beautiful too.
For one must make the poetry that matches one's nature.

Euripides, *Bacchae*

Pentheus: Release his hands. For he is in our net
and will not be so fast as to flee from me.
But your body is not unshapely, stranger,
at least for impressing women, for which purpose you are in Thebes.
For your hair is long, and not from wrestling,
and flows around your cheeks, full of desire.
You have pale, delicate skin from meticulous self-care,
not from the rays of the sun, but from time in the shadows,
hunting for Aphrodite with your beauty.

▪ ▪ ▪ ▪ ▪

Dionysus: Hey, you, the one so eager to see what is not meant to be seen,
the one pursuing what should not be pursued, I call on you, Pentheus.
Come out in front of the palace, let me see you,
wearing the dress of a woman, a maenad, a Bacchante,
a spy on your way to ambush your mother.
Your form seems just like any of the daughters of Cadmus.[8]

Πε. καὶ μὴν ὁρᾶν μοι δύο μὲν ἡλίους δοκῶ,
δισσὰς δὲ Θήβας καὶ πόλισμ᾽ ἑπτάστομον·
καὶ ταῦρος ἡμῖν πρόσθεν ἡγεῖσθαι δοκεῖς
καὶ σῶι κέρατα κρατὶ προσπεφυκέναι.
ἀλλ᾽ ἦ ποτ᾽ ἦσθα θήρ; τεταύρωσαι γὰρ οὖν.

Δι. ὁ θεὸς ὁμαρτεῖ, πρόσθεν ὢν οὐκ εὐμενής,
ἔνσπονδος ἡμῖν· νῦν δ᾽ ὁρᾶις ἃ χρή σ᾽ ὁρᾶν.

Πε. τί φαίνομαι δῆτ᾽; οὐχὶ τὴν Ἰνοῦς στάσιν
ἢ τὴν Ἀγαυῆς ἑστάναι, μητρός γ᾽ ἐμῆς;

Δι. αὐτὰς ἐκείνας εἰσορᾶν δοκῶ σ᾽ ὁρῶν.
ἀλλ᾽ ἐξ ἕδρας σοι πλόκαμος ἐξέστηχ᾽ ὅδε,
οὐχ ὡς ἐγώ νιν ὑπὸ μίτραι καθήρμοσα.

Πε. ἔνδον προσείων αὐτὸν ἀνασείων τ᾽ ἐγὼ
καὶ βακχιάζων ἐξ ἕδρας μεθώρμισα.

Δι. ἀλλ᾽ αὐτὸν ἡμεῖς, οἷς σε θεραπεύειν μέλει,
πάλιν καταστελοῦμεν· ἀλλ᾽ ὄρθου κάρα.

Pentheus: Why I seem to see two suns,
and a double Thebes, the seven-mouthed city.
And you seem to lead me onward like a bull
and to have grown horns on your head.
Were you a beast before? For now indeed you have
become a bull.

Dionysus: The god is with us. He was not favorably
disposed before,
but has entered a truce with us. And now you see what
you should see.

Pentheus: How do I look then? Do I not seem to stand
like Ino,
or even like Agauē, my mother?

Dionysus: When I look at you, it is like I'm actually
seeing them.
But, look, this hair has come loose from its place,
not as I had it tucked up under your headband.

Pentheus: Indeed when I was shaking up and down
and dancing like a Bacchante, I unmoored it from its
place!

Dionysus: But let us put it back again, for I am here to
serve.
Come, lift up your head.

Πε. ἰδού, σὺ κόσμει· σοὶ γὰρ ἀνακείμεσθα δή.

Δι. ζῶναί τέ σοι χαλῶσι κοὐχ ἑξῆς πέπλων
στολίδες ὑπὸ σφυροῖσι τείνουσιν σέθεν.

Πε. κἀμοὶ δοκοῦσι παρά γε δεξιὸν πόδα·
τἀνθένδε δ' ὀρθῶς παρὰ τένοντ' ἔχει πέπλος.

Δι. ἦ πού με τῶν σῶν πρῶτον ἡγήσῃ φίλων,
ὅταν παρὰ λόγον σώφρονας βάκχας ἴδῃς.

Πε. πότερα δὲ θύρσον δεξιᾶι λαβὼν χερὶ
ἢ τῇδε βάκχῃ μᾶλλον εἰκασθήσομαι;

Δι. ἐν δεξιᾶι χρὴ χἄμα δεξιῶι ποδὶ
αἴρειν νιν· αἰνῶ δ' ὅτι μεθέστηκας φρενῶν.

Pentheus: Yes, arrange it. For I am depending on you
completely.

Dionysus: Your girdle has gone slack, and the folds
of your dress are not spreading evenly around your
ankles.

Pentheus: They seem to be awry by my right foot,
but over here the dress flows just so, in a straight line.

Dionysus: You know, you will consider me your best
friend
when—contrary to your own word—you see how
modest the Bacchae are.

Pentheus: But should I hold the thyrsus in my right hand
or will I seem more like a Bacchante if it's in this one?[9]

Dionysus: You must have it your right hand, and at the
same time hold out
your right foot. I commend you on your change of heart.

189c–193d

Καὶ μήν, ὦ Ἐρυξίμαχε, εἰπεῖν τὸν Ἀριστοφάνη, ἄλλῃ γέ πῃ ἐν νῷ ἔχω λέγειν ἢ ᾗ σύ τε καὶ Παυσανίας εἰπέτην. ἐμοὶ γὰρ δοκοῦσιν ἄνθρωποι παντάπασι τὴν τοῦ ἔρωτος δύναμιν οὐκ ᾐσθῆσθαι, ἐπεὶ αἰσθανόμενοί γε μέγιστ' ἂν αὐτοῦ ἱερὰ κατασκευάσαι καὶ βωμούς, καὶ θυσίας ἂν ποιεῖν μεγίστας, οὐχ ὥσπερ νῦν τούτων οὐδὲν γίγνεται περὶ αὐτόν, δέον πάντων μάλιστα γίγνεσθαι.

ἔστι γὰρ θεῶν φιλανθρωπότατος, ἐπίκουρός τε ὢν τῶν ἀνθρώπων καὶ ἰατρὸς τούτων ὧν ἰαθέντων μεγίστη εὐδαιμονία ἂν τῷ ἀνθρωπείῳ γένει εἴη. ἐγὼ οὖν πειράσομαι ὑμῖν εἰσηγήσασθαι τὴν δύναμιν αὐτοῦ, ὑμεῖς δὲ τῶν ἄλλων διδάσκαλοι ἔσεσθε.

9 THE ORIGIN OF LOVE: HALVES AND HOLES

From Aristophanes, as portrayed in Plato's Symposium, *we receive a unique origin story of humankind, one that shows heteronormative love to be just one of several ways to feel devotion to one's "other half."*

Plato, *Symposium*

Indeed, Eryximachus, said Aristophanes, I have something rather different in mind to tell from what you and Pausanias have said.[1] For it seems to me to be the case that people entirely fail to understand the power of love, since if they did perceive it they would furnish Eros with the greatest of temples and altars, and offer him the greatest sacrifices, but, as it is now, nothing of this sort happens for him, though he is the most deserving of all.

He is the god who most loves humans, and acts as a helper for people and a healer for those wounds for which his cure is the greatest blessing that exists for the human race. I will try to explain his power to you, and then you can become teachers for others.

δεῖ δὲ πρῶτον ὑμᾶς μαθεῖν τὴν ἀνθρωπίνην φύσιν καὶ τὰ παθήματα αὐτῆς. ἡ γὰρ πάλαι ἡμῶν φύσις οὐχ αὑτὴ ἦν ἥπερ νῦν, ἀλλ' ἀλλοία. πρῶτον μὲν γὰρ τρία ἦν τὰ γένη τὰ τῶν ἀνθρώπων, οὐχ ὥσπερ νῦν δύο, ἄρρεν καὶ θῆλυ, ἀλλὰ καὶ τρίτον προσῆν κοινὸν ὂν ἀμφοτέρων τούτων, οὗ νῦν ὄνομα λοιπόν, αὐτὸ δὲ ἠφάνισται· ἀνδρόγυνον γὰρ ἓν τότε μὲν ἦν καὶ εἶδος καὶ ὄνομα ἐξ ἀμφοτέρων κοινὸν τοῦ τε ἄρρενος καὶ θήλεος, νῦν δὲ οὐκ ἔστιν ἀλλ' ἢ ἐν ὀνείδει ὄνομα κείμενον. ἔπειτα ὅλον ἦν ἑκάστου τοῦ ἀνθρώπου τὸ εἶδος στρογγύλον, νῶτον καὶ πλευρὰς κύκλῳ ἔχον, χεῖρας δὲ τέτταρας εἶχε, καὶ σκέλη τὰ ἴσα ταῖς χερσίν, καὶ πρόσωπα δύ' ἐπ' αὐχένι κυκλοτερεῖ, ὅμοια πάντῃ· κεφαλὴν δ' ἐπ' ἀμφοτέροις τοῖς προσώποις ἐναντίοις κειμένοις μίαν, καὶ ὦτα τέτταρα, καὶ αἰδοῖα δύο, καὶ τἆλλα πάντα ὡς ἀπὸ τούτων ἄν τις εἰκάσειεν.

ἐπορεύετο δὲ καὶ ὀρθὸν ὥσπερ νῦν, ὁποτέρωσε βουληθείη· καὶ ὁπότε ταχὺ ὁρμήσειεν θεῖν, ὥσπερ οἱ κυβιστῶντες καὶ εἰς ὀρθὸν τὰ σκέλη περιφερόμενοι κυβιστῶσι κύκλῳ, ὀκτὼ τότε οὖσι τοῖς μέλεσιν ἀπερειδόμενοι ταχὺ ἐφέροντο κύκλῳ. ἦν δὲ διὰ ταῦτα τρία τὰ γένη καὶ τοιαῦτα, ὅτι τὸ μὲν ἄρρεν ἦν τοῦ ἡλίου τὴν ἀρχὴν ἔκγονον, τὸ δὲ θῆλυ τῆς γῆς, τὸ δὲ ἀμφοτέρων μετέχον τῆς σελήνης, ὅτι καὶ ἡ σελήνη

First, it is necessary that you learn about human nature and what it has been through. For its nature in olden days was not the same as it is now, but quite different. For first there were three kinds of human, not two as now, male and female. There was also a third that had commonalities with both of these, and whose name still exists now, though the race itself has disappeared. For this was the "androgynous" one, both in form and name, which had elements in common with the male and the female, but is now just a name that is used as a slur. Back then, there was one whole form for each human that was spherical, which had its back and sides in a circle, and had four hands and an equal number of legs as it had hands, and two faces on its circular neck, which looked the same in every way. And each had one head with both faces looking in opposite directions, and four ears, and two sets of genitals. And everything else was just as one would guess from these things.

It walked upright, just like now, in whatever direction it wished. And whenever it would start to run quickly, just as acrobats who toss their legs straight up and rotate in a circle, so would they quickly turn about in cartwheels, supported by all eight limbs. There were three kinds of people, and they were the way they were because of the fact that the male was originally born from the sun, the female from the earth, and the one that partakes of both from the moon, since the moon too partakes of both the sun and earth. They were in fact spherical both in their

ἀμφοτέρων μετέχει· περιφερῆ δὲ δὴ ἦν καὶ αὐτὰ καὶ ἡ πορεία αὐτῶν διὰ τὸ τοῖς γονεῦσιν ὅμοια εἶναι.

ἦν οὖν τὴν ἰσχὺν δεινὰ καὶ τὴν ῥώμην, καὶ τὰ φρονήματα μεγάλα εἶχον, ἐπεχείρησαν δὲ τοῖς θεοῖς, καὶ ὃ λέγει Ὅμηρος περὶ Ἐφιάλτου τε καὶ Ὤτου, περὶ ἐκείνων λέγεται, τὸ εἰς τὸν οὐρανὸν ἀνάβασιν ἐπιχειρεῖν ποιεῖν, ὡς ἐπιθησομένων τοῖς θεοῖς. ὁ οὖν Ζεὺς καὶ οἱ ἄλλοι θεοὶ ἐβουλεύοντο ὅτι χρὴ αὐτοὺς ποιῆσαι, καὶ ἠπόρουν· οὔτε γὰρ ὅπως ἀποκτείναιεν εἶχον καὶ ὥσπερτοὺς γίγαντας κεραυνώσαντες τὸ γένος ἀφανίσαιεν—αἱ τιμαὶ γὰρ αὐτοῖς καὶ ἱερὰ τὰ παρὰ τῶν ἀνθρώπων ἠφανίζετο—οὔτε ὅπως ἐῷεν ἀσελγαίνειν. μόγις δὴ ὁ Ζεὺς ἐννοήσας λέγει ὅτι Δοκῶ μοι, ἔφη, ἔχειν μηχανήν, ὡς ἂν εἶέν τε ἄνθρωποι καὶ παύσαιντο τῆς ἀκολασίας ἀσθενέστεροι γενόμενοι. νῦν μὲν γὰρ αὐτούς, ἔφη, διατεμῶ δίχα ἕκαστον, καὶ ἅμα μὲν ἀσθενέστεροι ἔσονται, ἅμα δὲ χρησιμώτεροι ἡμῖν διὰ τὸ πλείους τὸν ἀριθμὸν γεγονέναι· καὶ βαδιοῦνται ὀρθοὶ ἐπὶ δυοῖν σκελοῖν. ἐὰν δ' ἔτι δοκῶσιν ἀσελγαίνειν καὶ μὴ 'θέλωσιν ἡσυχίαν ἄγειν, πάλιν αὖ, ἔφη, τεμῶ δίχα, ὥστ' ἐφ' ἑνὸς πορεύσονται σκέλους ἀσκωλιάζοντες.

ταῦτα εἰπὼν ἔτεμνε τοὺς ἀνθρώπους δίχα, ὥσπερ οἱ τὰ ὄα τέμνοντες καὶ μέλλοντες ταριχεύειν, ἢ ὥσπερ οἱ τὰ ᾠὰ ταῖς θριξίν· ὅντινα δὲ τέμοι, τὸν Ἀπόλλω ἐκέλευεν τό τε πρόσωπον μεταστρέφειν καὶ τὸ τοῦ αὐχένος ἥμισυ πρὸς

form and in their way of moving because of their likeness to their celestial progenitors.

They were awesome in strength and might, and so great was their pride that they made an attack on the gods, just as Homer says of Ephialtus and Otus when he tells that they tried to scale heaven so as to displace the gods. Then Zeus and the other gods deliberated on what they must do, and they were at a loss. For they did not want to kill them, using their thunderbolts to raze the race, as with the giants, for then too the honors and temples that come from humans would also disappear. But they also could not permit them to behave so outrageously. At last, when Zeus had thought it over, he said, "I think I've found a way for humans to exist and be prevented from their bad behavior, by being made weaker. For now," he said, "I will cut them through, each one into two, and they will simultaneously become weaker and more useful to us, since there will be more of them in number. And they will walk about upright on two legs. And if ever again they decide to behave outrageously and are not willing to keep the peace," he said, "then I will cut them apart again, so that they will have to get themselves around by hopping on one leg."

When he had said this, he cut the humans clean through in two, just as one might cut apples so as to preserve them, or the way a person cuts an egg in half with a hair. When he had cut each one, he ordered Apollo to turn the face around and part of the neck around toward the part that had been cut, so that seeing his stump, each person would be better

τὴν τομήν, ἵνα θεώμενος τὴν αὑτοῦ τμῆσιν κοσμιώτερος εἴη ὁ ἄνθρωπος, καὶ τἆλλα ἰᾶσθαι ἐκέλευεν. ὁ δὲ τό τε πρόσωπον μετέστρεφε, καὶ συνέλκων πανταχόθεν τὸ δέρμα ἐπὶ τὴν γαστέρα νῦν καλουμένην, ὥσπερ τὰ σύσπαστα βαλλάντια, ἓν στόμα ποιῶν ἀπέδει κατὰ μέσην τὴν γαστέρα, ὃ δὴ τὸν ὀμφαλὸν καλοῦσι. καὶ τὰς μὲν ἄλλας ῥυτίδας τὰς πολλὰς ἐξελέαινε καὶ τὰ στήθη διήρθρου, ἔχων τι τοιοῦτον ὄργανον οἷον οἱ σκυτοτόμοι περὶ τὸν καλάποδα λεαίνοντες τὰς τῶν σκυτῶν ῥυτίδας· ὀλίγας δὲ κατέλιπε, τὰς περὶ αὐτὴν τὴν γαστέρα καὶ τὸν ὀμφαλόν, μνημεῖον εἶναι τοῦ παλαιοῦ πάθους.

ἐπειδὴ οὖν ἡ φύσις δίχα ἐτμήθη, ποθοῦν ἕκαστον τὸ ἥμισυ τὸ αὑτοῦ συνῄει, καὶ περιβάλλοντες τὰς χεῖρας καὶ συμπλεκόμενοι ἀλλήλοις, ἐπιθυμοῦντες συμφῦναι, ἀπέθνῃσκον ὑπὸ λιμοῦ καὶ τῆς ἄλλης ἀργίας διὰ τὸ μηδὲν ἐθέλειν χωρὶς ἀλλήλων ποιεῖν. καὶ ὁπότε τι ἀποθάνοι τῶν ἡμίσεων, τὸ δὲ λειφθείη, τὸ λειφθὲν ἄλλο ἐζήτει καὶ συνεπλέκετο, εἴτε γυναικὸς τῆς ὅλης ἐντύχοι ἡμίσει—ὃ δὴ νῦν γυναῖκα καλοῦμεν—εἴτε ἀνδρός· καὶ οὕτως ἀπώλλυντο. ἐλεήσας δὲ ὁ Ζεὺς ἄλλην μηχανὴν πορίζεται, καὶ μετατίθησιν αὐτῶν τὰ αἰδοῖα εἰς τὸ πρόσθεν—τέως γὰρ καὶ ταῦτα ἐκτὸς εἶχον, καὶ ἐγέννων καὶ ἔτικτον οὐκ εἰς ἀλλήλους ἀλλ᾽ εἰς γῆν, ὥσπερ οἱ τέττιγες—μετέθηκέ τε οὖν οὕτω αὐτῶν εἰς τὸ πρόσθεν καὶ διὰ τούτων τὴν γένεσιν ἐν ἀλλήλοις ἐποίησεν, διὰ τοῦ ἄρρενος ἐν τῷ θήλει, τῶνδε ἕνεκα,

behaved. And he commanded that they should otherwise be healed. And so Apollo turned around the face of each one and drew together the skin from all over the body to what is now called the stomach, just as the drawstring on a bag, leaving one opening in the middle of the stomach, which is now called the navel. And he smoothed out the many other wrinkles and shaped the chest, using a certain tool that is like what shoemakers use to smooth out the wrinkles in leather around the bottoms of shoes. But he left a few wrinkles around the stomach and navel, to remind us of what happened long ago.

When our nature was first cut in two, each half was filled with longing and would come together with its other half. Throwing their arms around each other and intertwining, overwhelmed with the desire to grow back into one being, they would die from hunger and other kinds of neglect, since they did not wish to do anything without one another. And whenever one of the halves would die, and the other one be left, the one left behind would seek another and entwine itself, in case it might find half of the whole woman—what is now called a woman—or man. And in this way they perished. Zeus, pitying them, provided another solution, and moved their genitals to the front of their bodies. (For while they had had them on the outer parts, and they had conceived and birthed not with one another but on the earth, like cicadas.) He shifted these then to the front of their bodies, thusly, and brought them together to conceive, through the male in the female,

ἵνα ἐν τῇ συμπλοκῇ ἅμα μὲν εἰ ἀνὴρ γυναικὶ ἐντύχοι, γεννῷεν καὶ γίγνοιτο τὸ γένος, ἅμα δ' εἰ καὶ ἄρρην ἄρρενι, πλησμονὴ γοῦν γίγνοιτο τῆς συνουσίας καὶ διαπαύοιντο καὶ ἐπὶ τὰ ἔργα τρέποιντο καὶ τοῦ ἄλλου βίου ἐπιμελοῖντο.

ἔστι δὴ οὖν ἐκ τόσου ὁ ἔρως ἔμφυτος ἀλλήλων τοῖς ἀνθρώποις καὶ τῆς ἀρχαίας φύσεως συναγωγεὺς καὶ ἐπιχειρῶν ποιῆσαι ἓν ἐκ δυοῖν καὶ ἰάσασθαι τὴν φύσιν τὴν ἀνθρωπίνην. ἕκαστος οὖν ἡμῶν ἐστιν ἀνθρώπου σύμβολον, ἅτε τετμημένος ὥσπερ αἱ ψῆτται, ἐξ ἑνὸς δύο· ζητεῖ δὴ ἀεὶ τὸ αὑτοῦ ἕκαστος σύμβολον. ὅσοι μὲν οὖν τῶν ἀνδρῶν τοῦ κοινοῦ τμῆμά εἰσιν, ὃ δὴ τότε ἀνδρόγυνον ἐκαλεῖτο, φιλογύναικές τέ εἰσι καὶ οἱ πολλοὶ τῶν μοιχῶν ἐκ τούτου τοῦ γένους γεγόνασιν, καὶ ὅσαι αὖ γυναῖκες φίλανδροί τε καὶ μοιχεύτριαι ἐκ τούτου τοῦ γένους γίγνονται. ὅσαι δὲ τῶν γυναικῶν γυναικὸς τμῆμά εἰσιν, οὐ πάνυ αὗται τοῖς ἀνδράσι τὸν νοῦν προσέχουσιν, ἀλλὰ μᾶλλον πρὸς τὰς γυναῖκας τετραμμέναι εἰσί, καὶ αἱ ἑταιρίστριαι ἐκ τούτου τοῦ γένους γίγνονται. ὅσοι δὲ ἄρρενος τμῆμά εἰσι, τὰ ἄρρενα διώκουσι, καὶ τέως μὲν ἂν παῖδες ὦσιν, ἅτε τεμάχια ὄντα τοῦ ἄρρενος, φιλοῦσι τοὺς ἄνδρας καὶ χαίρουσι συγκατακείμενοι καὶ συμπεπλεγμένοι τοῖς ἀνδράσι, καί εἰσιν οὗτοι βέλτιστοι τῶν παίδων καὶ μειρακίων, ἅτε ἀνδρειότατοι ὄντες φύσει. φασὶ δὲ δή τινες αὐτοὺς ἀναισχύντους εἶναι, ψευδόμενοι· οὐ γὰρ ὑπ' ἀναισχυντίας τοῦτο δρῶσιν ἀλλ' ὑπὸ θάρρους καὶ ἀνδρείας καὶ ἀρρενωπίας, τὸ ὅμοιον αὐτοῖς

so that, by way of these adjustments, if a man should happen to embrace a woman, they might conceive and continue the species, or if a man together with a man, they might find satiety from being together and pause from it to turn to other tasks and otherwise take care of their livelihood.

It is from this then that desire for one another comes naturally to humans, both as the uniter of our ancient nature and in an attempt to make one from two and heal the wound that is human nature. Thus each of us is just a token[2] of a man, having been cut like flounder, two from one. And each is always searching for the matching token of himself. All men who are cuttings from the human who shared of both male and female, who then were called androgynous, are lovers of women; many lotharios come from this type. And, in turn, all the women who adore men and sleep around are from this kind of person too. Those women who are cuttings from the original women do not really have their hearts set on men, but rather are oriented toward women, and our lesbians come from this type of person. Those men who are cuttings of the original males pursue males, and while they are in their in youth, being chips off the old male block, they love men and enjoy lying together and embracing men. These are the best of boys and lads, for they are the most manly by nature. There are those who say that they are the most shameful, but they are liars. For it is not from shame that they do this, but from courage, manliness, and masculine bearing that attracts what is like to themselves. And here is sure proof of this: for when these

ἀσπαζόμενοι. μέγα δὲ τεκμήριον· καὶ γὰρ τελεωθέντες μόνοι ἀποβαίνουσιν εἰς τὰ πολιτικὰ ἄνδρες οἱ τοιοῦτοι. ἐπειδὰν δὲ ἀνδρωθῶσι, παιδεραστοῦσι καὶ πρὸς γάμους καὶ παιδοποιίας οὐ προσέχουσι τὸν νοῦν φύσει, ἀλλ' ὑπὸ τοῦ νόμου ἀναγκάζονται· ἀλλ' ἐξαρκεῖ αὐτοῖς μετ' ἀλλήλων καταζῆν ἀγάμοις. πάντως μὲν οὖν ὁ τοιοῦτος παιδεραστής τε καὶ φιλεραστὴς γίγνεται, ἀεὶ τὸ συγγενὲς ἀσπαζόμενος.

ὅταν μὲν οὖν καὶ αὐτῷ ἐκείνῳ ἐντύχῃ τῷ αὑτοῦ ἡμίσει καὶ ὁ παιδεραστὴς καὶ ἄλλος πᾶς, τότε καὶ θαυμαστὰ ἐκπλήττονται φιλίᾳ τε καὶ οἰκειότητι καὶ ἔρωτι, οὐκ ἐθέλοντες ὡς ἔπος εἰπεῖν χωρίζεσθαι ἀλλήλων οὐδὲ σμικρὸν χρόνον. καὶ οἱ διατελοῦντες μετ' ἀλλήλων διὰ βίου οὗτοί εἰσιν, οἳ οὐδ' ἂν ἔχοιεν εἰπεῖν ὅτι βούλονται σφίσι παρ' ἀλλήλων γίγνεσθαι. οὐδενὶ γὰρ ἂν δόξειεν τοῦτ' εἶναι ἡ τῶν ἀφροδισίων συνουσία, ὡς ἄρα τούτου ἕνεκα ἕτερος ἑτέρῳ χαίρει συνὼν οὕτως ἐπὶ μεγάλης σπουδῆς· ἀλλ' ἄλλο τι βουλομένη ἑκατέρου ἡ ψυχὴ δήλη ἐστίν, ὃ οὐ δύναται εἰπεῖν, ἀλλὰ μαντεύεται ὃ βούλεται, καὶ αἰνίττεται.

καὶ εἰ αὐτοῖς ἐν τῷ αὐτῷ κατακειμένοις ἐπιστὰς ὁ Ἥφαιστος, ἔχων τὰ ὄργανα, ἔροιτο· Τί ἔσθ' ὃ βούλεσθε, ὦ ἄνθρωποι, ὑμῖν παρ' ἀλλήλων γενέσθαι; καὶ εἰ ἀποροῦντας αὐτοὺς πάλιν ἔροιτο· Ἆρά γε τοῦδε ἐπιθυμεῖτε, ἐν τῷ αὐτῷ γενέσθαι ὅτι μάλιστα ἀλλήλοις, ὥστε καὶ νύκτα καὶ ἡμέραν μὴ ἀπολείπεσθαι ἀλλήλων; εἰ γὰρ τούτου ἐπιθυμεῖτε, θέλω ὑμᾶς συντῆξαι καὶ συμφυσῆσαι εἰς τὸ αὐτό, ὥστε δύ'

men reach maturity, they alone succeed in politics—such men as these. And when they reach manhood, they desire young men and have no thought of marriage and childbearing by nature, but simply are compelled to do these things by custom. But it would be enough for them just to live with one another, unmarried. In any case, such a man is born as a lover of young men and beloved to them, and always is welcoming to a like soul.

Thus whenever someone encounters his own other half, whether a lover of boys or anyone else at all, then they are struck most wondrously with love and intimacy and desire. They can hardly stand to be apart from each other for even a brief moment. And there are those who persevere through their lives with one another, who would not be able to say what it is they want from one another. For no one would think that this was merely a union of lust, or that on account of only this that each one delights in being with the other with such great zeal. But it is clear that the soul wants something else, something it cannot articulate but can only surmise and hint at.

But say Hephaestus were to appear before them as they lay together, holding his tools and say, "What is it that you want, humans, from one another?" And if he found them at a loss, and asked again, "Do you wish for this, to be in the same body with one another to the degree possible, so that neither night or day would you ever leave one another? For if you desire this, I am willing to fuse and weld you into the same being, so that though having been two you

ὄντας ἕνα γεγονέναι καὶ ἕως τ᾽ ἂν ζῆτε, ὡς ἕνα ὄντα, κοινῇ ἀμφοτέρους ζῆν, καὶ ἐπειδὰν ἀποθάνητε, ἐκεῖ αὖ ἐν Ἅιδου ἀντὶ δυοῖν ἕνα εἶναι κοινῇ τεθνεῶτε· ἀλλ᾽ ὁρᾶτε εἰ τούτου ἐρᾶτε καὶ ἐξαρκεῖ ὑμῖν ἂν τούτου τύχητε· ταῦτ᾽ ἀκούσας ἴσμεν ὅτι οὐδ᾽ ἂν εἷς ἐξαρνηθείη οὐδ᾽ ἄλλο τι ἂν φανείη βουλόμενος, ἀλλ᾽ ἀτεχνῶς οἴοιτ᾽ ἂν ἀκηκοέναι τοῦτο ὃ πάλαι ἄρα ἐπεθύμει, συνελθὼν καὶ συντακεὶς τῷ ἐρωμένῳ ἐκ δυοῖν εἷς γενέσθαι.

τοῦτο γάρ ἐστι τὸ αἴτιον, ὅτι ἡ ἀρχαία φύσις ἡμῶν ἦν αὕτη καὶ ἦμεν ὅλοι· τοῦ ὅλου οὖν τῇ ἐπιθυμίᾳ καὶ διώξει ἔρως ὄνομα. καὶ πρὸ τοῦ, ὥσπερ λέγω, ἓν ἦμεν, νυνὶ δὲ διὰ τὴν ἀδικίαν διῳκίσθημεν ὑπὸ τοῦ θεοῦ, καθάπερ Ἀρκάδες ὑπὸ Λακεδαιμονίων· φόβος οὖν ἔστιν, ἐὰν μὴ κόσμιοι ὦμεν πρὸς τοὺς θεούς, ὅπως μὴ καὶ αὖθις διασχισθησόμεθα, καὶ περίιμεν ἔχοντες ὥσπερ οἱ ἐν ταῖς στήλαις καταγραφὴν ἐκτετυπωμένοι, διαπεπρισμένοι κατὰ τὰς ῥῖνας, γεγονότες ὥσπερ λίσπαι.

ἀλλὰ τούτων ἕνεκα πάντ᾽ ἄνδρα χρὴ ἅπαντα παρακελεύεσθαι εὐσεβεῖν περὶ θεούς, ἵνα τὰ μὲν ἐκφύγωμεν, τῶν δὲ τύχωμεν, ὡς ὁ Ἔρως ἡμῖν ἡγεμὼν καὶ στρατηγός. ᾧ μηδεὶς ἐναντία πραττέτω—πράττει δ᾽ ἐναντία ὅστις θεοῖς ἀπεχθάνεται—φίλοι γὰρ γενόμενοι καὶ διαλλαγέντες τῷ θεῷ ἐξευρήσομέν τε καὶ ἐντευξόμεθα τοῖς παιδικοῖς τοῖς ἡμετέροις αὐτῶν, ὃ τῶν νῦν ὀλίγοι ποιοῦσι. καὶ μή μοι ὑπολάβῃ Ἐρυξίμαχος, κωμῳδῶν τὸν λόγον, ὡς Παυσανίαν

will become one for as long as you live, and so that, being one, you might both live together, and whenever you die, then in turn you will be dead in Hades as one together instead of two. But consider if you desire this and it would suffice for you to have it." Hearing this, we know that no one would refuse nor would seem to want anything else, but simply would think that he heard what he had wanted from the start, to come together and be fused by love from two people into one.

For the cause of this is that our ancient nature was to be whole and the same. And the name, therefore, for our desire for and pursuit of wholeness is love. For before this, as I said, we were one, but now because of our wrongdoing, we have been dispersed by the god, just as the Arcadians were by the Lacedemonians. And thus it is a matter of concern that if we do not behave well toward the gods, we may again be split apart, and wander about like those people molded by etching on gravestones and be sawed through at the nose, like split dice.

Rather, on account of these things, it is necessary to exhort every man to be pious toward the gods, so that we may escape such a fate, and meet with Eros as our leader and general. To him may no one be rebellious—since whoever is rebellious is hated by the gods—for we who become beloved and friends to the god will find and meet with our own beloveds, which very few in our time manage to do. And may Eryximachus not respond by making fun of my speech, since I can point to Pausanias

καὶ Ἀγάθωνα λέγω—ἴσως μὲν γὰρ καὶ οὗτοι τούτων τυγχάνουσιν ὄντες καί εἰσιν ἀμφότεροιτὴν φύσιν ἄρρενες—λέγω δὲ οὖν ἔγωγε καθ' ἁπάντων καὶ ἀνδρῶν καὶ γυναικῶν, ὅτι οὕτως ἂν ἡμῶν τὸ γένος εὔδαιμον γένοιτο, εἰ ἐκτελέσαιμεν τὸν ἔρωτα καὶ τῶν παιδικῶν τῶν αὑτοῦ ἕκαστος τύχοι εἰς τὴν ἀρχαίαν ἀπελθὼν φύσιν.

εἰ δὲ τοῦτο ἄριστον, ἀναγκαῖον καὶ τῶν νῦν παρόντων τὸ τούτου ἐγγυτάτω ἄριστον εἶναι· τοῦτο δ' ἐστὶ παιδικῶν τυχεῖν κατὰ νοῦν αὐτῷ πεφυκότων· οὗ δὴ τὸν αἴτιον θεὸν ὑμνοῦντες δικαίως ἂν ὑμνοῖμεν Ἔρωτα, ὃς ἔν τε τῷ παρόντι ἡμᾶς πλεῖστα ὀνίνησιν εἰς τὸ οἰκεῖον ἄγων, καὶ εἰς τὸ ἔπειτα ἐλπίδας μεγίστας παρέχεται, ἡμῶν παρεχομένων πρὸς θεοὺς εὐσέβειαν, καταστήσας ἡμᾶς εἰς τὴν ἀρχαίαν φύσιν καὶ ἰασάμενος μακαρίους καὶ εὐδαίμονας ποιῆσαι.

and Agathon,[3] for they perhaps are those who have come from the ones that were male in both parts of their nature. And so I say that for all men and women the way that our race may become similarly blessed is for us to achieve love and for each person to find their beloved in accordance with their ancient nature.

And if this really is best, then it is necessary for those present now to do the best thing that is most close at hand: this is to find our beloveds according to our own minds. When we praise the god responsible for these things, it is Eros that we justly praise, he who in the present blesses us most of all by leading us to our true selves, and for the future offers our greatest hopes. So let us offer reverence to the gods, that Eros may someday return us to our ancient nature and, in healing us, make us happy and blessed.

203a–207b

Ἐπορευόμην μὲν ἐξ Ἀκαδημείας εὐθὺ Λυκείου τὴν ἔξω τείχους ὑπ' αὐτὸ τὸ τεῖχος· ἐπειδὴ δ' ἐγενόμην κατὰ τὴν πυλίδα ᾗ ἡ Πάνοπος κρήνη, ἐνταῦθα συνέτυχον Ἱπποθάλει τε τῷ Ἱερωνύμου καὶ Κτησίππῳ τῷ Παιανιεῖ καὶ ἄλλοις μετὰ τούτων νεανίσκοις ἀθρόοις συνεστῶσι. καί με προσιόντα ὁ Ἱπποθάλης ἰδών, Ὦ Σώκρατες, ἔφη, ποῖ δὴ πορεύῃ καὶ πόθεν;

10 LUST FOR LIFE: WOOING BOYS

Both Plato in classical Athens in the fourth century BCE and Theocritus in Hellenistic Alexandria in the third century BCE show the hopes and tribulations of seeking a young man's love: overwhelming desire that causes one to blush, stammer, and compose reams of poetry in honor of the beloved. Plato's Lysis *portrays a certain man named Hippothales in a lovesick state and Socrates, who is the narrator, offering to help him do a better job of wooing his beloved, the handsome Lysis. Theocritus offers three poems (*Idylls *12, 28, and 29) in the voice of besotted male lovers, as well as an account of Heracles and his love and loss of the youth Hylas (*Idyll *13).*

Plato, *Lysis*

I was heading from the Academy straight to the Lyceum, outside the wall just under it. When I came to the little gate where the spring of Panops is, I ran into Hippothales, son of Hieronymus, and Ktesippus the Paianian and a few other young men standing about in a crowd. As I approached, Hippothales said, "Socrates, where are you going and where are you coming from?"

Ἐξ Ἀκαδημείας, ἦν δ' ἐγώ, πορεύομαι εὐθὺ Λυκείου.

Δεῦρο δή, ἦ δ' ὅς, εὐθὺ ἡμῶν. οὐ παραβάλλεις; ἄξιον μέντοι.

Ποῖ, ἔφην ἐγώ, λέγεις, καὶ παρὰ τίνας τοὺς ὑμᾶς;

Δεῦρο, ἔφη, δείξας μοι ἐν τῷ καταντικρὺ τοῦ τείχους περίβολόν τέ τινα καὶ θύραν ἀνεῳγμένην. διατρίβομεν δέ, ἦ δ' ὅς, αὐτόθι ἡμεῖς τε αὐτοὶ καὶ ἄλλοι πάνυ πολλοὶ καὶ καλοί.

Ἔστιν δὲ δὴ τί τοῦτο, καὶ τίς ἡ διατριβή;

Παλαίστρα, ἔφη, νεωστὶ ᾠκοδομημένη· ἡ δὲ διατριβὴ τὰ πολλὰ ἐν λόγοις, ὧν ἡδέως ἄν σοι μεταδιδοῖμεν.

Καλῶς γε, ἦν δ' ἐγώ, ποιοῦντες· διδάσκει δὲ τίς αὐτόθι;

Σὸς ἑταῖρός γε, ἦ δ' ὅς, καὶ ἐπαινέτης, Μίκκος.

Μὰ Δία, ἦν δ' ἐγώ, οὐ φαῦλός γε ἀνήρ, ἀλλ' ἱκανὸς σοφιστής.

Βούλει οὖν ἕπεσθαι, ἔφη, ἵνα καὶ ἴδῃς τοὺς ὄντας αὐτόθι [αὐτοῦ];

Πρῶτον ἡδέως ἀκούσαιμ' ἂν ἐπὶ τῷ καὶ εἴσειμι καὶ τίς ὁ καλός.

Ἄλλος, ἔφη, ἄλλῳ ἡμῶν δοκεῖ, ὦ Σώκρατες.

Σοὶ δὲ δὴ τίς, ὦ Ἱππόθαλες; τοῦτό μοι εἰπέ.

Καὶ ὃς ἐρωτηθεὶς ἠρυθρίασεν. καὶ ἐγὼ εἶπον· Ὦ παῖ Ἱερωνύμου Ἱππόθαλες, τοῦτο μὲν μηκέτι εἴπῃς, εἴτε ἐρᾷς

"From the Academy," I said. "And I'm heading to the Lyceum."[1]

"Come here," he said. "Join us. You're waving off? But it'd be worth your time!"

"Where are you saying I should go?" I asked. "And who are you with?"

"Here," he said and showed me an enclosure in the wall just across the way and a door that had been left open.

"We hang out at this spot," he continued. "Us and many others, a lot of guys—and good-looking ones."

"What is this place?" I asked. "What do you do here?"

"A wrestling school," he replied. "Just built. And we spend our time talking a lot, a pastime we would gladly share with you."

"How kind of you," I said. "Who is teacher in this place?"

"Your very own friend and admirer, Mikkus."

"By god," I said. "He's no amateur, but a very competent expert!"

"Do you wish to come," he said, "so that you can see them there for yourself?"

"First I would like to know into what sort of situation I'm entering, and also who is the good-looking one?"

"One man seems so to me, Socrates," he said. "And another seems handsome to someone else."

"And who seems so to you, Hippothales? Tell me that."

Thus interrogated, he blushed. I continued, "O Hippothales, child of Hieronymus, you need no longer tell me

του εἴτε μή· οἶδα γὰρ ὅτι οὐ μόνον ἐρᾷς, ἀλλὰ καὶ πόρρω ἤδη εἶ πορευόμενος τοῦ ἔρωτος. εἰμὶ δ' ἐγὼ τὰ μὲν ἄλλα φαῦλος καὶ ἄχρηστος, τοῦτο δέ μοί πως ἐκ θεοῦ δέδοται, ταχὺ οἵῳ τ' εἶναι γνῶναι ἐρῶντά τε καὶ ἐρώμενον.

Καὶ ὃς ἀκούσας πολὺ ἔτι μᾶλλον ἠρυθρίασεν. ὁ οὖν Κτήσιππος, Ἀστεῖόν γε, ἦ δ' ὅς, ὅτι ἐρυθριᾷς, ὦ Ἱππόθαλες, καὶ ὀκνεῖς εἰπεῖν Σωκράτει τοὔνομα· ἐὰν δ' οὗτος καὶ σμικρὸν χρόνον συνδιατρίψῃ σοι, παραταθήσεται ὑπὸ σοῦ ἀκούων θαμὰ λέγοντος. ἡμῶν γοῦν, ὦ Σώκρατες, ἐκκεκώφωκε τὰ ὦτα καὶ ἐμπέπληκε Λύσιδος· ἂν μὲν δὴ καὶ ὑποπίῃ, εὐμαρία ἡμῖν ἐστιν καὶ ἐξ ὕπνου ἐγρομένοις Λύσιδος οἴεσθαι τοὔνομα ἀκούειν. καὶ ἃ μὲν καταλογάδην διηγεῖται, δεινὰ ὄντα, οὐ πάνυ τι δεινά ἐστιν, ἀλλ' ἐπειδὰν τὰ ποιήματα ἡμῶν ἐπιχειρήσῃ καταντλεῖν καὶ συγγράμματα. καὶ ὅ ἐστιν τούτων δεινότερον, ὅτι καὶ ᾄδει εἰς τὰ παιδικὰ φωνῇ θαυμασίᾳ, ἣν ἡμᾶς δεῖ ἀκούοντας ἀνέχεσθαι. νῦν δὲ ἐρωτώμενος ὑπὸ σοῦ ἐρυθριᾷ.

Ἔστιν δέ, ἦν δ' ἐγώ, ὁ Λύσις νέος τις, ὡς ἔοικε· τεκμαίρομαι δέ, ὅτι ἀκούσας τοὔνομα οὐκ ἔγνων.

Οὐ γὰρ πάνυ, ἔφη, τὶ αὐτοῦ τοὔνομα λέγουσιν, ἀλλ' ἔτι πατρόθεν ἐπονομάζεται διὰ τὸ σφόδρα τὸν πατέρα γιγνώσκεσθαι αὐτοῦ. ἐπεὶ εὖ οἶδ' ὅτι πολλοῦ δεῖς τὸ εἶδος

whether you are in love or not. For I know now that not only are you in love, but that you have been taken rather far along in your passion. For I may be a feeble and useless man in other respects, but somehow this gift was given to me by the god, to perceive swiftly to what degree someone is in love or is loved."

Hearing this, he blushed much more than before. Then Ktesippus spoke, "How charmingly you blush, Hippothales, and shrink from saying the name to Socrates. But if he spends even a little time with you, he will be tortured by hearing you say it over and over and over again. I can tell you, Socrates, that he has quite deafened our ears by filling them full of 'Lysis.' And when he gets a little tipsy, you might easily wake from sleep thinking that you are hearing the name Lysis. And what he describes in conversation, though terrible, is not *so* entirely terrible as whenever he attempts to pour his poems over us as well as his speeches. And what is even more terrible than these is when he also sings on the topic of his darling in an incredible voice, which we must endure to hear. But now, when questioned by you, he blushes!"

"This Lysis is someone young," I said. "Or so it seems to me. For that much I can deduce, hearing a name that I do not recognize."

"That's because they don't usually call him by his own name, but rather still use the one from his father, since his father is well known. For I know well that you are not at

ἀγνοεῖν τοῦ παιδός· ἱκανὸς γὰρ καὶ ἀπὸ μόνου τούτου γιγνώσκεσθαι.

Λεγέσθω, ἦν δ' ἐγώ, οὗτινος ἔστιν.

Δημοκράτους, ἔφη, τοῦ Αἰξωνέως ὁ πρεσβύτατος ὑός.

Εἶεν, ἦν δ' ἐγώ, ὦ Ἱππόθαλες, ὡς γενναῖον καὶ νεανικὸν τοῦτον τὸν ἔρωτα πανταχῇ ἀνηῦρες· καί μοι ἴθι ἐπίδειξαι ἃ καὶ τοῖσδε ἐπιδείκνυσαι, ἵνα εἰδῶ εἰ ἐπίστασαι ἃ χρὴ ἐραστὴν περὶ παιδικῶν πρὸς αὐτὸν ἢ πρὸς ἄλλους λέγειν.

Τούτων δέ τι, ἔφη, σταθμᾷ, ὦ Σώκρατες, ὧν ὅδε λέγει;

Πότερον, ἦν δ' ἐγώ, καὶ τὸ ἐρᾶν ἔξαρνος εἶ οὗ λέγει ὅδε;

Οὐκ ἔγωγε, ἔφη, ἀλλὰ μὴ ποιεῖν εἰς τὰ παιδικὰ μηδὲ συγγράφειν.

Οὐχ ὑγιαίνει, ἔφη ὁ Κτήσιππος, ἀλλὰ ληρεῖ τε καὶ μαίνεται.

Καὶ ἐγὼ εἶπον· Ὦ Ἱππόθαλες, οὔ τι τῶν μέτρων δέομαι ἀκοῦσαι οὐδὲ μέλος εἴ τι πεποίηκας εἰς τὸν νεανίσκον, ἀλλὰ τῆς διανοίας, ἵνα εἰδῶ τίνα τρόπον προσφέρῃ πρὸς τὰ παιδικά.

Ὅδε δήπου σοι, ἔφη, ἐρεῖ· ἀκριβῶς γὰρ ἐπίσταται καὶ μέμνηται, εἴπερ, ὡς λέγει, ὑπ' ἐμοῦ ἀεὶ ἀκούων διατεθρύληται.

Νὴ τοὺς θεούς, ἔφη ὁ Κτήσιππος, πάνυ γε. καὶ γάρ ἐστι καταγέλαστα, ὦ Σώκρατες. τὸ γὰρ ἐραστὴν ὄντα καὶ διαφερόντως τῶν ἄλλων τὸν νοῦν προσέχοντα τῷ παιδὶ ἴδιον μὲν μηδὲν ἔχειν λέγειν ὃ οὐχὶ κἂν παῖς εἴποι, πῶς οὐχὶ

all lacking in knowledge of the appearance of the boy. For this alone is sufficient to know him."

"Tell me whose son he is," I said.

"Democratus's," he said. "The eldest son of Aixone."

"Well," I said. "Hippothales, how noble and young in every way is this love that you have discovered! Come and display for me what you have also shown them, so that I may know and understand what a lover ought to say about his darling, to him and to others."

"Do you lend any credence to what these men say, Socrates?" he asked.

"Do you deny that you are in love with the one he says?" I replied.

"I do not," he said. "But I do deny that I write poetry and speeches for my beloved."

"He is not in his right mind!" said Ktesippus. "Rather, he speaks nonsense and acts crazed!"

To this I said, "Hippothales, I do not need to hear any of your verses or songs, if you do write any poetry for your young man, but just their basic meaning, so that I may know the manner you adopt toward your beloved."

"He will doubtless tell you then," he said. "For he knows and remembers it all exactly, if, as he says, he has been constantly talked to death about it by me."

"Absolutely, by the gods!" said Ktesippus. "For indeed it is ridiculous, Socrates. For to be a lover and to turn one's mind apart from all others to one boy, privately, and then not to be able to say anything that even a child could say,

καταγέλαστον; ἃ δὲ ἡ πόλις ὅλη ᾄδει περὶ Δημοκράτους καὶ Λύσιδος τοῦ πάππου τοῦ παιδὸς καὶ πάντων πέρι τῶν προγόνων, πλούτους τε καὶ ἱπποτροφίας καὶ νίκας Πυθοῖ καὶ Ἰσθμοῖ καὶ Νεμέᾳ τεθρίπποις τε καὶ κέλησι, ταῦτα ποιεῖ τε καὶ λέγει, πρὸς δὲ τούτοις ἔτι τούτων κρονικώτερα. τὸν γὰρ τοῦ Ἡρακλέους ξενισμὸν πρῴην ἡμῖν ἐν ποιήματί τινι διῄει, ὡς διὰ τὴν τοῦ Ἡρακλέους συγγένειαν ὁ πρόγονος αὐτῶν ὑποδέξαιτο τὸν Ἡρακλέα, γεγονὼς αὐτὸς ἐκ Διός τε καὶ τῆς τοῦ δήμου ἀρχηγέτου θυγατρός, ἅπερ αἱ γραῖαι ᾄδουσι, καὶ ἄλλα πολλὰ τοιαῦτα, ὦ Σώκρατες· ταῦτ' ἐστὶν ἃ οὗτος λέγων τε καὶ ᾄδων ἀναγκάζει καὶ ἡμᾶς ἀκροᾶσθαι.

Καὶ ἐγὼ ἀκούσας εἶπον· Ὦ καταγέλαστε Ἱππόθαλες, πρὶν νενικηκέναι ποιεῖς τε καὶ ᾄδεις εἰς σαυτὸν ἐγκώμιον;

Ἀλλ' οὐκ εἰς ἐμαυτόν, ἔφη, ὦ Σώκρατες, οὔτε ποιῶ οὔτε ᾄδω.

Οὐκ οἴει γε, ἦν δ' ἐγώ.

Τὸ δὲ πῶς ἔχει; ἔφη.

Πάντων μάλιστα, εἶπον, εἰς σὲ τείνουσιν αὗται αἱ ᾠδαί. ἐὰν μὲν γὰρ ἕλῃς τὰ παιδικὰ τοιαῦτα ὄντα, κόσμος σοι ἔσται τὰ λεχθέντα καὶ ᾀσθέντα καὶ τῷ ὄντι ἐγκώμια ὥσπερ νενικηκότι, ὅτι τοιούτων παιδικῶν ἔτυχες· ἐὰν δέ σε διαφύγῃ, ὅσῳ ἂν μείζω σοι εἰρημένα ᾖ ἐγκώμια περὶ τῶν παιδικῶν, τοσούτῳ μειζόνων δόξεις καλῶν τε καὶ ἀγαθῶν ἐστερημένος καταγέλαστος εἶναι. ὅστις οὖν τὰ ἐρωτικά, ὦ

how is this not ridiculous? But what the whole city sings of—about Democratus and Lysis, the boy's grandfather, and all of his ancestors, their wealth and horse-breeding and victories at Pytho and Isthmus and Nemea in the four-horse chariot and single-horse races—it is these things about which he writes poetry and talks, and even more arcane tales than these. For even early this morning, he was recounting to us in a poem the tale of dinner with Heracles, since through kinship with Heracles their ancestor entertained Heracles himself, he having been born from Zeus and the daughter of the founder of the polity—such stories as old women sing, and many other such things, Socrates. This is what he says and sings, while forcing us to listen."

Hearing this I said, "Ridiculous Hippothales! Are you composing and singing a poem of praise for yourself before you have even won?"

"But it is not for myself that I compose and sing, Socrates," he said.

"You think not," I said.

"How is it then?" he said.

"To you most of all," I said, "do these songs pertain. For if you were to obtain a beloved such as this one, then the things you've said and sung will be a credit to you, truly an encomium as if you had conquered, whenever you should grasp such a beloved. But, if he eludes you, by so much as you have said in your encomium about your favorite will you seem to have lost in beauty and goodness, and you will seem absurd. Friend, whoever is wise in

φίλε, σοφός, οὐκ ἐπαινεῖ τὸν ἐρώμενον πρὶν ἂν ἕλῃ, δεδιὼς τὸ μέλλον ὅπῃ ἀποβήσεται. καὶ ἅμα οἱ καλοί, ἐπειδάν τις αὐτοὺς ἐπαινῇ καὶ αὔξῃ, φρονήματος ἐμπίμπλανται καὶ μεγαλαυχίας· ἢ οὐκ οἴει;

Ἔγωγε, ἔφη.

Οὐκοῦν ὅσῳ ἂν μεγαλαυχότεροι ὦσιν, δυσαλωτότεροι γίγνονται;

Εἰκός γε.

Ποῖός τις οὖν ἄν σοι δοκεῖ θηρευτὴς εἶναι, εἰ ἀνασοβοῖ θηρεύων καὶ δυσαλωτοτέραν τὴν ἄγραν ποιοῖ;

Δῆλον ὅτι φαῦλος.

Καὶ μὲν δὴ λόγοις τε καὶ ᾠδαῖς μὴ κηλεῖν ἀλλ' ἐξαγριαίνειν πολλὴ ἀμουσία· ἦ γάρ;

Δοκεῖ μοι.

Σκόπει δή, ὦ Ἱππόθαλες, ὅπως μὴ πᾶσι τούτοις ἔνοχον σαυτὸν ποιήσεις διὰ τὴν ποίησιν· καίτοι οἶμαι ἐγὼ ἄνδρα ποιήσει βλάπτοντα ἑαυτὸν οὐκ ἄν σε ἐθέλειν ὁμολογῆσαι ὡς ἀγαθός ποτ' ἐστὶν ποιητής, βλαβερὸς ὢν ἑαυτῷ.

Οὐ μὰ τὸν Δία, ἔφη· πολλὴ γὰρ ἂν ἀλογία εἴη. ἀλλὰ διὰ ταῦτα δή σοι, ὦ Σώκρατες, ἀνακοινοῦμαι, καὶ εἴ τι ἄλλο ἔχεις, συμβούλευε τίνα ἄν τις λόγον διαλεγόμενος ἢ τί πράττων προσφιλὴς παιδικοῖς γένοιτο.

Οὐ ῥᾴδιον, ἦν δ' ἐγώ, εἰπεῖν· ἀλλ' εἴ μοι ἐθελήσαις αὐτὸν ποιῆσαι εἰς λόγους ἐλθεῖν, ἴσως ἂν δυναίμην σοι ἐπιδεῖξαι

matters of love does not praise his beloved before he obtains him, for he is anxious about how the future will turn out. And also these good-looking men become full of pride and arrogance when someone praises and exalts them. Don't you think?"

"I do," he said.

"And by however much more they are arrogant, aren't they that much harder to catch?"

"It would seem so."

"What sort of hunter would a person seem to you then if, when hunting, he scared off the prey and made them harder to catch?"

"Clearly not a good one."

"And thus to praise in speech and song not to enchant but in fact to make savage is rather discordant, is it not?"

"So it seems to me."

"Watch out then, Hippothales, lest you make yourself liable to all these things through your poetry. Although I suppose you will not want to admit that a man who harms himself through his poetry could ever be a good poet, while he is harming himself."

"No, by Zeus," he said. "For that would be very illogical. But it is for these reasons, Socrates, that I have confided in you. If you have some other idea in mind, advise me on how to converse or what to do so that I may be endearing to my crush."

"It is not easy to explain," I said. "But if you are willing to make him come have a talk with me, perhaps I might be

ἃ χρὴ αὐτῷ διαλέγεσθαι ἀντὶ τούτων ὧν οὗτοι λέγειν τε καὶ ᾄδειν φασί σε.

Ἀλλ' οὐδέν, ἔφη, χαλεπόν. ἂν γὰρ εἰσέλθῃς μετὰ Κτησίππου τοῦδε καὶ καθεζόμενος διαλέγῃ, οἶμαι μὲν καὶ αὐτός σοι πρόσεισι—φιλήκοος γάρ, ὦ Σώκρατες, διαφερόντως ἐστίν, καὶ ἅμα, ὡς Ἑρμαῖα ἄγουσιν, ἀναμεμειγμένοι ἐν ταὐτῷ εἰσιν οἵ τε νεανίσκοι καὶ οἱ παῖδες—πρόσεισιν οὖν σοι. εἰ δὲ μή, Κτησίππῳ συνήθης ἐστὶν διὰ τὸν τούτου ἀνεψιὸν Μενέξενον· Μενεξένῳ μὲν γὰρ δὴ πάντων μάλιστα ἑταῖρος ὢν τυγχάνει. καλεσάτω οὖν οὗτος αὐτόν, ἐὰν ἄρα μὴ προσίῃ αὐτός.

Ταῦτα, ἦν δ' ἐγώ, χρὴ ποιεῖν. Καὶ ἅμα λαβὼν τὸν Κτήσιππον προσῇα εἰς τὴν παλαίστραν· οἱ δ' ἄλλοι ὕστεροι ἡμῶν ᾖσαν.

Εἰσελθόντες δὲ κατελάβομεν αὐτόθι τεθυκότας τε τοὺς παῖδας καὶ τὰ περὶ τὰ ἱερεῖα σχεδόν τι ἤδη πεποιημένα, ἀστραγαλίζοντάς τε δὴ καὶ κεκοσμημένους ἅπαντας. οἱ μὲν οὖν πολλοὶ ἐν τῇ αὐλῇ ἔπαιζον ἔξω, οἱ δέ τινες τοῦ ἀποδυτηρίου ἐν γωνίᾳ ἠρτίαζον ἀστραγάλοις παμπόλλοις, ἐκ φορμίσκων τινῶν προαιρούμενοι· τούτους δὲ περιέστασαν ἄλλοι θεωροῦντες.

ὧν δὴ καὶ ὁ Λύσις ἦν, καὶ εἱστήκει ἐν τοῖς παισί τε καὶ νεανίσκοις ἐστεφανωμένος καὶ τὴν ὄψιν διαφέρων, οὐ τὸ καλὸς εἶναι μόνον ἄξιος ἀκοῦσαι, ἀλλ' ὅτι καλός τε

able to demonstrate for you how it is best for you to talk to him, instead of saying the things that these men say you have been saying and singing."

"But that is no trouble," he said. "For if you go inside with Ktesippus here, and sit down to talk, I think he himself will probably come over to you, for he especially loves to listen to conversations. And also they are observing the Hermaea festival, the young men and the boys together, so he will come to you. But if he doesn't, still he associates with Ktesippus since he is cousins with Menexenus. Indeed, he has become a comrade to Menexenus most of all. Let him call him over, if he doesn't happen to approach on his own."

"This then is what I must do," I said. And taking Ktesippus along with me, I entered the palaestra.[2] The others followed after.

When we entered, we found there that the boys had already performed the sacrifice. With these sacred matters nearly done already, they were sitting around, playing dice and getting themselves adorned. Many of them sat in the courtyard, playing outside, but others were in the corner of the dressing room playing odds with a great number of dice, which they were taking from some little baskets. Others stood around watching them.

And one of them was Lysis. He stood among the boys and young men, wreathed and distinguished to behold, worthy not only of the reputation of good looks but also of a noble bearing. We made our way to the opposite side

κἀγαθός. καὶ ἡμεῖς εἰς τὸ καταντικρὺ ἀποχωρήσαντες ἐκαθεζόμεθα—ἦν γὰρ αὐτόθι ἡσυχία—καί τι ἀλλήλοις διελεγόμεθα. περιστρεφόμενος οὖν ὁ Λύσις θαμὰ ἐπεσκοπεῖτο ἡμᾶς, καὶ δῆλος ἦν ἐπιθυμῶν προσελθεῖν. τέως μὲν οὖν ἠπόρει τε καὶ ὤκνει μόνος προσιέναι, ἔπειτα ὁ Μενέξενος ἐκ τῆς αὐλῆς μεταξὺ παίζων εἰσέρχεται, καὶ ὡς εἶδεν ἐμέ τε καὶ τὸν Κτήσιππον, ᾔει παρακαθιζησόμενος· ἰδὼν οὖν αὐτὸν ὁ Λύσις εἵπετο καὶ συμπαρεκαθέζετο μετὰ τοῦ Μενεξένου. προσῆλθον δὴ καὶ οἱ ἄλλοι, καὶ δὴ καὶ ὁ Ἱπποθάλης, ἐπειδὴ πλείους ἑώρα ἐφισταμένους, τούτους ἐπηλυγισάμενος προσέστη ᾗ μὴ ᾤετο κατόψεσθαι τὸν Λύσιν, δεδιὼς μὴ αὐτῷ ἀπεχθάνοιτο· καὶ οὕτω προσεστὼς ἠκροᾶτο.

12

Ἤλυθες, ὦ φίλε κοῦρε· τρίτῃ σὺν νυκτὶ καὶ ἠοῖ
ἤλυθες· οἱ δὲ ποθεῦντες ἐν ἤματι γηράσκουσιν.
ὅσσον ἔαρ χειμῶνος, ὅσον μῆλον βραβίλοιο
ἥδιον, ὅσσον ὄις σφετέρης λασιωτέρη ἀρνός,
ὅσσον παρθενικὴ προφέρει τριγάμοιο γυναικός,
ὅσσον ἐλαφροτέρη μόσχου νεβρός, ὅσσον ἀηδών
συμπάντων λιγύφωνος ἀοιδοτάτη πετεηνῶν,

of the room and sat down—for it was quiet there—and spoke amongst ourselves. Lysis then often turned and glanced at us, and it was clear that he was eager to come over. For a while, though, he was apprehensive and hesitated to approach by himself. But then Menexenus came in from the courtyard from his game and, when he saw me and Ktesippus, came over and sat down with us. Then, when Lysis saw him, he followed and sat alongside Menexenus. And others came too, so that when Hippothales saw many of them standing there, he placed himself on their other side, as if they were a screen, in the hopes that Lysis would not catch sight of him, fearing lest he be annoyed. And there he stood and listened.

Theocritus, *Idylls*

You have come, o beloved youth. With the third night
 and dawn,
you have come. But those who feel desire age in a day.
By as much as spring is sweeter than winter, as much as
 the apple is sweeter
than the small sour grape, as much as the ewe has thicker
 wool
than the lamb, as much as a maiden surpasses a thrice-
 wedded woman,
as much as a fawn is more nimble than a calf, as much as
 the nightingale
with its shrill voice sings most sweetly of all winged
 creatures,

τόσσον ἔμ' εὔφρηνας σὺ φανείς, σκιερὴν δ' ὑπὸ φηγόν
ἠελίου φρύγοντος ὁδοιπόρος ἔδραμον ὥς τις.
εἴθ' ὁμαλοὶ πνεύσειαν ἐπ' ἀμφοτέροισιν Ἔρωτες
νῶιν, ἐπεσσομένοις δὲ γενοίμεθα πᾶσιν ἀοιδή·
δίω δή τινε τώδε μετὰ προτέροισι γενέσθην
φῶθ', ὃ μὲν εἴσπνηλος, φαίη χ' Ὡμυκλαϊάζων,
τὸν δ' ἕτερον πάλιν, ὥς κεν ὁ Θεσσαλὸς εἴποι, ἀίτην.
ἀλλήλους δ' ἐφίλησαν ἴσῳ ζυγῷ. ἦ ῥα τότ' ἦσαν
χρύσειοι πάλιν ἄνδρες, ὅτ' ἀντεφίλησ' ὁ φιληθείς.
εἰ γὰρ τοῦτο, πάτερ Κρονίδη, πέλοι, εἰ γάρ, ἀγήρῳ
ἀθάνατοι, γενεῇς δὲ διηκοσίῃσιν ἔπειτα
ἀγγείλειεν ἐμοί τις ἀνέξοδον εἰς Ἀχέροντα·
ἡ σὴ νῦν φιλότης καὶ τοῦ χαρίεντος ἀίτεω
πᾶσι διὰ στόματος, μετὰ δ' ἠιθέοισι μάλιστα.
ἀλλ' ἤτοι τούτων μὲν ὑπέρτεροι Οὐρανίωνες·
ἔσσεται ὡς ἐθέλουσιν. ἐγὼ δέ σε τὸν καλὸν αἰνέων
ψεύδεα ῥινὸς ὕπερθεν ἀραιῆς οὐκ ἀναφύσω.

by so much have you, appearing, gladdened me, and like
some traveler dashing
from the parching sun to the shade of an oak, I come
running.
If only Eros would breathe upon us both equally,
us two, and then we might become a song for all those
who come after:
"Quite divine were these two mortals above all those who
lived before,
the one the lover, as the Amyclaean would say,
and the other the one sought after, as the Thessalian
would put it.
They loved one another with an equal yoke. It was indeed
a golden age of men again, when the beloved loved the
lover."
Father Zeus and you immortals who do not age, if this
might be done,
then may it be that in two hundred generations
someone may bring a message to me in Acheron, whence
there is no exit:[3]
"Even now your love and that of your lovely beloved
is on the lips of all men, and most of all on that of young
men."
But of course these matters are in the care of the heavenly
gods on high.
It will be as they wish. But when I praise you as beautiful,
I will not grow any lies upon my nose.

ἣν γὰρ καί τι δάκῃς, τὸ μὲν ἀβλαβὲς εὐθὺς ἔθηκας,
διπλάσιον δ' ὤνησας, ἔχων δ' ἐπίμετρον ἀπῆλθον.
Νισαῖοι Μεγαρῆες, ἀριστεύοντες ἐρετμοῖς,
ὄλβιοι οἰκείοιτε, τὸν Ἀττικὸν ὡς περίαλλα
ξεῖνον ἐτιμήσασθε, Διοκλέα τὸν φιλόπαιδα.
αἰεί οἱ περὶ τύμβον ἀολλέες εἴαρι πρώτῳ
κοῦροι ἐριδμαίνουσι φιλήματος ἄκρα φέρεσθαι·
ὃς δέ κε προσμάξῃ γλυκερώτερα χείλεσι χείλη,
βριθόμενος στεφάνοισιν ἑὴν ἐς μητέρ' ἀπῆλθεν.
ὄλβιος ὅστις παισὶ φιλήματα κεῖνα διαιτᾷ.
ἦ που τὸν χαροπὸν Γανυμήδεα πόλλ' ἐπιβῶται
Λυδίῃ ἶσον ἔχειν πέτρῃ στόμα, χρυσὸν ὁποίῃ
πεύθονται, μὴ φαῦλος, ἐτήτυμον ἀργυραμοιβοί.

13

Οὐχ ἁμῖν τὸν Ἔρωτα μόνοις ἔτεχ', ὡς ἐδοκεῦμες,
Νικία, ᾧτινι τοῦτο θεῶν ποκα τέκνον ἔγεντο·
οὐχ ἁμῖν τὰ καλὰ πράτοις καλὰ φαίνεται ἦμεν,
οἳ θνατοὶ πελόμεσθα, τὸ δ' αὔριον οὐκ ἐσορῶμες·
ἀλλὰ καὶ Ἀμφιτρύωνος ὁ χαλκεοκάρδιος υἱός,
ὃς τὸν λῖν ὑπέμεινε τὸν ἄγριον, ἤρατο παιδός,

For though you snap a bit, you quickly take away the
hurt
and benefit me twice over, and I leave with something
extra.
Nisaean Megarians, best among rowers,
may you live blessed lives, since you honored above all
others
Diocles, the Attic stranger, who loved a boy.
Always at the start of spring, young men gather around
his tomb
and contend to take the top prize in kissing,
and whoever puts lips to lips most sweetly,
returns to his mother laden with wreathes.
Blessed is he who is the arbiter of these kisses for boys.
I suppose he often prays to bright-eyed Ganymede[4]
that his mouth be like to the Lydian stone on which
money-changers
discern gold, so that it not be deemed fake, but true.

. . . . .

Not only for us, as we once supposed, was Eros born,
Nicias, by whomever of the gods this child once was
begotten.[5]
Not for us first did his beauty appear as beauty,
we who are mortals and cannot see tomorrow.
But even the bronze-hearted son of Amphitryon,[6]
who survived the savage lion, adored a boy,

τοῦ χαρίεντος Ὕλα, τοῦ τὰν πλοκαμῖδα φορεῦντος,
καί νιν πάντ᾽ ἐδίδασκε, πατὴρ ὡσεὶ φίλον υἱόν,
ὅσσα μαθὼν ἀγαθὸς καὶ ἀοίδιμος αὐτὸς ἔγεντο·
χωρὶς δ᾽ οὐδέποκ᾽ ἦς, οὔτ᾽ εἰ μέσον ἆμαρ ὄροιτο,
οὔθ᾽ ὁπόχ᾽ ἁ λεύκιππος ἀνατρέχοι ἐς Διὸς Ἀώς,
οὔθ᾽ ὁπόκ᾽ ὀρτάλιχοι μινυροὶ ποτὶ κοῖτον ὁρῷεν,
σεισαμένας πτερὰ ματρὸς ἐπ᾽ αἰθαλόεντι πετεύρῳ,
ὡς αὐτῷ κατὰ θυμὸν ὁ παῖς πεποναμένος εἴη,
αὐτῷ δ᾽ εὖ ἕλκων ἐς ἀλαθινὸν ἄνδρ᾽ ἀποβαίη.
ἀλλ᾽ ὅτε τὸ χρύσειον ἔπλει μετὰ κῶας Ἰάσων
Αἰσονίδας, οἱ δ᾽ αὐτῷ ἀριστῆες συνέποντο
πασᾶν ἐκ πολίων προλελεγμένοι ὧν ὄφελός τι,
ἵκετο χὠ ταλαεργὸς ἀνὴρ ἐς ἀφνειὸν Ἰωλκόν,
Ἀλκμήνας υἱὸς Μιδεάτιδος ἡρωίνας,
σὺν δ᾽ αὐτῷ κατέβαινεν Ὕλας εὔεδρον ἐς Ἀργώ,
ἅτις κυανεᾶν οὐχ ἅψατο συνδρομάδων ναῦς,
ἀλλὰ διεξάιξε βαθὺν δ᾽ εἰσέδραμε Φᾶσιν,
αἰετὸς ὥς, μέγα λαῖτμα, ἀφ᾽ οὗ τότε χοιράδες ἔσταν.

Ἆμος δ᾽ ἀντέλλοντι Πελειάδες, ἐσχατιαὶ δέ
ἄρνα νέον βόσκοντι, τετραμμένου εἴαρος ἤδη,

the lovely Hylas, who wore his hair in curls.
And he taught him everything, just as a father does a
  beloved son,
all the things he'd learned in becoming noble and famous.
And he was never away from him—not when the sun
  rose to the middle
of the sky, nor when white-horsed dawn shot up to the
  house of Zeus,
nor when the whimpering little birds looked to their rest,
on their smoky perch as their mother shook out her wings—
so that the boy would be trained by him as he wished,
and, following well with him, would grow into a true man.
But when Jason son of Aeson went after the golden fleece,
and there followed with him the best of men,
chosen from every city as needed,
that much enduring man, the son of Alcmene, heroine
  of Midea,
came to wealthy Iolcus, and with him
Hylas went to the well-benched Argo,
which ship did not touch the dark clashing rocks,
but shot straight through and ran into deep Phasis
like an eagle at a huge expanse, and since then
the rocks have stood still.

When the Pleiades had risen, and the farthest lands
were pasturing their young lambs, and spring had just
  turned,

τᾶμος ναυτιλίας μιμνάσκετο θεῖος ἄωτος
ἡρώων, κοίλαν δὲ καθιδρυθέντες ἐς Ἀργώ
Ἑλλάσποντον ἵκοντο νότῳ τρίτον ἆμαρ ἀέντι,
εἴσω δ᾽ ὅρμον ἔθεντο Προποντίδος, ἔνθα Κιανῶν
αὔλακας εὐρύνοντι βόες τρίβοντες ἄροτρα.
ἐκβάντες δ᾽ ἐπὶ θῖνα κατὰ ζυγὰ δαῖτα πένοντο
δειελινοί, πολλοὶ δὲ μίαν στορέσαντο χαμεύναν.
λειμὼν γάρ σφιν ἔκειτο μέγα στιβάδεσσιν ὄνειαρ,
ἔνθεν βούτομον ὀξὺ βαθύν τ᾽ ἐτάμοντο κύπειρον.
κῴχεθ᾽ Ὕλας ὁ ξανθὸς ὕδωρ ἐπιδόρπιον οἴσων
αὐτῷ θ᾽ Ἡρακλῆι καὶ ἀστεμφεῖ Τελαμῶνι,
οἳ μίαν ἄμφω ἑταῖροι ἀεὶ δαίνυντο τράπεζαν,
χάλκεον ἄγγος ἔχων. τάχα δὲ κράναν ἐνόησεν
ἡμένῳ ἐν χώρῳ· περὶ δὲ θρύα πολλὰ πεφύκει,
κυάνεόν τε χελιδόνιον χλωρόν τ᾽ ἀδίαντον
καὶ θάλλοντα σέλινα καὶ εἰλιτενὴς ἄγρωστις.
ὕδατι δ᾽ ἐν μέσσῳ Νύμφαι χορὸν ἀρτίζοντο,
Νύμφαι ἀκοίμητοι, δειναὶ θεαὶ ἀγροιώταις,
Εὐνίκα καὶ Μαλὶς ἔαρ θ᾽ ὁρόωσα Νύχεια.
ἤτοι ὁ κοῦρος ἐπεῖχε ποτῷ πολυχανδέα κρωσσόν
βάψαι ἐπειγόμενος· ταὶ δ᾽ ἐν χερὶ πᾶσαι ἔφυσαν·
πασάων γὰρ ἔρως ἁπαλὰς φρένας ἐξεφόβησεν
Ἀργείῳ ἐπὶ παιδί. κατήριπε δ᾽ ἐς μέλαν ὕδωρ

then that divine flowering of heroes put their minds
to sailing, and sitting down in the Argo,
they entered the Hellespont on the third day by the south wind,
and they put into the harbor of Propontis, where the cattle
of the Cians carved broad furrows, wearing down their plows.
They came on shore and made their meal in pairs
at evening time, and many spread out one pallet.
For there was a big meadow that was good for their bed mats,
and there they cut down the sharp weeds and deep galingale.
Fair Hylas went off with a bronze jug to fetch water for the meal,
and with him went Heracles and steadfast Telamon,
two friends who always dined at the table together. Soon Hylas noticed
a spring in a settled place, and all around it rushes grew,
and dark swallow-wort and pale maidenhair
and blooming celery and marsh grasses.
In the middle of the water, the nymphs were dancing,
the sleepless nymphs, goddesses fearful to countryfolk,
Eunica and Malis and Nycheia, whose eyes see spring.
Here the lad reached out into the water with his wide-mouthed pail,
eager to dip it in. But all the nymphs grasped for his hand.
For desire for the Argive boy had struck

ἀθρόος, ὡς ὅτε πυρσὸς ἀπ᾽ οὐρανοῦ ἤριπεν ἀστήρ
ἀθρόος ἐν πόντῳ, ναύτας δέ τις εἶπεν ἑταίροις
κουφότερ᾽, ὦ παῖδες, ποιεῖσθ᾽ ὅπλα· πλευστικὸς οὖρος.
Νύμφαι μὲν σφετέροις ἐπὶ γούνασι κοῦρον ἔχοισαι
δακρυόεντ᾽ ἀγανοῖσι παρεψύχοντ᾽ ἐπέεσσιν·
Ἀμφιτρυωνιάδας δὲ ταρασσόμενος περὶ παιδί
ᾤχετο, Μαιωτιστὶ λαβὼν εὐκαμπέα τόξα
καὶ ῥόπαλον, τό οἱ αἰὲν ἐχάνδανε δεξιτερὰ χείρ.
τρὶς μὲν Ὕλαν ἄυσεν, ὅσον βαθὺς ἤρυγε λαιμός·
τρὶς δ᾽ ἄρ᾽ ὁ παῖς ὑπάκουσεν, ἀραιὰ δ᾽ ἵκετο φωνά
ἐξ ὕδατος, παρεὼν δὲ μάλα σχεδὸν εἴδετο πόρρω.
νεβροῦ φθεγξαμένας τις ἐν οὔρεσιν ὠμοφάγος λίς
ἐξ εὐνᾶς ἔσπευσεν ἑτοιμοτάταν ἐπὶ δαῖτα·
Ἡρακλέης τοιοῦτος ἐν ἀτρίπτοισιν ἀκάνθαις
παῖδα ποθῶν δεδόνητο, πολὺν δ᾽ ἐπελάμβανε χῶρον.
σχέτλιοι οἱ φιλέοντες, ἀλώμενος ὅσσ᾽ ἐμόγησεν
οὔρεα καὶ δρυμούς, τὰ δ᾽ Ἰάσονος ὕστερα πάντ᾽ ἧς.
ναῦς γέμεν ἄρμεν᾽ ἔχοισα μετάρσια τῶν παρεόντων,
ἱστία δ᾽ ἡμίθεοι μεσονύκτιον αὖτε καθαίρουν,
Ἡρακλῆα μένοντες. ὃ δ᾽ ᾇ πόδες ἆγον ἐχώρει
μαινόμενος· χαλεπὸς γὰρ ἔσω θεὸς ἧπαρ ἄμυσσεν.

their tender hearts. And he fell into the black water,
all at once, just as a burning star falls from the sky
all at once into the sea, and a sailor says to his comrades,
"Loosen the cables, boys. The wind is set for sailing."
While the nymphs, holding the lad in their laps,
tried to soothe him weeping with gentle words,
the son of Amphitryon, alarmed about the boy,
went out, taking his well-curved Scythian bow
and club, which his right hand always held.
Three times he called out "Hylas," as deeply as his throat
could roar.
Three times the boy replied, but his voice came
only softly through the water and, though he was very
nearby,
he sounded far away. A raw-eating lion, hearing a deer
cry out in the hills, will rush from rest to a ready meal;
thus was Heracles, in the untrodden thistles,
driven by longing for the boy, rushing all over the place.
Lovers are wretched! Such things he suffered as he
wandered
through mountains and forests, with all thoughts of Jason
left behind.
The ship was full, its rigging raised aloft by those who
were there,
and the heroes lowered the sails again at midnight,
awaiting Heracles. But he went where his feet took him,
maddened. For a harsh god was tearing his insides apart.

οὕτω μὲν κάλλιστος Ὕλας μακάρων ἀριθμεῖται·
Ἡρακλέην δ’ ἥρωες ἐκερτόμεον λιποναύταν,
οὕνεκεν ἠρώησε τριακοντάζυγον Ἀργώ,
πεζᾷ δ’ ἐς Κόλχους τε καὶ ἄξενον ἵκετο Φᾶσιν.

29

Οἶνος, ὦ φίλε παῖ, λέγεται, καὶ ἀλάθεα·
κἄμμε χρὴ μεθύοντας ἀλάθεας ἔμμεναι.
κἄγω μὲν τὰ φρένων ἐρέω κέατ’ ἐν μύχῳ·
οὐκ ὅλας φιλέην μ’ ἐθέλησθ’ ἀπὺ καρδίας.
γινώσκω· τὸ γὰρ αἴμισυ τὰς ζοΐας ἔχω
ζὰ τὰν σὰν ἰδέαν, τὸ δὲ λοῖπον ἀπώλετο·
κὤταν μὲν σὺ θέλῃς, μακάρεσσιν ἴσαν ἄγω
ἀμέραν· ὄτα δ’ οὐκ ἐθέλῃς σύ, μάλ’ ἐν σκότῳ.
πῶς ταῦτ’ ἄρμενα, τὸν φιλέοντ’ ὀνίαις δίδων;
ἀλλ’ αἴ μοί τι πίθοιο νέος προγενεστέρῳ,
τῷ κε λώιον αὖτος ἔχων ἔμ’ ἐπαινέσαις.
πόησαι καλίαν μίαν ἐνν ἔνι δενδρίῳ,
ὄππυι μηδὲν ἀπίξεται ἄγριον ὄρπετον.
νῦν δὲ τῶδε μὲν ἄματος ἄλλον ἔχῃς κλάδον,
ἄλλον δ’ αὔριον, ἐξ ἀτέρω δ’ ἄτερον μάτης·
καὶ μέν σευ τὸ κάλον τις ἴδων ῥέθος αἰνέσαι,

So it was that Hylas, so lovely, came to be counted among
the lost and blessed.
And the heroes mocked Heracles as a ship-deserter,
since he abandoned the thirty-benched Argo,
and came to the Colchians on foot and to inhospitable
Phasis.

. . . . .

"Wine and truth," as it is said, o beloved boy.
And so it is right for us too to be truthful when we're
drunk.
And I will say what is hidden in the marrow of my mind:
that you do not wish to love me from your whole heart.
I know. For I have only half a life left
due to your beauty, and the rest is lost.
Whenever you are willing, I lead a day like to the blessed
ones.
But when you do not wish it, I am the more in shadow.
How is this fitting, to give grief to your lover?
But if you, being young, would be persuaded by me,
for I am older, you would value me more and praise
me too.
Make just one nest in just one tree,
where no savage serpent will come.
But now on one day you have one branch, and another one
tomorrow, and from there you seek yet another.
And if someone sees you and praises your handsome face,

τῷ δ’ εὖθυς πλέον ἢ τριέτης ἐγένευ φίλος,
τὸν πρῶτον δὲ φίλεντα τρίταιον ἐθήκαο.
†ἄνδρων τῶν ὐπερανορέων δοκέης πνέην·
φίλη δ’, ἆς κε ζόης, τὸν ὔμοιον ἔχην ἄει.†
αἰ γὰρ ὧδε πόῃς, ἄγαθος μὲν ἀκούσεαι
ἐξ ἄστων· ὀ δέ τοί κ’ Ἔρος οὐ χαλέπως ἔχοι,
ὂς ἄνδρων φρένας εὐμαρέως ὐπαδάμναται
κἄμε μόλθακον ἐξ ἐπόησε σιδαρίω.
ἀλλὰ πὲρρ ἀπάλω στύματός σε πεδέρχομαι
ὀμνάσθην ὄτι πέρρυσιν ἦσθα νεώτερος,
κὤτι γηράλεοι πέλομεν πρὶν ἀπύπτυσαι
καὶ ῥύσσοι, νεότατα δ’ ἔχην παλινάγρετον
οὐκ ἔστι· πτέρυγας γὰρ ἐπωμαδίαις φόρει,
κἄμμες βαρδύτεροι τὰ ποτήμενα συλλάβην.
ταῦτα χρή σε νόεντα πέλην ποτιμώτερον
καί μοι τὠραμένῳ συνέραν ἀδόλως σέθεν,
ὅππως, ἄνικα τὰν γένυν ἀνδρεΐαν ἔχῃς,
ἀλλάλοισι πελώμεθ’ Ἀχιλλέιοι φίλοι.
αἰ δὲ ταῦτα φέρην ἀνέμοισιν ἐπιτρέπῃς,
ἐν θύμῳ δὲ λέγῃς, τί με, δαιμόνι’, ἐννόχλης;
νῦν μὲν κἀπὶ τὰ χρύσια μᾶλ’ ἔνεκεν σέθεν

straightaway you become a friend as if of more than
three years,
and make the one who loved you first a stranger of
three days.
You seem to breathe for overbearing men, but for
your life
it would be right to have one like-minded lover always.
For if you do this, you would be well spoken of
around town. And Eros would not be harsh to you,
who easily tames the minds of men
and softened even me from iron.
But by your tender mouth I beseech you
to remember that you were younger just a year ago,
and that before we can spit, we get old
and shriveled, and that youthfulness cannot be gotten
back
again. For it has wings on its shoulders,
and we are too slow to catch it as it flies away.
You must keep these things in mind
and be more kind to me and love me back
as simply as I love you, so that someday,
when you have a manly beard,
we may be to one another like Achillean lovers.
And if you throw these words of mine to the winds,
and say in your heart, "Why do you pester me,
strange man?"
then even though now I would gather the golden apples
for you

βαίην καὶ φύλακον νεκύων πεδὰ Κέρβερον,
τότα δ’ οὐδὲ κάλεντος ἐπ’ αὐλεΐαις θύραις
προμόλοιμί κε, παυσάμενος χαλέπω πόθω.

30

Ὤιαι τὼ χαλέπω καἰνομόρω τῶδε νοσήματος·
τετόρταιος ἔχει παῖδος ἔρος μῆνά με δεύτερον,
κάλω μὲν μετρίως, ἀλλ’ ὄποσον τῷ πόδι περρέχει
τὰς γᾶς, τοῦτο χάρις, ταὶς δὲ παραύαις γλύκυ μειδίαι.
καὶ νῦν μὲν τὸ κάκον ταῖς μὲν ἔχει ταῖς δ’ ὀν<ίησί με>,
τάχα δ’ οὐδ’ ὄσον ὔπνω ’πιτύχην ἔσσετ’ ἐρωία.
ἔχθες γὰρ παρίων ἔδρακε λέπτ’ ἄμμε δι’ ὀφρύων,
αἰδέσθεις προσίδην ἄντιος, ἠρεύθετο δὲ χρόα·
ἔμεθεν δὲ πλέον τὰς κραδίας ὦρος ἐδράξατο·
εἰς οἶκον δ’ ἀπέβαν ἔλκος ἔχων καῖνο<ν ἐν ἤπατι>.
πόλλα δ’ εἰσκαλέσαις θῦμον ἐμαύτῳ διελεξάμαν·
τί δῆτ’ αὖτε πόης; ἀλοσύνας τί ἔσχατον ἔσσεται;
λεύκαις οὐκέτ’ ἴσαισθ’ ὄττι φόρης ἐν κροτάφοις τρίχας;
ὥρα τοι φρονέην· μὴ <οὔτ>ι νέος τὰν ἰδέαν πέλων
πάντ’ ἔρδ’ ὄσσαπερ οἰ τὼν ἐτέων ἄρτι γεγεύμενοι.

or fetch Cerberus, guard-dog of the dead,
in that case I would not come to the courtyard door
even if you called, ceasing from this cruel desire.

▪ ▪ ▪ ▪ ▪

Oh, how cruel and doomed is my disease!
A quarterly love has held me for two months
for a boy who is just moderately good-looking, but excels
so much more
in grace right down to his toes, when he smiles sweetly
with his cheeks. Even now this affliction grips me
sometimes and at other times
releases me, but soon I will find no desired sleep.
For yesterday he looked at me delicately through his
eyelashes,
ashamed to look directly, and his face flushed.
And love grasped my heart even more,
and I went home with a fresh wound inside.
Summoning my soul, I argued on and on with myself:
"What are you doing all over again? What will be the end
of this madness?
Do you no longer know that you have white hairs at your
temples?
It is time for you to get smart. You are not at all young in
looks,
so stop doing all the things that men do when they're just
getting

καὶ μὰν ἄλλο σε λάθει· τὸ δ’ ἄρ’ ἦς λώιον ἔμμεναι
ξέννον τὼν χαλέπων παῖδος ἐρώ<των προγενέστερον>.
τῷ μὲν γὰρ βίος ἔρπει ἴσα γόννοις ἐλάφω θόας,
χαλάσει δ’ ἀτέρᾳ ποντοπόρην αὔριον ἄρμενα·
τὸ δ’ αὖτε γλυκέρας ἄνθεμον ἄβας πεδ’ ὐμαλίκων
μένει. τῷ δ’ ὀ πόθος καὶ τὸν ἔσω μύελον ἐσθίει
ὀμμιμνασκομένῳ, πόλλα δ’ ὄραι νύκτος ἐνύπνια,
παύσασθαι δ’ ἐνίαυτος χαλέπας οὐκ ἴ<κανος νόσω>.
ταῦτα κἄτερα πόλλα πρὸς ἔμον θῦμον ἐμεμψάμαν·
ὃ δὲ τοῦτ’ ἔφατ’· ὄττις δοκίμοι τὸν δολομάχανον
νικάσην Ἔρον, οὖτος δοκίμοι τοὶς ὐπὲρ ἀμμέων
εὔρην βραϊδίως ἄστερας ὀππόσσακιν ἔννεα.
καὶ νῦν, εἴτ’ ἐθέλω, χρή με μάκρον σχόντα τὸν ἄμφενα
ἔλκην τὸν ζύγον, εἴτ’ οὐκ ἐθέλω· ταῦτα γάρ, ὤγαθε,
βόλλεται θέος ὂς καὶ Δίος ἔσφαλε μέγαν νόον
καὔτας Κυπρογενήας· ἔμε μάν, φύλλον ἐπάμερον
σμίκρας δεύμενον αὔρας, ὀνέλων ὦκα φόρει <πνόᾳ>.

a taste of their years. And indeed you've forgotten
something else.
It is much better when you're older to be a stranger to the
cruel love
of a boy. For his life moves as if with the knees of a swift
deer,
and tomorrow he will let out his sails and move on to
somewhere else.
And again the flower of sweet youth likes to be with peers.
Whoever has desire eating into his marrow,
thinks back, and is haunted by dreams all night.
A year is not enough to stop his cruel disease."
With these and many other things I chided my heart.
And my soul replied, "Whoever thinks of defeating Eros
of wily devices
also thinks he can easily discover by how many more
times
than nine are the stars above. Even now,
whether I want it or not, it is necessary for me to hold
out my neck,
dragging the yoke. For these things, dear sir, are what the
god wishes,
Eros who has tripped up even the great mind of Zeus,
and also that of Cyprus-born Aphrodite. So too, like an
ephemeral leaf
lacking just a little breeze, he bears me away swiftly with
just a breath."

237a–241d

ΣΩ. Ἄγετε δή, ὦ Μοῦσαι, εἴτε δι᾽ ᾠδῆς εἶδος λίγειαι, εἴτε διὰ γένος μουσικὸν τὸ Λιγύων ταύτην ἔσχετ᾽ ἐπωνυμίαν, ξύμ μοι λάβεσθε τοῦ μύθου, ὅν με ἀναγκάζει ὁ βέλτιστος οὑτοσὶ λέγειν, ἵν᾽ ὁ ἑταῖρος αὐτοῦ, καὶ

11 THE WINGS OF LOVE: ADORING BOYS

There is no more eloquent discourse on the madness and passion of love than we find in Plato's Phaedrus. *(Phaedrus is the same person whose speech was excerpted from the* Symposium *in chapter 1.) In the parts included here, Socrates explains what* eros *is and gives two competing positions on whether young men should return the affections of those who feel true* eros *for them, or those who do not. (The first position is one he does* not *agree with, while the second is the one he does espouse.) Along the way, he offers a rapturous account of the blessings of* eros *for the soul: the madness of love, the power and pleasure of the gaze, and the sprouting of the wings of love.*

Plato, *Phaedrus*

Socrates: Come, o Muses, whether you have this name because you are clear-voiced or because you descend from the musical race of the Ligyans,[1] "stand by me" for my tale, which this most wonderful man compels

πρότερον δοκῶν τούτῳ σοφὸς εἶναι, νῦν ἔτι μᾶλλον δόξῃ.

Ἦν οὕτω δὴ παῖς, μᾶλλον δὲ μειρακίσκος, μάλα καλός· τούτῳ δὲ ἦσαν ἐρασταὶ πάνυ πολλοί. εἷς δέ τις αὐτῶν αἱμύλος ἦν, ὃς οὐδενὸς ἧττον ἐρῶν ἐπεπείκει τὸν παῖδα ὡς οὐκ ἐρῴη. καί ποτε αὐτὸν αἰτῶν ἔπειθεν τοῦτ᾽ αὐτό, ὡς μὴ ἐρῶντι πρὸ τοῦ ἐρῶντος δέοι χαρίζεσθαι, ἔλεγέν τε ὧδε—Περὶ παντός, ὦ παῖ, μία ἀρχὴ τοῖς μέλλουσι καλῶς βουλεύσεσθαι· εἰδέναι δεῖ περὶ οὗ ἂν ᾖ ἡ βουλή, ἢ παντὸς ἁμαρτάνειν ἀνάγκη. τοὺς δὲ πολλοὺς λέληθεν ὅτι οὐκ ἴσασι τὴν οὐσίαν ἑκάστου. ὡς οὖν εἰδότες οὐ διομολογοῦνται ἐν ἀρχῇ τῆς σκέψεως, προελθόντες δὲ τὸ εἰκὸς ἀποδιδόασιν· οὔτε γὰρ ἑαυτοῖς οὔτε ἀλλήλοις ὁμολογοῦσιν. ἐγὼ οὖν καὶ σὺ μὴ πάθωμεν ὃ ἄλλοις ἐπιτιμῶμεν, ἀλλ᾽ ἐπειδὴ σοὶ καὶ ἐμοὶ ὁ λόγος πρόκειται πότερα ἐρῶντι ἢ μὴ μᾶλλον εἰς φιλίαν ἰτέον, περὶ ἔρωτος οἷόν τ᾽ ἔστι καὶ ἣν ἔχει δύναμιν, ὁμολογίᾳ θέμενοι ὅρον, εἰς τοῦτο ἀποβλέποντες καὶ ἀναφέροντες τὴν σκέψιν ποιώμεθα εἴτε ὠφελίαν εἴτε βλάβην παρέχει.

me to deliver, so that I, his friend, having formerly seemed wise to him, may now seem even more so.

There was once a boy, or rather a youth, and he was very handsome. He had a great many admirers. There was a wily one among them who was no less in love than the others but persuaded the boy that he was not. And at some point, while wooing him, he convinced him of this too, that it was right to please someone who is not in love with him rather than someone who is. He said the following: "In general, boy, there is one rule for those hoping to make good decisions. It is necessary to know what the decision is really about, or one will be compelled to err. But most people aren't even aware that they don't know the reality of each thing and, then, thinking that they *do* know it, they don't even agree upon the premises of their investigation, and onward they go with exactly the sort of outcome you'd expect. For they do not even agree with themselves, let alone with one another. Therefore, let it be that you and I not suffer what we censure in others. Instead, since the question that lies before us is whether to the one who desires or the one who doesn't it is right to give affection, let us first come to a definition of *eros*—both what it is and what its power is—and having this in mind and referring to it as is needed, let us turn to our inquiry as to whether *eros* brings help or harm.

ὅτι μὲν οὖν δὴ ἐπιθυμία τις ὁ ἔρως, ἅπαντι δῆλον· ὅτι δ' αὖ καὶ μὴ ἐρῶντες ἐπιθυμοῦσι τῶν καλῶν, ἴσμεν. τῷ δὴ τὸν ἐρῶντά τε καὶ μὴ κρινοῦμεν; δεῖ αὖ νοῆσαι ὅτι ἡμῶν ἐν ἑκάστῳ δύο τινέ ἐστον ἰδέα ἄρχοντε καὶ ἄγοντε, οἷν ἑπόμεθα ᾗ ἂν ἄγητον, ἡ μὲν ἔμφυτος οὖσα ἐπιθυμία ἡδονῶν, ἄλλη δὲ ἐπίκτητος δόξα, ἐφιεμένη τοῦ ἀρίστου. τούτω δὲ ἐν ἡμῖν τοτὲ μὲν ὁμονοεῖτον, ἔστι δὲ ὅτε στασιάζετον· καὶ τοτὲ μὲν ἡ ἑτέρα, ἄλλοτε δὲ ἡ ἑτέρα κρατεῖ. δόξης μὲν οὖν ἐπὶ τὸ ἄριστον λόγῳ ἀγούσης καὶ κρατούσης τῷ κράτει σωφροσύνη ὄνομα· ἐπιθυμίας δὲ ἀλόγως ἑλκούσης ἐπὶ ἡδονὰς καὶ ἀρξάσης ἐν ἡμῖν τῇ ἀρχῇ ὕβρις ἐπωνομάσθη.

ὕβρις δὲ δὴ πολυώνυμον—πολυμελὲς γὰρ καὶ πολυμερές—καὶ τούτων τῶν ἰδεῶν ἐκπρεπὴς ἣ ἂν τύχῃ γενομένη, τὴν αὑτῆς ἐπωνυμίαν ὀνομαζόμενον τὸν ἔχοντα παρέχεται, οὔτε τινὰ καλὴν οὔτ' ἐπαξίαν κεκτῆσθαι. περὶ μὲν γὰρ ἐδωδὴν κρατοῦσα τοῦ λόγου τε τοῦ ἀρίστου καὶ τῶν ἄλλων ἐπιθυμιῶν ἐπιθυμία γαστριμαργία τε καὶ τὸν ἔχοντα ταὐτὸν τοῦτο κεκλημένον παρέξεται· περὶ δ' αὖ μέθας τυραννεύσασα, τὸν κεκτημένον ταύτῃ ἄγουσα, δῆλον οὗ τεύξεται προσρήματος· καὶ τἆλλα δὴ τὰ τούτων ἀδελφὰ καὶ ἀδελφῶν ἐπιθυμιῶν ὀνόματα τῆς ἀεὶ δυναστευούσης ᾗ προσήκει καλεῖσθαι πρόδηλον. ἧς δ' ἕνεκα πάντα τὰ πρόσθεν εἴρηται, σχεδὸν μὲν ἤδη

"Now, it is clear to all that *eros* is desire. And we know too that those who are not in love still desire whatever is beautiful. How then do we distinguish between the one who feels *eros* and the one who does not? We must discern that in each of us there are two ideas that rule and lead us, and which we follow wherever they go, these being, first, our own inborn desire for pleasure and, second, cultural influence to aim for whatever is best. Now, sometimes these two are in agreement within us, and sometimes they are at odds. Sometimes one is empowered, and at other times the other. When cultural influence leads and prevails toward the best end through reasoning, the name for it is 'moderation.' But when desire rules us and drags us to pleasure, its rule is called 'excess.'

"Excess has many names—for it has many limbs and many parts—and of these forms, the one that happens to be most prominent gives its name to the person who has this quality, and there's nothing beautiful or honorable about having it. So if desire for food wins over his better reasoning and other desires, it is called gluttony and the person who has this desire will be called a glutton. And, again, if desire for drink is dictating, then the excess will have that name and it is clear what he will be called. And it is clear that other similar names will be given for other such desires, whichever holds sway in each case. The cause of this should be evident by now

φανερόν, λεχθὲν δὲ ἢ μὴ λεχθὲν πάντως σαφέστερον· ἡ γὰρ ἄνευ λόγου δόξης ἐπὶ τὸ ὀρθὸν ὁρμώσης κρατήσασα ἐπιθυμία πρὸς ἡδονὴν ἀχθεῖσα κάλλους, καὶ ὑπὸ αὖ τῶν ἑαυτῆς συγγενῶν ἐπιθυμιῶν ἐπὶ σωμάτων κάλλος ἐρρωμένως ῥωσθεῖσα νικήσασα ἀγωγῇ, ἀπ᾽ αὐτῆς τῆς ῥώμης ἐπωνυμίαν λαβοῦσα, ἔρως ἐκλήθη.

Ἀτάρ, ὦ φίλε Φαῖδρε, δοκῶ τι σοί, ὥσπερ ἐμαυτῷ, θεῖον πάθος πεπονθέναι;

ΦΑΙ. Πάνυ μὲν οὖν, ὦ Σώκρατες, παρὰ τὸ εἰωθὸς εὔροιά τίς σε εἴληφεν.

ΣΩ. Σιγῇ τοίνυν μου ἄκουε. τῷ ὄντι γὰρ θεῖος ἔοικεν ὁ τόπος εἶναι, ὥστε ἐὰν ἄρα πολλάκις νυμφόληπτος προϊόντος τοῦ λόγου γένωμαι, μὴ θαυμάσῃς· τὰ νῦν γὰρ οὐκέτι πόρρω διθυράμβων φθέγγομαι.

ΦΑΙ. Ἀληθέστατα λέγεις.

ΣΩ. Τούτων μέντοι σὺ αἴτιος. ἀλλὰ τὰ λοιπὰ ἄκουε· ἴσως γὰρ κἂν ἀποτράποιτο τὸ ἐπιόν. ταῦτα μὲν οὖν θεῷ μελήσει, ἡμῖν δὲ πρὸς τὸν παῖδα πάλιν τῷ λόγῳ ἰτέον.

Εἶεν, ὦ φέριστε· ὃ μὲν δὴ τυγχάνει ὂν περὶ οὗ βουλευτέον, εἴρηταί τε καὶ ὥρισται, βλέποντες δὲ δὴ πρὸς αὐτὸ τὰ λοιπὰ λέγωμεν τίς ὠφελία ἢ βλάβη ἀπό τε ἐρῶντος καὶ μὴ τῷ χαριζομένῳ ἐξ εἰκότος

from all that has already been said, but anything spoken is altogether clearer than what is unspoken. For it is the case that desire that overpowers the influence of reason to do what's right and that leads to the pleasure of the beautiful and that, again, is vigorously strong-armed by similar desires toward the beauty of the body, and that wins out in the end—this desire takes its name from this very force and is called *eros*."

But, my beloved Phaedrus, do I not seem to you, as to myself, to be experiencing divine inspiration?

Phaedrus: Very much so, Socrates. A certain unusual fluency seems to have taken hold of you.

Socrates: Then listen in silence. For truly this place seems to be divine, so do not wonder if often while my speech proceeds I seem to become frenzied like someone seized by nymphs. For even now I am close to uttering dithyrambs!

Phaedrus: That's for sure.

Socrates: And indeed you are to blame for this! But hear the rest. For perhaps the approach of frenzy may be averted. In any case, let these things be a care to the god; we must turn our discussion to the boy once again.

"Well, my dearest, since we have spoken of and decided what our subject must be, let us keep our eye on the ball and discuss the remaining issue, that is, what good or harm is likely to follow from granting

συμβήσεται. τῷ δὴ ὑπὸ ἐπιθυμίας ἀρχομένῳ δουλεύοντί τε ἡδονῇ ἀνάγκη που τὸν ἐρώμενον ὡς ἥδιστον ἑαυτῷ παρασκευάζειν· νοσοῦντι δὲ πᾶν ἡδὺ τὸ μὴ ἀντιτεῖνον, κρεῖττον δὲ καὶ ἴσον ἐχθρόν. οὔτε δὴ κρείττω οὔτε ἰσούμενον ἑκὼν ἐραστὴς παιδικὰ ἀνέξεται, ἥττω δὲ καὶ ὑποδεέστερον ἀεὶ ἀπεργάζεται· ἥττων δὲ ἀμαθὴς σοφοῦ, δειλὸς ἀνδρείου, ἀδύνατος εἰπεῖν ῥητορικοῦ, βραδὺς ἀγχίνου.

τοσούτων κακῶν καὶ ἔτι πλειόνων κατὰ τὴν διάνοιαν ἐραστὴν ἐρωμένῳ ἀνάγκη γιγνομένων τε καὶ φύσει ἐνόντων [τῶν] μὲν ἥδεσθαι, τὰ δὲ παρασκευάζειν, ἢ στέρεσθαι τοῦ παραυτίκα ἡδέος. φθονερὸν δὴ ἀνάγκη εἶναι, καὶ πολλῶν μὲν ἄλλων συνουσιῶν ἀπείργοντα καὶ ὠφελίμων ὅθεν ἂν μάλιστ' ἀνὴρ γίγνοιτο, μεγάλης αἴτιον εἶναι βλάβης, μεγίστης δὲ τῆς ὅθεν ἂν φρονιμώτατος εἴη. τοῦτο δὲ ἡ θεία φιλοσοφία τυγχάνει ὄν, ἧς ἐραστὴν παιδικὰ ἀνάγκη πόρρωθεν εἴργειν, περίφοβον ὄντα τοῦ καταφρονηθῆναι·

favors to someone who is in love versus someone who is not. For someone who is ruled by desire and enslaved to pleasure, it will be a matter of necessity, I would think, that he procure from his beloved as much pleasure as he can for himself. For to someone who is sick, everything is sweet that cannot oppose him, but anything stronger or equal to him is an enemy. So he will not willingly endure that his darling be better than he or equal, but he will always work to make him less than and inferior. The ignorant man is inferior to the wise, the coward to the man of courage, the tongue-tied to the eloquent speaker, the slow-witted to the clever.

"Such evils of mind, and ones even worse than these, must be found by the lover in the beloved. Both those that are there by nature and those that he brings about are pleasing to him, but the lack of them is not immediately pleasurable for him. It is necessary that he be jealous, and that he keep the boy from any other society, especially whoever might be most beneficial to his becoming a man, and thus he is responsible for great harm, and the greatest as regards that which would make the lad most sensible. For this happens to be divine philosophy, the very thing from which the lover must keep his darling far removed due to his terrible fear of being looked upon with disdain.

τά τε ἄλλα μηχανᾶσθαι ὅπως ἂν ᾖ πάντα ἀγνοῶν καὶ πάντα ἀποβλέπων εἰς τὸν ἐραστήν, οἷος ὢν τῷ μὲν ἥδιστος, ἑαυτῷ δὲ βλαβερώτατος ἂν εἴη. τὰ μὲν οὖν κατὰ διάνοιαν ἐπίτροπός τε καὶ κοινωνὸς οὐδαμῇ λυσιτελὴς ἀνὴρ ἔχων ἔρωτα.

Τὴν δὲ τοῦ σώματος ἕξιν τε καὶ θεραπείαν οἵαν τε καὶ ὡς θεραπεύσει οὗ ἂν γένηται κύριος, ὃς ἡδὺ πρὸ ἀγαθοῦ ἠνάγκασται διώκειν, δεῖ μετὰ ταῦτα ἰδεῖν. ὀφθήσεται δὴ μαλθακόν τινα καὶ οὐ στερεὸν διώκων, οὐδ᾽ ἐν ἡλίῳ καθαρῷ τεθραμμένον ἀλλὰ ὑπὸ συμμιγεῖ σκιᾷ, πόνων μὲν ἀνδρείων καὶ ἱδρώτων ξηρῶν ἄπειρον, ἔμπειρον δὲ ἁπαλῆς καὶ ἀνάνδρου διαίτης, ἀλλοτρίοις χρώμασι καὶ κόσμοις χήτει οἰκείων κοσμούμενον, ὅσα τε ἄλλα τούτοις ἕπεται πάντα ἐπιτηδεύοντα, ἃ δῆλα καὶ οὐκ ἄξιον περαιτέρω προβαίνειν, ἀλλὰ ἓν κεφάλαιον ὁρισαμένους ἐπ᾽ ἄλλο ἰέναι· τὸ γὰρ τοιοῦτον σῶμα ἐν πολέμῳ τε καὶ ἄλλαις χρείαις ὅσαι μεγάλαι οἱ μὲν ἐχθροὶ θαρροῦσιν, οἱ δὲ φίλοι καὶ αὐτοὶ οἱ ἐρασταὶ φοβοῦνται.

Τοῦτο μὲν οὖν ὡς δῆλον ἐατέον, τὸ δ᾽ ἐφεξῆς ῥητέον, τίνα ἡμῖν ὠφελίαν ἢ τίνα βλάβην περὶ τὴν κτῆσιν ἡ τοῦ ἐρῶντος ὁμιλία τε καὶ ἐπιτροπεία παρέξεται. σαφὲς δὴ τοῦτό γε παντὶ μέν, μάλιστα δὲ τῷ ἐραστῇ, ὅτι τῶν φιλτάτων τε καὶ εὐνουστάτων καὶ θειοτάτων κτημάτων ὀρφανὸν πρὸ παντὸς εὔξαιτ᾽ ἂν

"And he will devise other things too so that the boy is ignorant of everything and looks to his lover for everything and becomes someone who is most pleasing to him, the lover, and most harmful to himself. As regards his mind, then, a man in love is not in any way a profitable steward or partner.

"It is necessary to consider next what sort of habits and service to the body such a master would provide, whoever is compelled to pursue the pleasurable rather than the good. He will clearly pursue someone soft, not firm, and not raised in the pure light of day but rather in the mottled shade, inexperienced in manly labors and dry sweats, but experienced in weak, unmanly activities, adorned with a complexion and cosmetics that are artificial (since he lacks his own tone), and who otherwise practices all that follows from these things, which are evident and not worth discussing any further. Having summed them up, it is better to move on to something else. For such a body in war and all great matters encourages a man's enemies, and strikes fear into the hearts of his friends and lovers.

"This, then, is self-evident and can be skipped, but we must speak about the next issue, which is what help or harm the companionship and guidance of such a lover will provide in regard to property. For it is clear to anyone, but to the lover most of all, that he would wish above all else for his beloved to be bereft

εἶναι τὸν ἐρώμενον· πατρὸς γὰρ καὶ μητρὸς καὶ συγγενῶν καὶ φίλων στέρεσθαι ἂν αὐτὸν δέξαιτο, διακωλυτὰς καὶ ἐπιτιμητὰς ἡγούμενος τῆς ἡδίστης πρὸς αὐτὸν ὁμιλίας. ἀλλὰ μὴν οὐσίαν γ' ἔχοντα χρυσοῦ ἤ τινος ἄλλης κτήσεως οὔτε εὐάλωτον ὁμοίως οὔτε ἁλόντα εὐμεταχείριστον ἡγήσεται· ἐξ ὧν πᾶσα ἀνάγκη ἐραστὴν παιδικοῖς φθονεῖν μὲν οὐσίαν κεκτημένοις, ἀπολλυμένης δὲ χαίρειν. ἔτι τοίνυν ἄγαμον, ἄπαιδα, ἄοικον ὅτι πλεῖστον χρόνον παιδικὰ ἐραστὴς εὔξαιτ' ἂν γενέσθαι, τὸ αὑτοῦ γλυκὺ ὡς πλεῖστον χρόνον καρποῦσθαι ἐπιθυμῶν.

Ἔστι μὲν δὴ καὶ ἄλλα κακά, ἀλλά τις δαίμων ἔμειξε τοῖς πλείστοις ἐν τῷ παραυτίκα ἡδονήν, οἷον κόλακι, δεινῷ θηρίῳ καὶ βλάβῃ μεγάλῃ, ὅμως ἐπέμειξεν ἡ φύσις ἡδονήν τινα οὐκ ἄμουσον, καί τις ἑταίραν ὡς βλαβερὸν ψέξειεν ἄν, καὶ ἄλλα πολλὰ τῶν τοιουτοτρόπων θρεμμάτων τε καὶ ἐπιτηδευμάτων, οἷς τό γε καθ' ἡμέραν ἡδίστοισιν εἶναι ὑπάρχει· παιδικοῖς δὲ ἐραστὴς πρὸς τῷ βλαβερῷ καὶ εἰς τὸ συνημερεύειν πάντων ἀηδέστατον. ἥλικα γὰρ δὴ καὶ ὁ παλαιὸς λόγος τέρπειν τὸν ἥλικα—ἡ γὰρ οἶμαι

of all the most lovely, thoughtful, and divine possessions. For he would even hope to receive him stripped of his father, mother, family, and friends, thinking that they might hinder or censure his sweetest couplings with the lad. But he will also think that someone who is wealthy, whether in gold or some other form of property, will not be easy to catch and, likewise, not easy to manage once caught. For all these reasons, there is every necessity for a lover to begrudge his darling the owning of wealth, and to rejoice in its loss. Even beyond this the lover would pray that his darling, for as long as possible, be unmarried, without children, and homeless, desiring to reap what is sweet for himself for as long as possible.

"And there are still other evils, but some god has mixed them up with the most momentary of pleasures, just as with a flatterer, a terrible creature and a source of great harm, but one in which nature has mixed in a certain pleasure that is not unharmonious. One might fault a prostitute as noxious, and there are many other such creatures and practices in which the experience while it lasts is most pleasant. But a lover is not only harmful to his darling but the most unpleasant of all to spend time with. For indeed the old proverb says that 'like likes like'—and I think this means that closeness in age leads to similar pleasures and, through this similarity, provides

χρόνου ἰσότης ἐπ᾽ ἴσας ἡδονὰς ἄγουσα δι᾽ ὁμοιότητα φιλίαν παρέχεται—ἀλλ᾽ ὅμως κόρον γε καὶ ἡ τούτων συνουσία ἔχει. καὶ μὴν τό γε ἀναγκαῖον αὖ βαρὺ παντὶ περὶ πᾶν λέγεται· ὃ δὴ πρὸς τῇ ἀνομοιότητι μάλιστα ἐραστὴς πρὸς παιδικὰ ἔχει. νεωτέρῳ γὰρ πρεσβύτερος συνὼν οὔθ᾽ ἡμέρας οὔτε νυκτὸς ἑκὼν ἀπολείπεται, ἀλλ᾽ ὑπ᾽ ἀνάγκης τε καὶ οἴστρου ἐλαύνεται, ὃς ἐκείνῳ μὲν ἡδονὰς ἀεὶ διδοὺς ἄγει, ὁρῶντι, ἀκούοντι, ἁπτομένῳ, καὶ πᾶσαν αἴσθησιν αἰσθανομένῳ τοῦ ἐρωμένου, ὥστε μεθ᾽ ἡδονῆς ἀραρότως αὐτῷ ὑπηρετεῖν·

τῷ δὲ δὴ ἐρωμένῳ ποῖον παραμύθιον ἢ τίνας ἡδονὰς διδοὺς ποιήσει τὸν ἴσον χρόνον συνόντα μὴ οὐχὶ ἐπ᾽ ἔσχατον ἐλθεῖν ἀηδίας—ὁρῶντι μὲν ὄψιν πρεσβυτέραν καὶ οὐκ ἐν ὥρᾳ, ἑπομένων δὲ τῶν ἄλλων ταύτῃ, ἃ καὶ λόγῳ ἐστὶν ἀκούειν οὐκ ἐπιτερπές, μὴ ὅτι δὴ ἔργῳ ἀνάγκης ἀεὶ προσκειμένης μεταχειρίζεσθαι, φυλακάς τε δὴ καχυποτόπους φυλαττομένῳ διὰ παντὸς καὶ πρὸς ἅπαντας, ἀκαίρους τε ἐπαίνους καὶ ὑπερβάλλοντας ἀκούοντι, ὡς δ᾽ αὔτως ψόγους νήφοντος μὲν οὐκ ἀνεκτούς, εἰς δὲ μέθην ἰόντος πρὸς τῷ μὴ ἀνεκτῷ ἐπαισχεῖς, παρρησίᾳ κατακορεῖ καὶ ἀναπεπταμένῃ χρωμένου;

Καὶ ἐρῶν μὲν βλαβερός τε καὶ ἀηδής, λήξας δὲ τοῦ ἔρωτος εἰς τὸν ἔπειτα χρόνον ἄπιστος, εἰς ὃν πολλὰ καὶ μετὰ πολλῶν ὅρκων τε καὶ δεήσεων ὑπισχνούμενος μόγις κατεῖχε τήν γ᾽ ἐν τῷ τότε συνουσίαν

friendship—but nonetheless the time spent together by these men becomes sour. For constraint of any kind is said to become heavy for everyone, and indeed the lover, being quite dissimilar, becomes most of all a constraint on his darling. For the one being much older than the other does not willingly leave him day or night, but is driven by the sting of compulsion, which always gives him pleasures, whether through seeing, hearing, touching, or feeling his beloved through any other sense, so that with pleasure he does him service constantly.

"But by offering what respite or pleasures to his beloved will he make passing this same amount of time with him not hit the very outer reaches of unpleasantness—as he looks upon his old face, no longer in its prime, with all the rest of him in similar shape, which is not even pleasant to hear about, let alone to be in fact always forced to touch? And meanwhile he is guarded suspiciously in every way against everyone, listening to ill-timed and overdone praise or likewise to unbearable reproaches when the lover is sober, and when he is drunk to comments that are shameful as well an unendurable, with his insatiable outspokenness on full display.

"And if while he is in love he is harmful and unpleasant, when he has ceased to feel love he will then become faithless to the very one he scarcely held on to with entreaties and promises to endure a

ἐπίπονον οὖσαν φέρειν δι' ἐλπίδα ἀγαθῶν. τότε δὴ δέον ἐκτίνειν, μεταβαλὼν ἄλλον ἄρχοντα ἐν αὑτῷ καὶ προστάτην, νοῦν καὶ σωφροσύνην ἀντ' ἔρωτος καὶ μανίας, ἄλλος γεγονὼς λέληθεν τὰ παιδικά. καὶ ὁ μὲν αὐτὸν χάριν ἀπαιτεῖ τῶν τότε, ὑπομιμνῄσκων τὰ πραχθέντα καὶ λεχθέντα, ὡς τῷ αὐτῷ διαλεγόμενος· ὁ δὲ ὑπ' αἰσχύνης οὔτε εἰπεῖν τολμᾷ ὅτι ἄλλος γέγονεν, οὔθ' ὅπως τὰ τῆς προτέρας ἀνοήτου ἀρχῆς ὁρκωμόσιά τε καὶ ὑποσχέσεις ἐμπεδώσῃ ἔχει, νοῦν ἤδη ἐσχηκὼς καὶ σεσωφρονηκώς, ἵνα μὴ πράττων ταὐτὰ τῷ πρόσθεν ὅμοιός τε ἐκείνῳ καὶ ὁ αὐτὸς πάλιν γένηται.

φυγὰς δὴ γίγνεται ἐκ τούτων, καὶ ἀπεστερηκὼς ὑπ' ἀνάγκης ὁ πρὶν ἐραστής, ὀστράκου μεταπεσόντος, ἵεται φυγῇ μεταβαλών· ὁ δὲ ἀναγκάζεται διώκειν ἀγανακτῶν καὶ ἐπιθεάζων, ἠγνοηκὼς τὸ ἅπαν ἐξ ἀρχῆς, ὅτι οὐκ ἄρα ἔδει ποτὲ ἐρῶντι καὶ ὑπ' ἀνάγκης ἀνοήτῳ χαρίζεσθαι, ἀλλὰ πολὺ μᾶλλον μὴ ἐρῶντι καὶ νοῦν ἔχοντι· εἰ δὲ μή, ἀναγκαῖον εἴη ἐνδοῦναι αὑτὸν ἀπίστῳ, δυσκόλῳ, φθονερῷ, ἀηδεῖ,

painful companionship then in the hopes of future benefits. But since then it is indeed necessary to pay up, he has switched to a new ruler and leader within himself and has turned to sense and sensibility in place of *eros* and madness. Unbeknownst to his darling, he has become another person. And the young man asks for favors in return, reminding him of all that was said and done, as if he were still dealing with the same man. And, out of shame, the lover does not dare to admit that he has become a different person, nor is he able to make good on the oaths and promises made under the prior, mindless rule now that he is back in his right and sound mind, lest by doing the same things as before he becomes like to the way he was again.

"Indeed he is a fugitive from these things and by necessity the former lover has become a defrauder. The shoe is on the other foot, and he turns tail and runs. And now the young man is compelled to pursue him with accusations and imprecations, not realizing at all from the start that he ought never to have to have looked with favor upon someone struck by *eros*, someone necessarily out of his mind, but that it would have been far better to be with someone who was not in love and was in his right mind. For in that case he would not have given himself over to someone faithless, ill-tempered, jealous, and unpleasant, both harmful to his wealth and harmful to the

βλαβερῷ μὲν πρὸς οὐσίαν, βλαβερῷ δὲ πρὸς τὴν τοῦ σώματος ἕξιν, πολὺ δὲ βλαβερωτάτῳ πρὸς τὴν τῆς ψυχῆς παίδευσιν, ἧς οὔτε ἀνθρώποις οὔτε θεοῖς τῇ ἀληθείᾳ τιμιώτερον οὔτε ἔστιν οὔτε ποτὲ ἔσται.

ταῦτά τε οὖν χρή, ὦ παῖ, συννοεῖν, καὶ εἰδέναι τὴν ἐραστοῦ φιλίαν ὅτι οὐ μετ' εὐνοίας γίγνεται, ἀλλὰ σιτίου τρόπον, χάριν πλησμονῆς, ὡς λύκοι ἄρνας ἀγαπῶσιν, ὣς παῖδα φιλοῦσιν ἐρασταί.

Τοῦτ' ἐκεῖνο, ὦ Φαῖδρε. οὐκέτ' ἂν τὸ πέρα ἀκούσαις ἐμοῦ λέγοντος, ἀλλ' ἤδη σοι τέλος ἐχέτω ὁ λόγος.

244a–b

ΣΩ. Ποῦ δή μοι ὁ παῖς πρὸς ὃν ἔλεγον; ἵνα καὶ τοῦτο ἀκούσῃ, καὶ μὴ ἀνήκοος ὢν φθάσῃ χαρισάμενος τῷ μὴ ἐρῶντι.

ΦΑΙ. Οὗτος παρά σοι μάλα πλησίον ἀεὶ πάρεστιν, ὅταν σὺ βούλῃ.

ΣΩ. Οὑτωσὶ τοίνυν, ὦ παῖ καλέ, ἐννόησον, ὡς ὁ μὲν πρότερος ἦν λόγος Φαίδρου τοῦ Πυθοκλέους, Μυρρινουσίου ἀνδρός· ὃν δὲ μέλλω λέγειν, Στησιχόρου τοῦ Εὐφήμου, Ἱμεραίου. λεκτέος δὲ ὧδε, ὅτι Οὐκ ἔστ' ἔτυμος λόγος ὃς ἂν παρόντος ἐραστοῦ τῷ μὴ ἐρῶντι μᾶλλον φῇ δεῖν χαρίζεσθαι, διότι δὴ ὁ μὲν μαίνεται, ὁ δὲ σωφρονεῖ. εἰ μὲν γὰρ ἦν ἁπλοῦν τὸ

state of his body, and by far the most harmful to the education of his soul, of which, in truth, there is among neither gods nor men anything of higher worth, nor will there ever be.

"My boy, you must keep these things in mind and know that the affection of a lover is not derived from goodwill but rather is like a desire for food for the sake of satisfaction. Just as wolves love lambs, so do lovers adore their lad."

That's it, Phaedrus. Do not listen to me anymore, but here let my speech finds its end.

▪ ▪ ▪ ▪ ▪

Socrates: Where is that boy to whom I was speaking before? It is important that he hear this too, lest before hearing it he first give favor to someone who is not in love with him.

Phaedrus: He is right here, always by your side whenever you wish.

Socrates: Know this then, handsome lad, that that prior speech was by Phaedrus, son of Pythocles, man of Myrrinousious. But the one I am about to give is by Stesichorus, son of Euphemus of Himeraius. And it must be said that *that* speech is not true, the one that says that, though a person who is in love is available, one should rather pay favor to the person not in love, because the lover is mad and the other is in his right

μανίαν κακὸν εἶναι, καλῶς ἂν ἐλέγετο· νῦν δὲ τὰ μέγιστα τῶν ἀγαθῶν ἡμῖν γίγνεται διὰ μανίας, θείᾳ μέντοι δόσει διδομένης. ἥ τε γὰρ δὴ ἐν Δελφοῖς προφῆτις αἵ τ' ἐν Δωδώνῃ ἱέρειαι μανεῖσαι μὲν πολλὰ δὴ καὶ καλὰ ἰδίᾳ τε καὶ δημοσίᾳ τὴν Ἑλλάδα ἠργάσαντο, σωφρονοῦσαι δὲ βραχέα ἢ οὐδέν· καὶ ἐὰν δὴ λέγωμεν Σίβυλλάν τε καὶ ἄλλους, ὅσοι μαντικῇ χρώμενοι ἐνθέῳ πολλὰ δὴ πολλοῖς προλέγοντες εἰς τὸ μέλλον ὤρθωσαν, μηκύνοιμεν ἂν δῆλα παντὶ λέγοντες.

245b–c

Τοσαῦτα μέν σοι καὶ ἔτι πλείω ἔχω μανίας γιγνομένης ἀπὸ θεῶν λέγειν καλὰ ἔργα. ὥστε τοῦτό γε αὐτὸ μὴ φοβώμεθα, μηδέ τις ἡμᾶς λόγος θορυβείτω δεδιττόμενος ὡς πρὸ τοῦ κεκινημένου τὸν σώφρονα δεῖ προαιρεῖσθαι φίλον· ἀλλὰ τόδε πρὸς ἐκείνῳ δείξας φερέσθω τὰ νικητήρια, ὡς οὐκ ἐπ' ὠφελίᾳ ὁ ἔρως τῷ ἐρῶντι καὶ τῷ ἐρωμένῳ ἐκ θεῶν ἐπιπέμπεται. ἡμῖν δὲ ἀποδεικτέον αὖ τοὐναντίον, ὡς ἐπ' εὐτυχίᾳ τῇ μεγίστῃ παρὰ θεῶν ἡ τοιαύτη μανία δίδοται· ἡ δὲ δὴ ἀπόδειξις ἔσται δεινοῖς μὲν ἄπιστος, σοφοῖς δὲ πιστή. δεῖ οὖν πρῶτον ψυχῆς φύσεως πέρι θείας τε καὶ

mind. For if it were simply the case that madness is bad, then this would be well spoken. But the fact is that the greatest of benefits comes to us through madness, or at least the kind given by divine grace. For indeed the prophetess at Delphi and the priestesses at Dodona when maddened have conferred the greatest goods upon Greece in private and public matters, but when in their right minds have done little or nothing. And if we should speak of the Sibyl and others who by inspired prophecy foretold many things for many people and thus sent them on a straight path into the future, it is clear to anyone that we would have to speak at great length.

▪ ▪ ▪ ▪ ▪

Such things, and still more, are the beautiful deeds from the gods that I can tell you come from madness. So do not be afraid of this in and of itself, and let no speech confuse or alarm us by saying that one ought to prefer a levelheaded friend to someone who is impassioned. But in addition to this, let that speaker carry off the prizes of victory only if he can show that *eros* is not sent by the gods for the benefit of the lover and the beloved. For we must demonstrate the opposite, that such madness is given by the gods for the greatest of fortune. This proof will not be convincing to those who are just clever, but will be believed by whomever is wise. We must, then, first

ἀνθρωπίνης ἰδόντα πάθη τε καὶ ἔργα τἀληθὲς νοῆσαι· ἀρχὴ δὲ ἀποδείξεως ἥδε. Ψυχὴ πᾶσα ἀθάνατος.

251a–252c

ὁ δὲ ἀρτιτελής, ὁ τῶν τότε πολυθεάμων, ὅταν θεοειδὲς πρόσωπον ἴδῃ κάλλος εὖ μεμιμημένον ἤ τινα σώματος ἰδέαν, πρῶτον μὲν ἔφριξε καί τι τῶν τότε ὑπῆλθεν αὐτὸν δειμάτων, εἶτα προσορῶν ὡς θεὸν σέβεται, καὶ εἰ μὴ ἐδεδίει τὴν τῆς σφόδρα μανίας δόξαν, θύοι ἂν ὡς ἀγάλματι καὶ θεῷ τοῖς παιδικοῖς. ἰδόντα δ' αὐτὸν οἷον ἐκ τῆς φρίκης μεταβολή τε καὶ ἱδρὼς καὶ θερμότης ἀήθης λαμβάνει· δεξάμενος γὰρ τοῦ κάλλους τὴν ἀπορροὴν διὰ τῶν ὀμμάτων ἐθερμάνθη ᾗ ἡ τοῦ πτεροῦ φύσις ἄρδεται, θερμανθέντος δὲ ἐτάκη τὰ περὶ τὴν ἔκφυσιν, ἃ πάλαι ὑπὸ σκληρότητος συμμεμυκότα εἶργε μὴ βλαστάνειν, ἐπιρρυείσης δὲ τῆς τροφῆς ᾤδησέ τε καὶ ὥρμησε φύεσθαι ἀπὸ τῆς ῥίζης ὁ τοῦ πτεροῦ καυλὸς ὑπὸ πᾶν τὸ τῆς ψυχῆς εἶδος· πᾶσα γὰρ ἦν τὸ πάλαι πτερωτή.

ζεῖ οὖν ἐν τούτῳ ὅλη καὶ ἀνακηκίει, καὶ ὅπερ τὸ τῶν ὀδοντοφυούντων πάθος περὶ τοὺς ὀδόντας γίγνεται ὅταν ἄρτι φύωσιν, κνῆσίς τε καὶ ἀγανάκτησις περὶ τὰ οὖλα, ταὐτὸν δὴ πέπονθεν ἡ τοῦ πτεροφυεῖν ἀρχομένου ψυχή· ζεῖ τε καὶ ἀγανακτεῖ καὶ γαργαλίζεται φύουσα τὰ πτερά. ὅταν μὲν οὖν βλέπουσα

truly consider the nature of the soul, both divine and human, looking at what it feels and does. This is the start of our argument: Every soul is immortal.

. . . . .

Take someone just initiated who has beheld many of these things. When he sees a godlike face or a certain kind of body that truly mimics absolute beauty, at first he shudders and some part of his former fears steal over him. Then, gazing upon him, he worships him as a god and, if he didn't fear being thought completely mad, he would even sacrifice to his darling as to an icon or a god. And a change from his shuddering takes hold of him as he gazes, a sudden sweat and an unusual warmth. For, as he receives this flow of beauty through his eyes, he is warmed and the roots of his feathers are refreshed. As he is warmed, the area around the roots is softened, which for so long was scarred over and stiff so that it could not grow. But, as nourishment flows in, the stem swells up and starts to sprout from the roots all over the form of his soul. For the entire soul was once feathered.

The whole of it then seethes and throbs, and just as for children who are teething there is pain whenever a new tooth is coming up as it first breaks through, and there is itching and irritation in the gums, so does the soul suffer the same pain when the feathers begin to grow. The growing feathers make it

πρὸς τὸ τοῦ παιδὸς κάλλος, ἐκεῖθεν μέρη ἐπιόντα καὶ ῥέοντ'—ἃ δὴ διὰ ταῦτα ἵμερος καλεῖται—δεχομένη [τὸν ἵμερον] ἄρδηταί τε καὶ θερμαίνηται, λωφᾷ τε τῆς ὀδύνης καὶ γέγηθεν· ὅταν δὲ χωρὶς γένηται καὶ αὐχμήσῃ, τὰ τῶν διεξόδων στόματα ᾗ τὸ πτερὸν ὁρμᾷ, συναυαινόμενα μύσαντα ἀποκλῄει τὴν βλάστην τοῦ πτεροῦ, ἡ δ' ἐντὸς μετὰ τοῦ ἱμέρου ἀποκεκλῃμένη, πηδῶσα οἷον τὰ σφύζοντα, τῇ διεξόδῳ ἐγχρίει ἑκάστη τῇ καθ' αὑτήν, ὥστε πᾶσα κεντουμένη κύκλῳ ἡ ψυχὴ οἰστρᾷ καὶ ὀδυνᾶται, μνήμην δ' αὖ ἔχουσα τοῦ καλοῦ γέγηθεν.

ἐκ δὲ ἀμφοτέρων μεμειγμένων ἀδημονεῖ τε τῇ ἀτοπίᾳ τοῦ πάθους καὶ ἀποροῦσα λυττᾷ, καὶ ἐμμανὴς οὖσα οὔτε νυκτὸς δύναται καθεύδειν οὔτε μεθ' ἡμέραν οὗ ἂν ᾖ μένειν, θεῖ δὲ ποθοῦσα ὅπου ἂν οἴηται ὄψεσθαι τὸν ἔχοντα τὸ κάλλος· ἰδοῦσα δὲ καὶ ἐποχετευσαμένη ἵμερον ἔλυσε μὲν τὰ τότε συμπεφραγμένα, ἀναπνοὴν δὲ λαβοῦσα κέντρων τε καὶ ὠδίνων ἔληξεν, ἡδονὴν δ' αὖ ταύτην γλυκυτάτην ἐν τῷ παρόντι καρποῦται. ὅθεν δὴ ἑκοῦσα εἶναι οὐκ ἀπολείπεται, οὐδέ τινα τοῦ καλοῦ περὶ πλείονος ποιεῖται, ἀλλὰ μητέρων τε καὶ ἀδελφῶν καὶ ἑταίρων πάντων λέλησται, καὶ οὐσίας δι' ἀμέλειαν ἀπολλυμένης παρ' οὐδὲν τίθεται, νομίμων δὲ καὶ εὐσχημόνων,

seethe and feel vexed and irritated. Whenever, therefore, the soul looks upon the beauty of the boy, receiving thence this rush and flow of bits of beauty—and it is for this reason that desire is said to "rush" up[2]—the soul is refreshed and warmed. It is freed from suffering and feels joy. But whenever the soul is apart from the boy and dries up, then the openings of the passages where the feathers might sprout become parched and closed, and this bars the budding of feathers. And the buds, shut inside with desire, leap like throbbing veins and pierce the opening where each one is, so that the entire soul, pricked all over, is stung and pained; but, then, again remembering the lovely one, it feels joy.

And so, from both feelings mixed up together, the soul is sorely troubled by the strangeness of its emotions and finds itself at a loss and in a fury, so maddened that it cannot sleep at night nor stay still during the day but rushes about, longing to see the one it thinks holds beauty. And when it does see him and is overwhelmed by rivers of passion, it loosens the formerly blocked up passages, has respite from the pricks, ceases from pain, and reaps again the very sweetest pleasure in that moment. Wherefore the soul is not willing to be left behind, and holds nothing as more important than the boy it loves, and forgets mothers, brothers, and all friends, and property too, through neglect, valuing these at nothing. And all rules of decency, in which the soul was invested

οἷς πρὸ τοῦ ἐκαλλωπίζετο, πάντων καταφρονήσασα δουλεύειν ἑτοίμη καὶ κοιμᾶσθαι ὅπου ἂν ἐᾷ τις ἐγγυτάτω τοῦ πόθου· πρὸς γὰρ τῷ σέβεσθαι τὸν τὸ κάλλος ἔχοντα ἰατρὸν ηὕρηκε μόνον τῶν μεγίστων πόνων.

τοῦτο δὲ τὸ πάθος, ὦ παῖ καλέ, πρὸς ὃν δή μοι ὁ λόγος, ἄνθρωποι μὲν ἔρωτα ὀνομάζουσιν, θεοὶ δὲ ὃ καλοῦσιν ἀκούσας εἰκότως διὰ νεότητα γελάσῃ. λέγουσι δὲ οἶμαί τινες Ὁμηριδῶν ἐκ τῶν ἀποθέτων ἐπῶν δύο ἔπη εἰς τὸν Ἔρωτα, ὧν τὸ ἕτερον ὑβριστικὸν πάνυ καὶ οὐ σφόδρα τι ἔμμετρον· ὑμνοῦσι δὲ ὧδε—

τὸν δ' ἤτοι θνητοὶ μὲν Ἔρωτα καλοῦσι ποτηνόν,
ἀθάνατοι δὲ Πτέρωτα, διὰ πτεροφύτορ' ἀνάγκην.

τούτοις δὴ ἔξεστι μὲν πείθεσθαι, ἔξεστιν δὲ μή· ὅμως δὲ ἥ γε αἰτία καὶ τὸ πάθος τῶν ἐρώντων τοῦτο ἐκεῖνο τυγχάνει ὄν.

255a–e

ἅτε οὖν πᾶσαν θεραπείαν ὡς ἰσόθεος θεραπευόμενος οὐχ ὑπὸ σχηματιζομένου τοῦ ἐρῶντος ἀλλ' ἀληθῶς τοῦτο πεπονθότος, καὶ αὐτὸς ὢν φύσει φίλος τῷ θεραπεύοντι, ἐὰν ἄρα καὶ ἐν τῷ πρόσθεν ὑπὸ συμφοιτητῶν ἤ τινων ἄλλων διαβεβλημένος ᾖ, λεγόντων ὡς αἰσχρὸν ἐρῶντι πλησιάζειν, καὶ διὰ τοῦτο ἀπωθῇ τὸν ἐρῶντα, προϊόντος δὲ ἤδη τοῦ

before, it now disdains, ready to be enslaved and to lie down wherever it may be closest to the object of its desire. For only by worshipping the one who has beauty is it able to find a cure for its greatest sufferings.

This experience, dear boy, the subject of this discourse, is called *eros* by men, but as for what the gods call it—well, when you hear it, perhaps because of how young you are, you will laugh. Some of the Homeric poets, I think, quote two verses on Eros from verses that have been athetized, of which the second is completely absurd and not even metrical. They sing as follows,

> Truly mortals call Eros winged, but immortals
> call him Wingeros,[3] due to his wing-growing force.

You may or may not believe in these verses, to be sure. In any case, the cause and experience of lovers happens to be precisely this.

▪ ▪ ▪ ▪ ▪

Since, therefore, the beloved boy is attended upon in every way, as if he were a god, by the lover who is not pretending but is truly feeling this love, and since he himself is naturally affectionate to someone so attentive to him—even if before by his school friends or some others, he had been deceived by their saying that it would be shameful to consort with a lover and because of this had always rejected him—now, with

χρόνου ἥ τε ἡλικία καὶ τὸ χρεὼν ἤγαγεν εἰς τὸ προσέσθαι αὐτὸν εἰς ὁμιλίαν· οὐ γὰρ δήποτε εἵμαρται κακὸν κακῷ φίλον οὐδ' ἀγαθὸν μὴ φίλον ἀγαθῷ εἶναι.

προσεμένου δὲ καὶ λόγον καὶ ὁμιλίαν δεξαμένου, ἐγγύθεν ἡ εὔνοια γιγνομένη τοῦ ἐρῶντος ἐκπλήττει τὸν ἐρώμενον διαισθανόμενον ὅτι οὐδ' οἱ σύμπαντες ἄλλοι φίλοι τε καὶ οἰκεῖοι μοῖραν φιλίας οὐδεμίαν παρέχονται πρὸς τὸν ἔνθεον φίλον. ὅταν δὲ χρονίζῃ τοῦτο δρῶν καὶ πλησιάζῃ μετὰ τοῦ ἅπτεσθαι ἔν τε γυμνασίοις καὶ ἐν ταῖς ἄλλαις ὁμιλίαις, τότ' ἤδη ἡ τοῦ ῥεύματος ἐκείνου πηγή, ὃν ἵμερον Ζεὺς Γανυμήδους ἐρῶν ὠνόμασε, πολλὴ φερομένη πρὸς τὸν ἐραστήν, ἡ μὲν εἰς αὐτὸν ἔδυ, ἡ δ' ἀπομεστουμένου ἔξω ἀπορρεῖ· καὶ οἷον πνεῦμα ἤ τις ἠχὼ ἀπὸ λείων τε καὶ στερεῶν ἁλλομένη πάλιν ὅθεν ὡρμήθη φέρεται, οὕτω τὸ τοῦ κάλλους ῥεῦμα πάλιν εἰς τὸν καλὸν διὰ τῶν ὀμμάτων ἰόν, ᾗ πέφυκεν ἐπὶ τὴν ψυχὴν ἰέναι ἀφικόμενον καὶ ἀναπτερῶσαν, τὰς διόδους τῶν πτερῶν ἄρδει τε καὶ ὥρμησε πτεροφυεῖν τε καὶ τὴν τοῦ ἐρωμένου αὖ ψυχὴν ἔρωτος ἐνέπλησεν.

ἐρᾷ μὲν οὖν, ὅτου δὲ ἀπορεῖ· καὶ οὔθ' ὅτι πέπονθεν οἶδεν οὐδ' ἔχει φράσαι, ἀλλ' οἷον ἀπ' ἄλλου ὀφθαλμίας ἀπολελαυκὼς πρόφασιν εἰπεῖν οὐκ ἔχει, ὥσπερ δὲ ἐν

time marching on, his maturity and expedience lead him to admit his lover into his company. For never has it yet been fated for an evil man to be friends with an evil man nor for a good man to not be friends with a good one.

And when the lover has been admitted to conversation and company, his good intent so near at hand astounds the beloved boy as he perceives that none of his other friends or family members offers him any such portion of affection as his lover who is inspired by the gods. And as he spends time with him and is near to him to the point that they touch while at the gymnasium and in other social settings, then the flowing water of that rushing river—which Zeus when in love with Ganymede called the "rush" of desire[4]—washes over the lover, and some of it settles within him, while some of it overflows and streams forth into the world. And just as wind or a certain echo can be bounced from smooth or rough surfaces and pushed back out again, so does the flow of beauty going out from the eyes enter the beautiful one again, and by this return it arrives again at the soul as it becomes winged, and warms the openings for the feathers and spurs their growth and fills the soul of the beloved boy with love.

He then is in love but he is at a loss as to whom he loves. He does not understand what he is feeling nor is he able to articulate it, but like a person who has

κατόπτρῳ ἐν τῷ ἐρῶντι ἑαυτὸν ὁρῶν λέληθεν. καὶ ὅταν μὲν ἐκεῖνος παρῇ, λήγει κατὰ ταὐτὰ ἐκείνῳ τῆς ὀδύνης, ὅταν δὲ ἀπῇ, κατὰ ταὐτὰ αὖ ποθεῖ καὶ ποθεῖται, εἴδωλον ἔρωτος ἀντέρωτα ἔχων· καλεῖ δὲ αὐτὸν καὶ οἴεται οὐκ ἔρωτα ἀλλὰ φιλίαν εἶναι. ἐπιθυμεῖ δὲ ἐκείνῳ παραπλησίως μέν, ἀσθενεστέρως δέ, ὁρᾶν, ἅπτεσθαι, φιλεῖν, συγκατακεῖσθαι· καὶ δή, οἷον εἰκός, ποιεῖ τὸ μετὰ τοῦτο ταχὺ ταῦτα.

caught an eye infection from someone else, he cannot give the cause of it and, seeing himself in his lover, he does not realize that he is like someone looking in a mirror. Whenever he is near him, in the same way as his lover he ceases to feel pain, but whenever the lover is away, in the same way too he longs for him and is longed for in return, for he now feels *eros* in return, an image of *eros*. Yet he names and thinks of it not as *eros* but as friendship. But he desires to be near to his lover, if not quite as forcefully, to see him, to touch him, to kiss him, to lie with him. And indeed, in all likelihood, these things are soon accomplished.

12 WHO WANTS TO LIVE FOREVER: KILLER QUEEN

In the long history of ancient Athens, one man above all stands for the pleasure and perils of beauty, lust, and the queer paths of desire. This is Alcibiades—possessed of a stunning charisma, in love with and loved by many, adored and feared, passionate and resolute. In this final section, we look at his speech in Plato's Symposium *in which he expounds upon his unrequited desire for the much older Socrates, a dynamic that flips the conventional man/boy, lover/beloved equation on its head (on which, see chapter 1, note 1). The volume ends with a view from later in antiquity, that of Plutarch, an author from the first-to-second century CE. Plutarch's* Life of Alcibiades *focuses on the extraordinary beauty and charm of Alcibiades, his impassioned life of desire for (and from) a multitude of men and women, and his flamboyant lifestyle. If there's one thing to say about Alcibiades, it is that he lived just as he chose.*

216d–219e

εὖ γὰρ ἴστε ὅτι οὐδεὶς ὑμῶν τοῦτον γιγνώσκει· ἀλλὰ ἐγὼ δηλώσω, ἐπείπερ ἠρξάμην. ὁρᾶτε γὰρ ὅτι Σωκράτης ἐρωτικῶς διάκειται τῶν καλῶν καὶ ἀεὶ περὶ τούτους ἐστὶ καὶ ἐκπέπληκται, καὶ αὖ ἀγνοεῖ πάντα καὶ οὐδὲν οἶδεν. ὡς τὸ σχῆμα αὐτοῦ τοῦτο οὐ σιληνῶδες; σφόδρα γε. τοῦτο γὰρ οὗτος ἔξωθεν περιβέβληται, ὥσπερ ὁ γεγλυμμένος σιληνός· ἔνδοθεν δὲ ἀνοιχθεὶς πόσης οἴεσθε γέμει, ὦ ἄνδρες συμπόται, σωφροσύνης; ἴστε ὅτι οὔτε εἴ τις καλός ἐστι μέλει αὐτῷ οὐδέν, ἀλλὰ καταφρονεῖ τοσοῦτον ὅσον οὐδ᾽ ἂν εἷς οἰηθείη, οὔτ᾽ εἴ τις πλούσιος, οὔτ᾽ εἰ ἄλλην τινὰ τιμὴν ἔχων τῶν ὑπὸ πλήθους μακαριζομένων· ἡγεῖται δὲ πάντα ταῦτα τὰ κτήματα οὐδενὸς ἄξια καὶ ἡμᾶς οὐδὲν εἶναι—λέγω ὑμῖν—εἰρωνευόμενος δὲ καὶ παίζων πάντα τὸν βίον πρὸς τοὺς ἀνθρώπους διατελεῖ. σπουδάσαντος δὲ αὐτοῦ καὶ ἀνοιχθέντος οὐκ οἶδα εἴ τις ἑώρακεν τὰ ἐντὸς ἀγάλματα·

ἀλλ᾽ ἐγὼ ἤδη ποτ᾽ εἶδον, καί μοι ἔδοξεν οὕτω θεῖα καὶ χρυσᾶ εἶναι καὶ πάγκαλα καὶ θαυμαστά, ὥστε ποιητέον εἶναι ἔμβραχυ ὅτι κελεύοι Σωκράτης. ἡγούμενος δὲ αὐτὸν ἐσπουδακέναι ἐπὶ τῇ ἐμῇ ὥρᾳ ἕρμαιον ἡγησάμην εἶναι καὶ εὐτύχημα ἐμὸν θαυμαστόν, ὡς ὑπάρχον μοι χαρισαμένῳ Σωκράτει πάντ᾽ ἀκοῦσαι ὅσαπερ οὗτος ᾔδει· ἐφρόνουν

Plato, *Symposium*

Know well that none of you really knows Socrates. But I will reveal him, seeing that I have already begun. For note how Socrates is amorously disposed toward beautiful people and is always hanging around them in a passionate state and, again, that he acts ignorant about all things and like he knows nothing. And isn't his manner just like that of Silenus?[1] Exactly so. For he cloaks himself in this ignorance on the outside, just like a carving of Silenus. But if you opened up his insides, o fellow drinkers, can you imagine how full of temperance he is? Know that if someone is handsome it doesn't mean anything to him at all, but that in fact he disdains him to a degree that no one would imagine, and so too if he is rich, or if he has any other honor of those considered blessings by most people. He thinks all of these possessions to be worth nothing and us to be worth nothing, I tell you. In fact, he passes his whole life dissembling and making fun of men. I do not know whether he was ever serious and open with any others so that they could see the glories within.

But I saw them once and to me they seemed so divine and golden and entirely beautiful and wondrous that it was necessary for me to do, in short, whatever Socrates bid. And thinking him to be serious about my youthful bloom, I felt myself to have godsent and wondrous good fortune, and I embarked upon gratifying Socrates so as to learn all the things he knew. For I considered myself to be quite

γὰρ δὴ ἐπὶ τῇ ὥρᾳ θαυμάσιον ὅσον. ταῦτα οὖν διανοηθείς, πρὸ τοῦ οὐκ εἰωθὼς ἄνευ ἀκολούθου μόνος μετ᾽ αὐτοῦ γίγνεσθαι, τότε ἀποπέμπων τὸν ἀκόλουθον μόνος συνεγιγνόμην—δεῖ γὰρ πρὸς ὑμᾶς πάντα τἀληθῆ εἰπεῖν· ἀλλὰ προσέχετε τὸν νοῦν, καὶ εἰ ψεύδομαι, Σώκρατες, ἐξέλεγχε—συνεγιγνόμην γάρ, ὦ ἄνδρες, μόνος μόνῳ, καὶ ᾤμην αὐτίκα διαλέξεσθαι αὐτόν μοι ἅπερ ἂν ἐραστὴς παιδικοῖς ἐν ἐρημίᾳ διαλεχθείη, καὶ ἔχαιρον.

τούτων δ᾽ οὐ μάλα ἐγίγνετο οὐδέν, ἀλλ᾽ ὥσπερ εἰώθει διαλεχθεὶς ἄν μοι καὶ συνημερεύσας ᾤχετο ἀπιών. μετὰ ταῦτα συγγυμνάζεσθαι προυκαλούμην αὐτὸν καὶ συνεγυμναζόμην, ὥς τι ἐνταῦθα περανῶν. συνεγυμνάζετο οὖν μοι καὶ προσεπάλαιεν πολλάκις οὐδενὸς παρόντος· καὶ τί δεῖ λέγειν; οὐδὲν γάρ μοι πλέον ἦν. ἐπειδὴ δὲ οὐδαμῇ ταύτῃ ἤνυτον, ἔδοξέ μοι ἐπιθετέον εἶναι τῷ ἀνδρὶ κατὰ τὸ καρτερὸν καὶ οὐκ ἀνετέον, ἐπειδήπερ ἐνεκεχειρήκη, ἀλλὰ ἰστέον ἤδη τί ἐστι τὸ πρᾶγμα.

προκαλοῦμαι δὴ αὐτὸν πρὸς τὸ συνδειπνεῖν, ἀτεχνῶς ὥσπερ ἐραστὴς παιδικοῖς ἐπιβουλεύων. καί μοι οὐδὲ τοῦτο ταχὺ ὑπήκουσεν, ὅμως δ᾽ οὖν χρόνῳ ἐπείσθη. ἐπειδὴ δὲ ἀφίκετο τὸ πρῶτον, δειπνήσας ἀπιέναι ἐβούλετο. καὶ τότε μὲν αἰσχυνόμενος ἀφῆκα αὐτόν· αὖθις δ᾽ ἐπιβουλεύσας, ἐπειδὴ ἐδεδειπνήκεμεν διελεγόμην ἀεὶ πόρρω τῶν νυκτῶν,

marvelous in my youthful charms. And with these things in mind, though previously it had not been customary for me to be alone with him without my attendant, at that point I sent the attendant away and was alone—for it is necessary to tell you all the whole truth. But pay attention and, if I lie, Socrates, refute me! Anyway, boys, I was alone with him who was also alone, and I expected that right away he would converse with me in the manner that a lover does with his darling when they are in a private place, and I was glad.

But nothing of the kind occurred. Rather, he talked with me as usual. When we had spent the day together, he departed. After this, I invited him to work out at the gymnasium with me, and I worked out with him, thinking I'd get the job done there. And he did work out with me and even wrestled with me frequently when no one else was present. But what is there to say? For there was nothing else in it for me. Since I was getting nowhere in this way, it seemed to me that I must make a strong push for this man and not let up, having embarked upon this, and that really I should know already what the situation was.

So I invited him to dinner, exactly as a lover would make designs upon his darling. And he did not agree to this immediately, but nonetheless in time he was persuaded. The first time he came, he wished to depart as soon as he had eaten. And, on that occasion, I felt ashamed and let him go. Then I contrived to have him back again and, when we had dined and talked ever later into the night and he got up to

καὶ ἐπειδὴ ἐβούλετο ἀπιέναι, σκηπτόμενος ὅτι ὀψὲ εἴη, προσηνάγκασα αὐτὸν μένειν. ἀνεπαύετο οὖν ἐν τῇ ἐχομένῃ ἐμοῦ κλίνῃ, ἐν ᾗπερ ἐδείπνει, καὶ οὐδεὶς ἐν τῷ οἰκήματι ἄλλος καθηῦδεν ἢ ἡμεῖς.

μέχρι μὲν οὖν δὴ δεῦρο τοῦ λόγου καλῶς ἂν ἔχοι καὶ πρὸς ὁντινοῦν λέγειν· τὸ δ᾽ ἐντεῦθεν οὐκ ἄν μου ἠκούσατε λέγοντος, εἰ μὴ πρῶτον μέν, τὸ λεγόμενον, οἶνος ἄνευ τε παίδων καὶ μετὰ παίδων ἦν ἀληθής, ἔπειτα ἀφανίσαι Σωκράτους ἔργον ὑπερήφανον εἰς ἔπαινον ἐλθόντα ἄδικόν μοι φαίνεται. ἔτι δὲ τὸ τοῦ δηχθέντος ὑπὸ τοῦ ἔχεως πάθος κἄμ᾽ ἔχει. φασὶ γάρ πού τινα τοῦτο παθόντα οὐκ ἐθέλειν λέγειν οἷον ἦν πλὴν τοῖς δεδηγμένοις, ὡς μόνοις γνωσομένοις τε καὶ συγγνωσομένοις εἰ πᾶν ἐτόλμα δρᾶν τε καὶ λέγειν ὑπὸ τῆς ὀδύνης. ἐγὼ οὖν δεδηγμένος τε ὑπὸ ἀλγεινοτέρου καὶ τὸ ἀλγεινότατον ὧν ἄν τις δηχθείη—τὴν καρδίαν γὰρ ἢ ψυχὴν ἢ ὅτι δεῖ αὐτὸ ὀνομάσαι πληγείς τε καὶ δηχθεὶς ὑπὸ τῶν ἐν φιλοσοφίᾳ λόγων, οἳ ἔχονται ἐχίδνης ἀγριώτερον, νέου ψυχῆς μὴ ἀφυοῦς ὅταν λάβωνται, καὶ ποιοῦσι δρᾶν τε καὶ λέγειν ὁτιοῦν—καὶ ὁρῶν αὖ Φαίδρους, Ἀγάθωνας, Ἐρυξιμάχους, Παυσανίας, Ἀριστοδήμους τε καὶ Ἀριστοφάνας· Σωκράτη δὲ αὐτὸν τί δεῖ λέγειν, καὶ ὅσοι ἄλλοι; πάντες γὰρ κεκοινωνήκατε τῆς φιλοσόφου μανίας τε καὶ βακχείας—διὸ πάντες ἀκούσεσθε· συγγνώσεσθε γὰρ τοῖς τε τότε πραχθεῖσι καὶ τοῖς νῦν λεγομένοις. οἱ δὲ οἰκέται, καὶ εἴ τις ἄλλος ἐστὶν βέβηλός τε καὶ ἄγροικος, πύλας πάνυ μεγάλας τοῖς ὠσὶν ἐπίθεσθε.

go, I made a pretext of how late it was, and prevailed upon him to stay. Then he lay down on the couch next to me, the one where he had rested for dinner, and there was no one else sleeping in the room aside from us.

My story thus far could well have been told to anyone. But from here on out, you could not have heard me saying this, if not first, as it is said, wine is truth (with or without servants present) and second since it seems to me that to allow this magnificent deed of Socrates to remain unseen while praising him would be unjust. And, furthermore, I suffer like someone bitten by a snake. For they say that someone who has suffered this does not wish to speak of it at all except to others who have been bitten, since they alone know and understand all that he might venture to do and say in his pain. I, then, have been bitten by a more painful snake and in the most painful way a person can be bitten, for I have been struck and bitten in my heart, or my soul, or whatever it is called, by the words of philosophy, which have taken hold of me more savagely than a serpent. And since they seized my young and unschooled soul, they make me do and say whatever they want. And I look around again and see Phaedrus, Agathon, Eryximachus, Pausanias, Aristodemus, and Aristophanes (and why is it necessary to mention Socrates?), and indeed as many others as there are. For all of you share in common this mania and frenzy for philosophy, and because of this, you will all hear the rest. For you will forgive me for the things that were done then and said now. As for you domestics, and

Ἐπειδὴ γὰρ οὖν, ὦ ἄνδρες, ὅ τε λύχνος ἀπεσβήκει καὶ οἱ παῖδες ἔξω ἦσαν, ἔδοξέ μοι χρῆναι μηδὲν ποικίλλειν πρὸς αὐτόν, ἀλλ' ἐλευθέρως εἰπεῖν ἅ μοι ἐδόκει· καὶ εἶπον κινήσας αὐτόν, Σώκρατες, καθεύδεις;

Οὐ δῆτα, ἦ δ' ὅς.

Οἶσθα οὖν ἅ μοι δέδοκται;

Τί μάλιστα, ἔφη.

Σὺ ἐμοὶ δοκεῖς, ἦν δ' ἐγώ, ἐμοῦ ἐραστὴς ἄξιος γεγονέναι μόνος, καί μοι φαίνῃ ὀκνεῖν μνησθῆναι πρός με. ἐγὼ δὲ οὑτωσὶ ἔχω· πάνυ ἀνόητον ἡγοῦμαι εἶναι σοὶ μὴ οὐ καὶ τοῦτο χαρίζεσθαι καὶ εἴ τι ἄλλο ἢ τῆς οὐσίας τῆς ἐμῆς δέοιο ἢ τῶν φίλων τῶν ἐμῶν. ἐμοὶ μὲν γὰρ οὐδέν ἐστι πρεσβύτερον τοῦ ὡς ὅτι βέλτιστον ἐμὲ γενέσθαι, τούτου δὲ οἶμαί μοι συλλήπτορα οὐδένα κυριώτερον εἶναι σοῦ. ἐγὼ δὴ τοιούτῳ ἀνδρὶ πολὺ μᾶλλον ἂν μὴ χαριζόμενος αἰσχυνοίμην τοὺς φρονίμους, ἢ χαριζόμενος τούς τε πολλοὺς καὶ ἄφρονας.

Καὶ οὗτος ἀκούσας μάλα εἰρωνικῶς καὶ σφόδρα ἑαυτοῦ τε καὶ εἰωθότως ἔλεξεν Ὦ φίλε Ἀλκιβιάδη, κινδυνεύεις τῷ ὄντι οὐ φαῦλος εἶναι, εἴπερ ἀληθῆ τυγχάνει ὄντα ἃ λέγεις περὶ ἐμοῦ, καί τις ἔστ' ἐν ἐμοὶ δύναμις δι' ἧς ἂν σὺ γένοιο ἀμείνων· ἀμήχανόν τοι κάλλος ὁρῴης ἂν ἐν ἐμοὶ καὶ τῆς παρὰ σοὶ εὐμορφίας πάμπολυ διαφέρον. εἰ δὴ καθορῶν

anyone else who is impure or boorish, cover your ears with strong doors!

For, my good men, when the lamp had gone out and the servants departed, it seemed right to me not to beat around the bush with him, but to say freely what I thought. And so, rousing him, I said, "Socrates, are you asleep?"

"Not at all," he said.

"Do you know, then, what I have determined?"

"What indeed?" he asked.

"It seems to me," I said, "that you alone are worthy of being my lover, and yet it appears that you hesitate to mention it to me. But I think this: I think it would be very stupid of me *not* to gratify you in this way and in whatever other way you might need, whether in regard to my money or my friends. For, to my mind, there is nothing more important than for me to become as good as I can, and I think that there is no partner who could be a better authority in this than you. Thus I would be more ashamed before intelligent people if I did not gratify such a man than I would before the many stupid ones if I do."

When he had heard me, he took on his usual ironic manner, but even more so, and said, "O my dear Alcibiades, you are likely to be in truth no common person if these things you are saying about me are true and this power exists within me through which you might become better. How irresistible must be the beauty you see in me, so very much better than the beauty of your own looks! Indeed, if having observed this, you are trying to partner up with me

αὐτὸ κοινώσασθαί τέ μοι ἐπιχειρεῖς καὶ ἀλλάξασθαι κάλλος ἀντὶ κάλλους, οὐκ ὀλίγῳ μου πλεονεκτεῖν διανοῇ, ἀλλ' ἀντὶ δόξης ἀλήθειαν καλῶν κτᾶσθαι ἐπιχειρεῖς καὶ τῷ ὄντι χρύσεα χαλκείων διαμείβεσθαι νοεῖς. ἀλλ', ὦ μακάριε, ἄμεινον σκόπει, μή σε λανθάνω οὐδὲν ὤν. ἥ τοι τῆς διανοίας ὄψις ἄρχεται ὀξὺ βλέπειν ὅταν ἡ τῶν ὀμμάτων τῆς ἀκμῆς λήγειν ἐπιχειρῇ· σὺ δὲ τούτων ἔτι πόρρω.

Κἀγὼ ἀκούσας, Τὰ μὲν παρ' ἐμοῦ, ἔφην, ταῦτά ἐστιν, ὧν οὐδὲν ἄλλως εἴρηται ἢ ὡς διανοοῦμαι· σὺ δὲ αὐτὸς οὕτω βουλεύου ὅτι σοί τε ἄριστον καὶ ἐμοὶ ἡγῇ.

Ἀλλ', ἔφη, τοῦτό γ' εὖ λέγεις· ἐν γὰρ τῷ ἐπιόντι χρόνῳ βουλευόμενοι πράξομεν ὃ ἂν φαίνηται νῷν περί τε τούτων καὶ περὶ τῶν ἄλλων ἄριστον.

Ἐγὼ μὲν δὴ ταῦτα ἀκούσας τε καὶ εἰπών, καὶ ἀφεὶς ὥσπερ βέλη, τετρῶσθαι αὐτὸν ᾤμην· καὶ ἀναστάς γε, οὐδ' ἐπιτρέψας τούτῳ εἰπεῖν οὐδὲν ἔτι, ἀμφιέσας τὸ ἱμάτιον τὸ ἐμαυτοῦ τοῦτον—καὶ γὰρ ἦν χειμών—ὑπὸ τὸν τρίβωνα κατακλινεὶς τὸν τουτουί, περιβαλὼν τὼ χεῖρε τούτῳ τῷ δαιμονίῳ ὡς ἀληθῶς καὶ θαυμαστῷ, κατεκείμην τὴν νύκτα ὅλην. καὶ οὐδὲ ταῦτα αὖ, ὦ Σώκρατες, ἐρεῖς ὅτι ψεύδομαι. ποιήσαντος δὲ δὴ ταῦτα ἐμοῦ οὗτος τοσοῦτον περιεγένετό τε καὶ κατεφρόνησεν καὶ κατεγέλασεν τῆς ἐμῆς ὥρας καὶ ὕβρισεν—καὶ περὶ ἐκεῖνό γε ᾤμην τὶ εἶναι, ὦ ἄνδρες δικασταί· δικασταὶ γάρ ἐστε τῆς Σωκράτους ὑπερηφανίας—εὖ γὰρ ἴστε μὰ θεούς, μὰ θεάς, οὐδὲν περιττότερον

and exchange beauty for beauty, then you intend to grasp no small thing from me but are trying to possess true beauty in exchange for just its reputation and intend truly to get 'gold for bronze.'[2] But, o blessed man, be on guard in case I turn out to be worth nothing at all. For the vision of the mind begins to look sharp only when that of the eyes starts to abate from its peak. You are still far from this."

Hearing this, I said, "What I have said, this exactly and not otherwise, is what I have in mind. So it is for you yourself to decide what you think is best for you and me."

"On that," he said, "you have spoken well. In the time to come, taking counsel, we will do what seems best to ourselves concerning these and other things."

When I had said and heard these things and let fly my arrows, as it were, I thought him to have been duly wounded. And so I stood up and, not permitting him to say anything else, I wrapped my coat around him—for it was winter—and lay beneath his own thin cloak, like so, putting my arms around this truly devilish and wondrous man. I lay there all night. And in these things, again, Socrates, you cannot say that I am lying! For when I had indeed done all that, this man showed himself to be utterly superior and to hold my youth in contempt, mockery, and insult—and in regard to the very thing in which I thought I was really something, o gentlemen of the jury. For you are the judges of Socrates' arrogance! Know well by the gods and goddesses, that when I arose in the morning I had no more

καταδεδαρθηκὼς ἀνέστην μετὰ Σωκράτους, ἢ εἰ μετὰ πατρὸς καθηῦδον ἢ ἀδελφοῦ πρεσβυτέρου.

Τὸ δὴ μετὰ τοῦτο τίνα οἴεσθέ με διάνοιαν ἔχειν, ἡγούμενον μὲν ἠτιμάσθαι, ἀγάμενον δὲ τὴν τούτου φύσιν τε καὶ σωφροσύνην καὶ ἀνδρείαν, ἐντετυχηκότα ἀνθρώπῳ τοιούτῳ οἵῳ ἐγὼ οὐκ ἂν ᾤμην ποτ' ἐντυχεῖν εἰς φρόνησιν καὶ εἰς καρτερίαν; ὥστε οὔθ' ὅπως οὖν ὀργιζοίμην εἶχον καὶ ἀποστερηθείην τῆς τούτου συνουσίας, οὔτε ὅπῃ προσαγαγοίμην αὐτὸν ηὐπόρουν. εὖ γὰρ ᾔδη ὅτι χρήμασί γε πολὺ μᾶλλον ἄτρωτος ἦν πανταχῇ ἢ σιδήρῳ ὁ Αἴας, ᾧ τε ᾤμην αὐτὸν μόνῳ ἁλώσεσθαι, διεπεφεύγει με. ἠπόρουν δή, καταδεδουλωμένος τε ὑπὸ τοῦ ἀνθρώπου ὡς οὐδεὶς ὑπ' οὐδενὸς ἄλλου περιῇα.

1.3–2.2

Περὶ μὲν οὖν τοῦ κάλλους οὐδὲν ἴσως δεῖ λέγειν, πλὴν ὅτι καὶ παῖδα καὶ μειράκιον καὶ ἄνδρα πάσῃ συνανθῆσαν τῇ ἡλικίᾳ καὶ ὥρᾳ τοῦ σώματος ἐράσμιον καὶ ἡδὺν παρέσχεν. οὐ γάρ, ὡς Εὐριπίδης ἔλεγε, πάντων τῶν καλῶν καὶ τὸ μετόπωρον καλόν ἐστιν, ἀλλὰ τοῦτ' Ἀλκιβιάδῃ μετ' ὀλίγων ἄλλων δι' εὐφυΐαν καὶ ἀρετὴν τοῦ σώματος ὑπῆρξε. τῇ δὲ φωνῇ καὶ τὴν τραυλότητα συμπρέψαι λέγουσι καὶ τῷ λάλῳ πιθανότητα παρασχεῖν χάριν ἐπιτρέχουσαν. μέμνηται δὲ καὶ Ἀριστοφάνης αὐτοῦ τῆς τραυλότητος ἐν οἷς ἐπισκώπτει Θέωρον·

had relations with Socrates than I would have had I slept with my own father or older brother.

Well, after this you can imagine what state of mind I was in, feeling myself to have been slighted, and yet wondering at the nature of this man, both his self-restraint and his manliness. I had encountered such a man as I had never thought I would meet, both in mind and in fortitude. So the result was that I could not be angry and deprive myself of his company, nor could I find a way to seduce him. For I knew well that he would be even more invulnerable to money in every way than Ajax was to iron, and that the only way by which I'd thought to catch him he had eluded. So I was at a loss, and went about more enslaved to this man than anyone has ever been to anyone.

Plutarch, *Life of Alcibiades*

Concerning the beauty of Alcibiades, it is perhaps not necessary to say anything except that it was in bloom when he was a child, a young man, and also in his prime, and made him lovely and appealing in every age and season of his body. For it is not the case that, as Euripides says, the autumn of all beautiful people is beautiful, but it *was* true for Alcibiades along with just a few others, due to the natural shapeliness and excellence of his body. As to his voice, it is also said that he was known for having a lisp that lent his speech a certain persuasiveness and charm. Even Aristophanes mentions his lisp in the lines where he mocks Theorus:

Εἶτ' Ἀλκιβιάδης εἶπε πρός με τραυλίσας·
ὁλᾷς Θέωλον; τὴν κεφαλὴν κόλακος ἔχει.

ὀρθῶς γε τοῦτ' Ἀλκιβιάδης ἐτραύλισε.

καὶ Ἄρχιππος τὸν υἱὸν τοῦ Ἀλκιβιάδου σκώπτων, βαδίζει, φησί, διακεχλιδώς, θοἰμάτιον ἕλκων, ὅπως ἐμφερὴς μάλιστα τῷ πατρὶ δόξειεν εἶναι, κλασαυχενεύεταί τε καὶ τραυλίζεται.

Τὸ δ' ἦθος αὐτοῦ πολλὰς μὲν ὕστερον, ὡς εἰκὸς ἐν πράγμασι μεγάλοις καὶ τύχαις πολυτρόποις, ἀνομοιότητας πρὸς αὑτὸ καὶ μεταβολὰς ἐπεδείξατο. φύσει δὲ πολλῶν ὄντων καὶ μεγάλων παθῶν ἐν αὐτῷ τὸ φιλόνικον ἰσχυρότατον ἦν καὶ τὸ φιλόπρωτον, ὡς δῆλόν ἐστι τοῖς παιδικοῖς ἀπομνημονεύμασιν. ἐν μὲν γὰρ τῷ παλαίειν πιεζούμενος, ὑπὲρ τοῦ μὴ πεσεῖν ἀναγαγὼν πρὸς τὸ στόμα τὰ ἅμματα τοῦ πιεζοῦντος οἷος ἦν διαφαγεῖν τὰς χεῖρας. ἀφέντος οὖν τὴν λαβὴν ἐκείνου καὶ εἰπόντος· δάκνεις ὦ Ἀλκιβιάδη καθάπερ αἱ γυναῖκες.

οὐκ ἔγωγε, εἶπεν, ἀλλ' ὡς οἱ λέοντες.

3.1–6.2

Ἐν δὲ ταῖς Ἀντιφῶντος λοιδορίαις γέγραπται, ὅτι παῖς ὢν ἐκ τῆς οἰκίας ἀπέδρα πρὸς Δημοκράτην τινὰ τῶν ἐραστῶν, βουλομένου δ' αὐτὸν ἐπικηρύττειν Ἀρίφρονος, Περικλῆς οὐκ εἴασεν εἰπών, εἰ μὲν τέθνηκεν, ἡμέρᾳ μιᾷ διὰ τὸ κήρυγμα φανεῖσθαι πρότερον, εἰ δὲ σῶς ἐστιν, ἄσωστον

Then Alcibiades said to me in his lisp,
"do you thee Theowus? He has the head of a cwow!"

Alcibiades lisped that right at least.[3]

And Archippus, mocking the son of Alcibiades, said, "he walks with a strut, dragging his robes, so that he might seem exactly like his father, tipping his head back and lisping."[4]

His character later in life showed many inconsistences and changes, which made sense given his great enterprises and varied fortunes. But by nature he had many strong passions, of which his competitiveness and his love of winning were the strongest, as is clear even in the reminiscences from his childhood. For in one, when he was pinned down while wrestling, in order to keep himself from falling, he put his mouth on the grip of the boy pinning him and was able to bite his hands. Then the other boy, letting go his hold, said, "Alcibiades, you bite like a woman!"

"Not I," he said, "but like a lion."

▪ ▪ ▪ ▪ ▪

Among the fabrications of Antiphon,[5] it was written that when Alcibiades was a boy he ran away from home to Democrates, one of his lovers, and that Ariphron wanted him publicly disinherited as dead, but that Pericles would not allow it and said, "if he has died, it will be clear only a day sooner thanks to the public announcement, but if he is alive, then he will be past recovery for the rest of his life."

αὐτῷ τὸν λοιπὸν βίον ἔσεσθαι, καὶ ὅτι τῶν ἀκολούθων τινὰ κτείνειεν ἐν τῇ Σιβυρτίου παλαίστρᾳ ξύλῳ πατάξας. ἀλλὰ τούτοις μὲν οὐκ ἄξιον ἴσως πιστεύειν, ἅ γε λοιδορεῖσθαί τις αὐτῷ δι' ἔχθραν ὁμολογῶν εἶπεν.

Ἤδη δὲ πολλῶν καὶ γενναίων ἀθροιζομένων καὶ περιεπόντων, οἱ μὲν ἄλλοι καταφανεῖς ἦσαν αὐτοῦ τὴν λαμπρότητα τῆς ὥρας ἐκπεπληγμένοι καὶ θεραπεύοντες, ὁ δὲ Σωκράτους ἔρως μέγα μαρτύριον ἦν τῆς πρὸς ἀρετὴν εὐφυΐας τοῦ παιδός, ἣν ἐμφαινομένην τῷ εἴδει καὶ διαλάμπουσαν ἐνορῶν, φοβούμενος δὲ τὸν πλοῦτον καὶ τὸ ἀξίωμα καὶ τὸν προκαταλαμβάνοντα κολακείαις καὶ χάρισιν ἀστῶν καὶ ξένων καὶ συμμάχων ὄχλον, οἷος ἦν ἀμύνειν καὶ μὴ περιορᾶν ὥσπερ φυτὸν ἐν ἄνθει τὸν οἰκεῖον καρπὸν ἀποβάλλον καὶ διαφθεῖρον. οὐδένα γὰρ ἡ τύχη περιέσχεν ἔξωθεν οὐδὲ περιέφραξε τοῖς λεγομένοις ἀγαθοῖς τοσοῦτον ὥστ' ἄτρωτον ὑπὸ φιλοσοφίας γενέσθαι καὶ λόγοις ἀπρόσιτον παρρησίαν καὶ δηγμὸν ἔχουσιν·

ὡς Ἀλκιβιάδης εὐθὺς ἐξ ἀρχῆς θρυπτόμενος καὶ ἀποκλειόμενος ὑπὸ τῶν πρὸς χάριν ἐξομιλούντων εἰσακοῦσαι τοῦ νουθετοῦντος καὶ παιδεύοντος, ὅμως ὑπ' εὐφυΐας ἐγνώρισε Σωκράτη καὶ προσήκατο, διασχὼν τοὺς πλουσίους καὶ ἐνδόξους ἐραστάς. ταχὺ δὲ ποιησάμενος συνήθη καὶ λόγων ἀκούσας οὐχ ἡδονὴν ἄνανδρον ἐραστοῦ θηρεύοντος οὐδὲ φιλήματα καὶ ψαύσεις προσαιτοῦντος, ἀλλ'

Antiphon also said that he killed one of his servants in the palaestra of Sibyrtius by beating him with a stick. But it is probably not worth believing these things, since this slander was spoken by someone who admitted that he hated him.

Before long, there were many highborn men going around with him and following him about, and others were clearly struck by the brilliance of this youth and attended on him. But the love of Socrates is the greatest proof of the natural goodness and excellence of the boy. When Socrates saw these virtues, evident in him and shining forth, he feared that wealth, rank, and crowds of citizens, foreigners, and allies alike would overtake the boy with flattery and charms. He intended to protect him and not allow for this plant in flower, as it were, to cast away and destroy its native fruit. For there is no one whom fortune can embrace from without or fortify with so many supposed goods such that he will not be wounded by philosophy or be invulnerable to its arguments that hold such frankness and such bite.

Thus, though Alcibiades was corrupted from the start and barred by the companions who sought his favor from hearing from anyone who would advise and educate him, still because of his good disposition he came to know Socrates and submitted to him, distancing himself from his wealthy and influential lovers. And quickly he became close to Socrates. For once he had heard the words of someone who loved him, someone not seeking unmanly pleasure or

ἐλέγχοντος τὰ σαθρὰ τῆς ψυχῆς αὐτοῦ καὶ πιεζοῦντος τὸν κενὸν καὶ ἀνόητον τῦφον, ἔπτηξ' ἀλέκτωρ δοῦλος ὣς κλίνας πτερόν.

καὶ τὸ μὲν Σωκράτους ἡγήσατο πρᾶγμα τῷ ὄντι θεῶν ὑπηρεσίαν εἰς νέων ἐπιμέλειαν εἶναι καὶ σωτηρίαν, καταφρονῶν δ' αὐτὸς ἑαυτοῦ, θαυμάζων δ' ἐκεῖνον, ἀγαπῶν δὲ τὴν φιλοφροσύνην, αἰσχυνόμενος δὲ τὴν ἀρετήν, ἐλάνθανεν εἴδωλον ἔρωτος, ὥς φησιν ὁ Πλάτων, ἀντέρωτα κτώμενος, ὥστε θαυμάζειν ἅπαντας ὁρῶντας αὐτὸν Σωκράτει μὲν συνδειπνοῦντα καὶ συμπαλαίοντα καὶ συσκηνοῦντα, τοῖς δ' ἄλλοις ἐρασταῖς χαλεπὸν ὄντα καὶ δυσχείρωτον, ἐνίοις δὲ καὶ παντάπασι σοβαρῶς προσφερόμενον, ὥσπερ Ἀνύτῳ τῷ Ἀνθεμίωνος.

ἐτύγχανε μὲν γὰρ ἐρῶν τοῦ Ἀλκιβιάδου, ξένους δέ τινας ἑστιῶν ἐκάλει κἀκεῖνον ἐπὶ τὸ δεῖπνον. ὁ δὲ τὴν μὲν κλῆσιν ἀπείπατο, μεθυσθεὶς δ' οἴκοι μετὰ τῶν ἑταίρων, ἐκώμασε πρὸς τὸν Ἄνυτον, καὶ ταῖς θύραις ἐπιστὰς τοῦ ἀνδρῶνος καὶ θεασάμενος ἀργυρῶν ἐκπωμάτων καὶ χρυσῶν πλήρεις τὰς τραπέζας, ἐκέλευσε τοὺς παῖδας τὰ ἡμίση λαβόντας οἴκαδε κομίζειν πρὸς ἑαυτόν, εἰσελθεῖν δ' οὐκ ἠξίωσεν, ἀλλ' ἀπῆλθε ταῦτα πράξας. τῶν οὖν ξένων δυσχεραινόντων καὶ λεγόντων, ὡς ὑβριστικῶς καὶ ὑπερηφάνως εἴη τῷ Ἀνύτῳ κεχρημένος ὁ Ἀλκιβιάδης, ἐπιεικῶς μὲν οὖν ὁ Ἄνυτος ἔφη καὶ φιλανθρώπως· ἃ γὰρ ἐξῆν αὐτῷ λαβεῖν ἅπαντα, τούτων ἡμῖν τὰ ἡμίση καταλέλοιπεν.

begging for kisses or caresses, but who rather censured the decaying parts of his soul and stifled his empty and thoughtless conceit, "though a cock, he crouched like a slave, resting his wings."[6]

He even considered the work of Socrates to be truly in the service of the gods for the care and salvation of young men, and despising himself, he was in awe of Socrates. In admiring his kindness and feeling ashamed before his virtue, he unknowingly acquired an image of love in return for love, as Plato says,[7] such that everyone marveled to see him with Socrates eating, training at the gym, and sharing his tent, since with his other lovers he had been difficult and defiant, and with some of them he was even insolently disposed, as with Anytus, son of Anthemion.

For Anytus had fallen in love with Alcibiades, and invited some friends to his home to dine. Alcibiades refused the invitation, but after getting drunk at home with some companions, took the party to Anytus's place. As he was standing by the doors to the banqueting hall, he noticed that the tables were full of silver and gold cups and ordered his servants to take half of them and bring them to his house for himself. Nor did he deem it worth entering but, having done this much, he departed. Naturally, Anytus's guests were angry and said that Alcibiades had behaved outrageously and rudely to Anytus, but Anytus said rather that he had acted reasonably and generously, "since he could have taken all of the cups but instead left behind half of them for us."

Οὕτω δὲ καὶ τοῖς ἄλλοις ἐρασταῖς ἐχρῆτο, πλὴν ἕνα μετοικικὸν ὥς φασιν ἄνθρωπον, οὐ πολλὰ κεκτημένον, ἀποδόμενον δὲ πάντα καὶ τὸ συναχθὲν εἰς ἑκατὸν στατῆρας τῷ Ἀλκιβιάδῃ προσφέροντα καὶ δεόμενον λαβεῖν, γελάσας καὶ ἡσθεὶς ἐκάλεσεν ἐπὶ δεῖπνον. ἑστιάσας δὲ καὶ φιλοφρονηθεὶς τό τε χρυσίον ἀπέδωκεν αὐτῷ καὶ προσέταξε τῇ ὑστεραίᾳ τοὺς ὠνουμένους τὰ τέλη τὰ δημόσια ταῖς τιμαῖς ὑπερβάλλειν ἀντωνούμενον. παραιτουμένου δὲ τοῦ ἀνθρώπου διὰ τὸ πολλῶν ταλάντων εἶναι τὴν ὠνήν, ἠπείλησε μαστιγώσειν εἰ μὴ ταῦτα πράττοι· καὶ γὰρ ἐτύγχανεν ἐγκαλῶν τι τοῖς τελώναις ἴδιον. ἕωθεν οὖν προελθὼν ὁ μέτοικος εἰς ἀγορὰν ἐπέθηκε τῇ ὠνῇ τάλαντον. ἐπεὶ δ' οἱ τελῶναι συστρεφόμενοι καὶ ἀγανακτοῦντες ἐκέλευον ὀνομάζειν ἐγγυητήν, ὡς οὐκ ἂν εὑρόντος, θορυβουμένου τοῦ ἀνθρώπου καὶ ἀναχωροῦντος ἑστὼς ὁ Ἀλκιβιάδης ἄπωθεν πρὸς τοὺς ἄρχοντας ἐμὲ γράψατε εἶπεν, ἐμὸς φίλος ἐστίν, ἐγγυῶμαι. τοῦτ' ἀκούσαντες οἱ τελῶναι πάντες ἐξηπορήθησαν. εἰωθότες γὰρ ἀεὶ ταῖς δευτέραις ὠναῖς χρεωλυτεῖν τὰς πρώτας, οὐχ ἑώρων ἀπαλλαγὴν οὖσαν αὐτοῖς τοῦ πράγματος. ἐδέοντο δὴ τοῦ ἀνθρώπου διδόντες ἀργύριον· ὁ δ' Ἀλκιβιάδης οὐκ εἴα λαβεῖν ἔλαττον ταλάντου. διδόντων δὲ τὸ τάλαντον ἐκέλευσεν ἀποστῆναι λαβόντα. κἀκεῖνον μὲν οὕτως ὠφέλησεν.

And that's how he treated all his other lovers except, they say, for one man who was a metic,[8] who did not have much money. This man sold everything he had and, bringing the hundred staters[9] he had earned, offered it all to Alcibiades and begged him to take it. Alcibiades laughed, delighted, and invited him to dinner. After he had entertained him and treated him kindly, he returned his gold to him, and enjoined him to counterbid on the public projects the next day, and to outbid all the other contractors. When the man declined, because the cost for this was many talents, Alcibiades threatened to flog him if he did not do it. For he happened to have a private quarrel of some kind with the contractors. So the metic went to the marketplace at dawn and made a bid of a talent. When the contractors gathered together, angry, and ordered him to name his guarantor, thinking he would find none, the man became confused and drew back. At this point, Alcibiades stood up, from some distance, and said to the magistrates, "Write down my name. He is my friend. I pledge myself as his guarantor." When the contractors heard this, they all realized they were in trouble. For it was their custom to pay down one set of debts with the payment for the next, and they did not see any escape for themselves from this situation. So they beseeched the man, offering him money to back down from his bid, and Alcibiades would not allow him to take less than a talent. And when they had given him the talent, Alcibiades ordered him to take it and depart. And that is how he aided him.

Ὁ δὲ Σωκράτους ἔρως πολλοὺς ἔχων καὶ μεγάλους ἀνταγωνιστὰς πῇ μὲν ἐκράτει τοῦ Ἀλκιβιάδου, δι' εὐφυΐαν ἁπτομένων τῶν λόγων αὐτοῦ καὶ τὴν καρδίαν στρεφόντων καὶ δάκρυα ἐκχεόντων, ἔστι δ' ὅτε καὶ τοῖς κόλαξι πολλὰς ἡδονὰς ὑποβάλλουσιν ἐνδιδοὺς ἑαυτόν, ἀπωλίσθανε τοῦ Σωκράτους καὶ δραπετεύων ἀτεχνῶς ἐκυνηγεῖτο, πρὸς μόνον ἐκεῖνον ἔχων τὸ αἰδεῖσθαι καὶ τὸ φοβεῖσθαι, τῶν δ' ἄλλων ὑπερορῶν.

16.1–3

Ἐν δὲ τοῖς τοιούτοις πολιτεύμασι καὶ λόγοις καὶ φρονήματι καὶ δεινότητι πολλὴν αὖ πάλιν τὴν τρυφὴν τῆς διαίτης καὶ περὶ πότους καὶ ἔρωτας ὑβρίσματα, καὶ θηλύτητας ἐσθήτων ἁλουργῶν ἑλκομένων δι' ἀγορᾶς, καὶ πολυτέλειαν ὑπερήφανον, ἐκτομάς τε καταστρωμάτων ἐν ταῖς τριήρεσιν, ὅπως μαλακώτερον ἐγκαθεύδοι, κειρίαις, ἀλλὰ μὴ σανίσι, τῶν στρωμάτων ἐπιβαλλομένων, ἀσπίδος τε διαχρύσου ποίησιν οὐδὲν ἐπίσημον τῶν πατρίων ἔχουσαν, ἀλλ' Ἔρωτα κεραυνοφόρον [ἅπερ] ὁρῶντες, οἱ μὲν ἔνδοξοι μετὰ τοῦ βδελύττεσθαι καὶ δυσχεραίνειν ἐφοβοῦντο τὴν ὀλιγωρίαν αὐτοῦ καὶ παρανομίαν ὡς τυραννικὰ καὶ ἀλλόκοτα, τοῦ δὲ δήμου τὸ πάθος τὸ πρὸς αὐτὸν οὐ κακῶς ἐξηγούμενος ὁ Ἀριστοφάνης ταῦτ' εἴρηκε Ποθεῖ μέν, ἐχθαίρει δέ, βούλεται δ' ἔχειν, ἔτι δὲ μᾶλλον τῇ ὑπονοίᾳ πιέζων·

But his love for Socrates, though it had many great rivals, somehow conquered Alcibiades, due to his naturally good disposition, and Socrates' words touched him and turned his heart and made him weep. Still there were times when he gave himself over to his flatterers, who cast before him many pleasures, and would slip away from Socrates. Then, having run away, he would end up being chased down by him again, since only for him did he feel respect and fear, while he despised all the others.

▪ ▪ ▪ ▪ ▪

For all his political shrewdness, command of language, intelligence, and wit, he always returned again to his luxurious way of life, his excesses of drinking and desire, his effeminacy in clothes, wearing long purple robes to the marketplace, and his overweening extravagance. Thus he had parts of the decks on his triremes cut away so that he could sleep more softly with his bedding spread out on cords rather than planks. He also had a shield of gold made for himself that had no device of his ancestors on it all, but rather an image of Eros bearing a thunderbolt. The upper classes looked upon all these things with disgust and displeasure, and feared his contemptuous behavior and lawlessness as tyrannical and bizarre. As to the feelings of the common people toward him, Aristophanes explained it rather well when he wrote this: "they desire him, they despise him, and they long to have him." And, even more so, he weighs in on their deeper feelings with these lines,

μάλιστα μὲν λέοντα μὴ 'ν πόλει τρέφειν·
ἢν δ' ἐκτρέφῃ τις, τοῖς τρόποις ὑπηρετεῖν.

ἐπιδόσεις γὰρ καὶ χορηγίαι καὶ φιλοτιμήματα πρὸς τὴν πόλιν ὑπερβολὴν μὴ ἀπολείποντα καὶ δόξα προγόνων καὶ λόγου δύναμις καὶ σώματος εὐπρέπεια καὶ ῥώμη μετ' ἐμπειρίας τῶν πολεμικῶν καὶ ἀλκῆς πάντα τἆλλα συγχωρεῖν ἐποίει καὶ φέρειν μετρίως τοὺς Ἀθηναίους, ἀεὶ τὰ πρᾳότατα τῶν ὀνομάτων τοῖς ἁμαρτήμασι τιθεμένους, παιδιὰς καὶ φιλοτιμίας.

Most of all do not raise a lion in the city.
But if someone does raise one, he must serve his
moods.[10]

In the end, his civic contributions, his service as *choregos*,[11] his magnificent acts, his unsurpassed extravagance toward the city, the repute of his forebears, the power of his speech, and the beauty and strength of his body, along with his experience and courage in war, made the Athenians yield to him in all matters and bear him patiently. They always placed only the most mild of labels on his faults, as if they were just youthfulness or ambition.

NOTES

Introduction

1. Those interested in reading more about ancient Greek sexuality will find a full library, starting with the work of Michel Foucault, Sir Kenneth Dover, David Halperin, John Winkler, Giulia Sissa, Kirk Ormand, Andrew Lear, James Davidson, and many more.
2. Eve Kosofsky Sedgwick, 1993, "Queer and Now," in *Tendencies*, Durham, NC: Duke University Press, pp. 1–20, 8.
3. *Plutarch's Lives IV: Alcibiades and Coriolanus, Lysander and Sulla*, translated by Bernadotte Perrin, Cambridge, MA: Harvard University Press, 1950. *Theocritus, Moschus, Bion*, edited and translated by Neil Hopkinson, Cambridge, MA: Harvard University Press, 2015. *Xenophon IV: Memorabilia, Oeconomicus*, translated by E. C. Marchant, *Symposium, Apology*, translated by O. J. Todd, revised by Jeffrey Henderson, Cambridge, MA: Harvard University Press, 2013.

Chapter 1. Two of Us

1. This point is about the relationship between the "lover" (*erastes*) and the "beloved" (*eromenos*). As can be seen throughout this volume, a common trope of erotic relationships in ancient Greece was that the older party to an affair was the active agent of love or desire, while the younger party was its passive recipient.

Chapter 2. Come and Get Your Love

1. According to myth, Tantalus was king of Sipylus and his son was Pelops. As Pindar tells it, Pelops was "whisked away" to become the beloved of Poseidon, much as Ganymede was snatched up by Zeus. Later in the poem, we see that this act of rape becomes the basis for an ongoing relationship of reciprocity, as Pelops asks Poseidon's help in winning the woman he wishes to marry.

Chapter 3. I'm Coming Out

1. The names of the two leading maiden dancers are "Agido" and "Hagesichora," which mean "woman from the Agiad family" and "leader of the chorus," respectively. Some scholars consider these names to be generic titles for the roles of the two leading dancers in any given iteration of this song and dance. Their identities, if they were real people, are not otherwise attested, and many of the references and practices in the song are opaque to modern readers. The imagery of horses is thought to be erotic.
2. As with Alcman 1, many of the names and rites described here remain mysterious to modern readers, and the text itself is very fragmented.

NOTES

Chapter 5. Crash into Me

1. For Sappho 94 and 96, I have used elements of different editions of the text, including *Poetarum Lesbiorum Fragmenta*, edited by Edgar Lobel and Denys Page, Oxford: Clarendon Press, 1955 (which supplies most of the Greek text for Sappho in this volume), and *Greek Lyric I: Sappho and Alcaeus*, translated by David Campbell, Cambridge, MA: Harvard University Press, 1982.

Chapter 6. Boy's Gone Crazy

1. This poem turns on a syntactical joke, whereby the name "Cleoboulus" appears in three different oblique cases, meaning that it is an object of desire in every grammatical way possible.
2. The Panathenaea was the most important festival at Athens, held annually in honor of the goddess Athena.
3. The pankration was an athletic competition that involved a mixture of boxing and wrestling.
4. The Greek word is *sōphrosunē*, which denotes a concept that ranges from what we think of as "temperance," as I have translated it here, to "moderation," "chastity," or "self-control." I have chosen to translate it as seems appropriate in each place. For the history of *sōphrosunē*, see Christopher Moore, 2023, *The Virtue of Agency. Sōphrosunē and Self-Constitution in Classical Greece*, Oxford: Oxford University Press.
5. Satyr plays were a form of drama produced in Athens. They had comedic elements but were also connected to tragedy. Each satyr play featured a chorus representing satyrs, also called sileni. These were mythic characters who

had some aspects of animals and some of men; each featured a large phallus as part of his costume. This comment by Xenophon seems to be a reference to Alcibiades' extended comparison of Socrates to a statue of Silenus (who was also a particular satyr) in Plato's *Symposium* (215b–c).

6. Alexander is another name for Paris of Troy. He was tasked with judging among Aphrodite, Athena, and Hera.

Chapter 7. Don't Do Me Like That

1. The goddess of the Underworld, whose house is death.
2. Aphrodite, also called "Cypris" and "Cytherea."
3. On Zeus's snatching of Ganymede, see chapter 2.

Chapter 8. The Wild Side

1. Minor female goddesses associated with loose sexual mores.
2. A lost tetralogy by Aeschylus.
3. An ancient scholar on the play posits that this question, *podapos ho gunnis*, is a quote from Aeschylus's lost work that referred to Dionysus, "the female male."
4. Euripides, Sophocles, and Aeschylus all wrote plays based on the story of Phaedra, and Euripides wrote two; since the character Phaedra in his extant *Hippolytus* does not behave in a particularly licentious way, we might conjecture that the Phaedra in his lost play does.
5. This is first extant use in Greek of the word *mimesis* in regard to theatrical practice.
6. See chapter 6, note 4.

7. Cf. chapter 6 on Ibycus and Anacreon. Alcaeus was a poet from Lesbos and roughly a contemporary of Sappho. Phrynicus was an early tragedian, of whom we have no surviving plays.
8. Cadmus is the founder of Thebes and grandfather to both Pentheus and Dionysus; thus Pentheus and Dionysus are first cousins.
9. A *thyrsus* is a staff wrapped at the top with leaves of ivy or another plant. It was considered an instrument of Dionysiac worship.

Chapter 9. The Origin of Love

1. Along with Phaedrus, quoted here in chapter 1, Eryximachus and Pausanias were other earlier speakers at the gathering.
2. In this context, *sumbolon* means a kind of token broken into two pieces with which two people could prove their identities to one another.
3. Pausanias and Agathon, both present at the gathering, were known as longtime lovers. Agathon is the same man as the one comically portrayed by Aristophanes in the *Thesmophoriazusae*, quoted here in chapter 8.

Chapter 10. Lust for Life

1. The Academy and Lyceum were both schools in classical Athens for philosophy and other kinds of training.
2. A wrestling school and gymnasium.
3. The Acheron was a river thought to flow into the Underworld.
4. See chapter 2.

5. There are several stories in Greek mythology on the origin of Eros.
6. This is Heracles (known in Rome as "Hercules"), who was also considered the son of Zeus. Later in the poem, he is referred to also as the son of Alcmene, his mother.

Chapter 11. The Wings of Love

1. This is a pun: the name "Ligyans" sounds like *ligus*, the Greek word for "clear" or "shrill."
2. In the Greek, there is a pun on the word for "rushing" or "flowing" (used here in the form *rheont'*) and a particular word for "desire" (*himeros*).
3. The Greek neologism is *Pterōta*—that is, *pteros* ("winged") plus *erōs.*
4. On Ganymede and Zeus, see chapter 2. On the pun in "rush of desire," see earlier in this passage.

Chapter 12. Who Wants to Live Forever

1. See chapter 6 for Xenophon's later comparison of Socrates to a Silenus, and chapter 6, note 4 on Alcibiades' longer description of Socrates in this light in Plato's text.
2. A proverbial expression for a comically bad trade made by Glaucus in the *Iliad*, book 6, when he traded his gold armor for Diomedes' bronze armor.
3. A lisped form of "see Theorus" and "crow." This passage is a quote from Aristophanes' *Wasps* (44–46).
4. Kock, *Comicorum atticorum fragmenta i*, p. 688.
5. Antiphon of Rhamnus was a fifth-century orator.
6. A poetic quote whose source is unknown.

7. Plutarch uses Plato's *Phaedrus* and *Symposium* as sources for information in this passage.
8. Metics were foreigners living in Athens, who paid some taxes and received some privileges, but did not have the rights of citizens.
9. A hundred staters was a fairly small amount of money, whereas a "talent," mentioned later in this passage, was quite a lot—thousands of dollars in today's money.
10. These lines and the line just above are both quotes about Alcibiades from Aristophanes' *Frogs* (1425 and 1431–32).
11. A *choregos* was a role taken on each year by a wealthy Athenian whereby he would pay for the mounting of theatrical productions at the Dionysian festivals.